Praise for
Modern Parents, Vintage Values

"Melissa and Sissy are women who have spent a lifetime caring for adolescents and their parents. Their ministry is unquestionably one of the premier bridge building tools between teens and their families. Their life passion is to see young men and women grow up in the maturity of Jesus Christ."

—Dan B. Allender, Ph.D., author and president of Mars Hill Graduate School

"This is it! The book I've been waiting for as a mom! *Modern Parents, Vintage Values* answers every question I've thought about as a concerned and invested parent, giving practical and biblical solutions to each situation. Raising three children in today's technology driven world isn't an easy task. Teaching and maintaining the values I was taught as a child is even harder. But today, my life just got a little easier. I need two copies of this book. One for my nightstand and one for my purse."

—Candace Cameron Bure, actress, author, *Reshaping It All*

"Like an ice-cold glass of lemonade taken from your rocker on a scorching hot summer day, this book refreshes a parent's heart and gives them permission to return to what God meant us to spend our time doing all along: instill virtues into our children. You'll love the practical ideas! I did."

—Dannah Gresh, author, *Secret Keeper Girl*, and coauthor, *Lies Young Women Believe*

"*Modern Parents, Vintage Values* is a treasure of a resource and I recommend it to anyone with children. We need to know what they're up against! Thank you, Melissa and Sissy, for being beacons for us mommies who want to know what we're up against."

—Angie Smith, author, *I Will Carry You*

"As a mom, I'm glad to read a book from authors who recognize the dangers to children of new media, pop culture, and more. As a blogger, I also appreciate Melissa and Sissy's awareness of those media benefits. *Modern Parents, Vintage Values* will help parents protect their children by developing their character, thereby preparing them to be good stewards of the technologies of today and beyond."

—Candice Watters, author, *Start Your Family*, FamilyMaking.com

"In their mission to help kids and their families, Sissy Goff and Melissa Trevathan have a history of success. Their expertise in helping children through tough times on their way to adulthood, through a psychological and spiritual approach, has been proven time and time again."

—Michael McDonald, songwriter and recording artist

"Through the years of knowing Melissa and Sissy, I have seen their constant commitment to the emotional healing of teens and their families. They offer 'real' love and hope in a day and time when no one's life goes untouched by tragedies—big or small. The passion they share is contagious, their wisdom life changing!"

—Kim Hill, recording artist

Modern
PARENTS,
Vintage
VALUES

Modern PARENTS, Vintage VALUES

Instilling Character in Today's Kids

MELISSA TREVATHAN & SISSY GOFF

B&H
PUBLISHING GROUP

Nashville, Tennessee

978-1-4336-6881-4

Published by B&H Publishing Group
Nashville, Tennessee

Dewey Decimal Classification: 649
Subject Heading: CHARACTER \ CHILD
REARING \ VALUES

1 2 3 4 5 6 7 8 • 14 13 12 11 10

This book is written in honor of the vintage characters whose stories have influenced ours: Margaret Trevathan, Robbie Stamps, Otie Trevathan, Hedy Patterson, Robert Goff, Marian Goff, and Dorothy Goff. It is also written in memory of our treasured friends, Noel and Molasses.

Acknowledgments

Gratitude is one value that we have in abundance. We are grateful to a group of people who have helped us to dream up, write out, and put into print this book including: David and Amy Huffman, our skilled and winsome managers; Jennifer Lyell, our wise and profoundly encouraging editor and new friend; the fabulous folks at Daystar with whom we have the blessing of sharing vintage values in the lives of kids: David Thomas, Jeremy Shapiro, David Denton, Chris Roberts, Tracy Kouns, Heather Flener, Heather James, Mary Berndt, Lynne Fleet, and Pat McCurdy. And to our dear friends Mimi, Pace, Cindy, Pepper, Mary Katharine, Belle, Jackie, Robbie, and Nita who speak values and truth into our lives on a daily basis. And, finally, to our families . . . Kathleen, Helen, Bob, Margaret, and Robbie, who remind us of God's faithfulness and love.

Contents

Foreword

*R*ecently my husband and I took a short day-trip to a quaint small town about an hour's drive from our home base in the big city. We had lunch at a little café known for its peach tea and meringue pies and then made our way to the antique shops on the town square. While strolling through one antique shop in particular, I couldn't help but be transported back in time. It was a bit surreal to see some of the familiar mementos of my past covered with a light layer of dust and staring back at me from an antique store shelf. Vintage Barbies, Pet Rocks, AM/FM transistor radios, and even a Partridge Family record album! (Proud member of the David Cassidy fan club here.) In spite of my pleas, my husband refused to allow me to rescue the poor Felix the Cat wall clock and hang it in our bedroom in a last-ditch effort to return it back to its glory days. Never mind that I always found it a bit unnerving that Felix's eyes creepily shifted back and forth with each and every tick-tock and seemed to follow me wherever I went. On second thought, he's better off on the wall in the store!

On another aisle we found a shelf filled with old rotary dial phones. (If you are under the age of thirty and reading this, you may have to Google it to get an idea of what I'm talking about.) Of course, I couldn't resist the urge to put my finger in the "zero" and give it a sample dial. Oh, the patience it took to dial a number filled with "9's" and "0's"! Your family was on the cutting edge of technology if it was among the first to get the push button model when it released. As I stood there looking at the phones, I thought about my kids, armed with touch screen "smart phones" that keep them connected around the clock to friends, family, and the World Wide Web. I found myself wishing for simpler times when phones were tethered to living room walls and moms and dads were the great and mighty gatekeepers to all things incoming. It seemed annoying at the time to share a single phone line, but now as a parent, I can certainly see the value.

As I read through the manuscript of *Modern Parent, Vintage Values,* I thought about my visit to the antique store. While vintage mementos from my past were worth only a fraction of their original price, the vintage values many of us were raised with have become rare and priceless qualities among today's youth. Values like kindness, compassion, integrity, responsibility, patience, gratitude, confidence, forgiveness, and the near-extinct good manners, are timeless for every generation. Sissy and Melissa do an outstanding job of unpacking these vintage values from the old cedar chest and bringing them back to life.

I've had the amazing privilege of doing many events with Sissy and Melissa. Over the years we've served on a dozen or so Q&A panels for parents, and when the tough questions come, I often defer to them. They have shared their gift of relevant insight and wisdom with both young people and their parents for many years. Their wisdom is always encouraging and filled with hope. Most importantly they are faithful to point parents right back to Scripture and the Author of all things of eternal value, vintage or otherwise.

It's time parents get back to the business of teaching their children the timeless, vintage values laid forth in God's Word. Several decades from now, antique stores will be filled with Nintendo Wii game consoles, iPhones, Justin Bieber posters, and Hannah Montana lunch pails—cast aside as vintage, valueless junk. I don't know about you, but I want to leave my children a legacy of vintage values that stand the test of time . . . long after that creepy Felix the Cat clock ticks its last and final tick-tock.

—Vicki Courtney

Dear Reader,

"You are the only you this world will ever know." These words are the beginning to one of our favorite quotes of Dan Allender's that we use often when speaking to kids and parents alike. You are the only you. You are also the only mom, or dad, or Papa, Aunt Robbie, or godmother your child will ever know. And you will impact the life and heart of that child in ways that no one else ever will.

This book is one that, we hope, will help you make that impact with more understanding, more clarity and hope. As counselors with more than sixty years of combined experience with kids, these pages are filled with truths we have learned from the parents and kids whose paths have crossed ours. We say often that we're not experts . . . we just have the privilege of sitting with parents and kids of all ages who are wrestling through this topic of raising children and growing up in our modern world.

So, as you read these pages, know that not every child will face the issues we cover in the first part of the book. Your child may not ever have to deal with some of these struggles, but statistics show that they'll know someone who does. We want to help not only equip you, but also help you equip your child. The vintage values and timeless truths sections, however, are ones we believe will speak to the hopes and prayers you have for each of your children.

Thank you for picking up this book. We are honored to come alongside you as you love your children. You are the only you, and you're already well on your way to helping your child become the only him (or her) this world will ever know.

An Introduction

*I*magine a warm summer day. You're sitting outside drinking iced tea. Your children are in the yard laughing and playing, seemingly without a care in the world. They've got umbrellas out, and they're dancing in the water falling from the sprinkler. You can barely hear the strains of B. J. Thomas singing "Raindrops Keep Falling on My Head." What year do you think this is?

As much as it sounds like the summer of 1970, you're almost forty years off. These kids were at Camp Hopetown, the summer camp we run for kids involved in our counseling ministry. Allow us to introduce ourselves. We are two counselors who work with kids and have been doing so for a combined experience of more than sixty years, although most of those years are Melissa's. My name is Sissy, and I was barely born when B. J. was crooning about the falling raindrops.

We are part of a counseling ministry called Daystar. Our office is housed in a little yellow house with a big front porch. One seven-year-old boy called it, "the little yellow house that helps people." Our dogs, Lucy, the Havanese, and Blueberry, the old English sheepdog, help us counsel the kids and families who come to Daystar. Our offices house eight counselors and see more than two hundred kids per week between individual and group counseling. We offer summer camps and parenting classes both in the community and beyond. We believe in offering

1

hope to families in any situation, and we believe in vintage values in this modern world.

Actually, we just like the whole idea of vintage in general. On most days we have spiced tea brewing in our lobby. There is a checkers table in one of the waiting rooms with typically two or three kids gathered around it. At our camps the kids play chess, learn to water-ski (not just wakeboard), and help cook the meals. We sing old-timey hymns along with worship choruses and talk about the rich meaning behind the words. We even have Christmas at camp and take the kids to a town made up of one row of antique stores. They have three dollars to buy a gift for the person whose name they drew. The gifts are symbolic, like a boy who gave a counselor an old walking stick because he said she helped people stand who were struggling. We like vintage and believe it brings out good in the lives of kids.

This book is divided into three sections. In the first, which we call "Modern Parents," we tackle a few of the topics we hear most often from parents in our counseling offices. We talk about technology, entitlement, respect, anxiety, and eating disorders, to name a few—issues that are coming at parents with more frequency and intensity than ever before. Many of these issues will be around for years to come, and yet we know that new challenges will also emerge. So, we encourage you to go to www.modernparentsvintagevalues.com for updates and downloads about issues facing modern parents.

In the second section we introduce the idea of "Vintage Values." We outline nine values including compassion, gratitude, kindness, patience, manners, and several others. We break each section down into children and teenagers and talk, not just about what those values look like but specifically how to instill them in both ages. And in each chapter of the first two sections, we end with something called "A Sunday Drive."

Do you remember going on Sunday drives with your family? After church and lunch, you'd pile in the car and just drive. You didn't have a time frame. You didn't really have anywhere you were going. You just spent time together. We hope these chapters can serve the same purpose. In them we give some practical suggestions you can do as a family not just to learn about but to experience the ideas we've discussed in the previous chapter.

The last section of our book is called "Timeless Truths." In it we share some final ideas of not just what but who enables us to parent in these times. The job is daunting. We're battling terrorism and technology, attitudes and entitlement like our grandparents never could have imagined. But you can . . . and often do. We're guessing your imagination, however, causes you even more fear. What if I let her text and she sends someone an inappropriate picture? What if I let him spend the night out and his friend's parents don't watch him like I do? How do I shelter her and keep her from harm? Why is he acting like this?

We want this book to be a journey for you and your family. We hope that, in its pages, you will learn more about your child and more about yourself. We hope you will be reminded of truth and inspired to parent with more life and more freedom. Basically, our hope is that you'll find hope for who God is creating your child to be and that you will find comfort in knowing it was in His image that your child was created and it is by His grace and goodness that you can seek to instill these good and godly characteristics. And finally, we hope that you'll close this book knowing a little more of the ultimate truth of God's love in the life of your family.

Part 1

Modern Parents

The Age of Anonymity

Technology promises to give us control over the earth and over other people. But the promise is not fulfilled: lethal automobiles, ugly buildings and ponderous bureaucracies ravage the earth and empty lives of meaning. Structures become more important than the people who use them. We care more for our possessions with which we hope to make our way in the world than with our thoughts and dreams which tell us who we are in the world.

—Eugene Peterson, *A Long Obedience in the Same Direction*[1]

SUP
HW PIR
K BFN LOL
Y2K

Confused? If you're anything like the two of us, the answer would be yes. The above letters look just as much like some type of computer code to prevent the world from collapsing at Y2K as they do nonsense. Actually, this is a text message conversation. In normal language it reads as follows:

What's up?

Homework. Parents in room.

Okay. Bye for now. Laugh out loud (or lots of love, depending on sender).

You're too kind.

Normal language here may be the operative phrase. If someone had mentioned the words Facebook, sexting, Skype, Wi-Fi, video upload, YouTube, even Internet to you twenty years ago, you would potentially have thought they were speaking a different language. That language is what this chapter is about. We do need to say, at the outset, that none of the sections in this chapter are exhaustive. We wish they were, but there is simply too much information to cover on each topic. So we'll do our best to touch on what we feel is most helpful to you in raising kids with vintage values—in not just a modern but a technologically savvy generation.

A mom of a fifteen-year-old recently said, "I feel like I'm an analog parent in a digital world." Join the club. Analog parents, grandparents, teachers, and counselors. We're typically playing catchup as we're trying to set boundaries and limits on things we barely even understand ourselves. And, even as we set the boundaries, our kids are saying things like: "You just don't understand. Everyone texts/Facebooks/Skypes today. It's just a different world from when you grew up."

And so it is. A different world with a different language. In this chapter we'll try to explain both, in regard to the six technological issues we hear kids and parents talk about the most. In the section called "A Different World," we'll define the technology and discuss the trends among kids and teenagers today. In "A Deeper Look," we'll uncover why exactly kids are so drawn to each of these items and the concerns associated with them. "What's a Modern Parent to Do?" will give you specific ideas in how to set boundaries and respond to your children's foray into the technological world. And, finally, our "Sunday Drive" section will give analog parents a chance to connect with their digital children away from batteries and Wi-Fi.

Cell Phones

A Different World

"My daughter sends more than two hundred text messages per day." This figure may sound astronomical to you. But we have heard this exact sentence countless times in our offices from concerned parents. According to a Nielsen study in August 2009, the average number of teen texts per month has increased by 566 percent from 2007 to 2009. The average teen texts 2,899 times per month while making only 191 calls.

In terms of general cell phone use, Nielsen also found that 77 percent of teens have cell phones, with an extra 11 percent regularly borrowing one (uh-oh). Eighty-three percent of those teens use text messaging. Fifty-six percent use picture messaging (sending a picture via their cell phone). Forty-five percent play games on their phones. Forty percent instant message, and 37 percent use the Internet on their phones.[2]

It's spilling over to children, as well. You may have your son or daughter as young as six years old asking for a cell phone. As of 2007, according to C&R Research, 22 percent of children aged six to nine owned their own cell phone; 60 percent of tweens, aged ten to fourteen. There is no question that those statistics have risen exponentially since then.[3]

As a pilot group two Texas elementary schools are handing out "smart phones" to fifth-grade classrooms.[4] These children will use them to gain access to Internet, listen to podcasts, even complete work sheets. But they won't be able to make or receive calls or texts. Verizon Wireless is providing these devices free of charge. Of course.

Let's face it. Not only do kids and teens tell us *often* that their cell phones are the one possession they can't imagine their lives without; they credit them as their link to the outer world and the foundation of their social lives. Cell phones are here to stay . . . that is, until they're replaced by something that makes conversations move faster and require even less energy (or social skills).

A Deeper Look

One of the main benefits of cell phones for children or teens is safety related. We know where they are. They are accessible (as long as they answer their phones, which we'll get to in the next section). If your daughter takes off with two friends for the evening, you can check in with her at any given point. If you are in a divorce situation, you can get in touch with her when she is at the other parent's home for visitation. It makes communication much more convenient.

With phones today equipped with GPS capabilities, it also can give us up to the minute information as to where they are. A young man (seventeen years old) was brought in for counseling because of lying repeatedly to his parents. The downside was that he was good at it. The upside was that his parents had his number . . . because that number, or phone, had a GPS device embedded inside. So, when he claimed to be at the "library," they knew he was at his girlfriend's house. When he went to the "movie," they knew he had gone to a party instead. Not that you want to maintain a CIA-like parenting style in terms of your child's whereabouts, but there are definitely situations where it can come in handy to find out exactly where they are.

Cell phones can also be great teachers of responsibility. Learning to stay within the given minutes or text messages of a plan, keeping up with the phone itself, not dropping it in a glass of water—or toilet. These are great incentives for getting and keeping that social foundation they want so desperately. Allow the cell phone not only to be a privilege to receive but also one to keep as they learn the responsibility that comes with owning one.

The cell phone phenomenon of our culture offers many other positives. We can find out immediately if a child has been in an accident. If your son is driving and gets lost, he can call you instead of stopping in an unfamiliar or even unsafe part of town. You know if your daughter gets sick. If you need to pick children up from school earlier, you can text a quick message (that they will receive during school hours).

Let's talk about the concerns. And there are quite a few. Maybe the first and foremost is the lack of social skills required to text. According to statistics, texting is the preferred communication method among kids today. When sending an abbreviated message, kids lose the social niceties we used to have to communicate over the phone. Remember how your parents taught you to answer the phone? "Smith's house, this is John." They don't even have to say "hi" or "how are you." They just jump right in. "SUP?"

Sexting has also become a tremendous concern for today's parents. According to a recent survey by the National Campaign to Prevent Teen and Unplanned Pregnancy, 39 percent of all teens have sent or posted online sexually suggestive messages. Forty-eight percent have received these kinds of messages. In addition, 20 percent of teens ages thirteen to nineteen have sent or posted online nude or seminude pictures of themselves.[5]

We have seen quite a few of these kids in our offices, boys and girls. They are naive (believing the pictures won't be passed on), naive (not thinking that the pictures sent into cyberspace *stay* in cyberspace), and naive (having no thought about the effects these messages can have on their reputation). The boys send and ask for messages because they are driven both by hormones and by peer pressure (all the other guys are talking about girls they have sexted with). The girls sext often because they either are asked or are hoping the guy they like will pay more attention to them if they do. Basically the same reasons any teen or preteen becomes involved in a real-life sexual relationship can cause them to become involved in a phone sexual relationship. In their minds, however, sexting is even better because they haven't actually committed the act.

Thankfully authorities are becoming involved. As we've said already, we adults are usually playing catch up. Sexting went on for several years without our having a name for it or even really knowing it was going on. Today teens are facing charges from misdemeanors to felonies for distributing child pornography. It's always nice to have another voice speaking into the lives of our kids, and a voice that carries the law and consequences can be one that breaks through some of the naivete that accompanies these acts.

The legal system is also joining the ranks of parents and other adults who are concerned about kids who are using their cell phones while driving. With more and more phones having Internet accessibility, kids can drive and text, check Facebook, and maybe actually even talk, if all else fails. As of October 2009 seven states have made it illegal to talk on cell phones while driving. Eighteen states and the District of Columbia have banned driving and texting.[6] Fortunately we do have other voices, and voices with often a little more of an intimidation factor, in the lives of our kids.

Cell phones have become a permanent fixture in our lives, and the lives of our children. While the convenience makes it easier for us to get in touch with them, we may very well be raising a generation of children and teens with underdeveloped communication skills accompanied by a lack of respect for others and even their bodies. They become more comfortable and adept at relating in a two-dimensional world of words and buttons than with three-dimensional people, with feelings and consequences.

What's a Modern Parent to Do?

- Be aware of your own sense of peer pressure. Your child does not need a phone just because the "cool parents" have bought phones for their children. It sounds silly, but it is easy to fall into pressure, even as adults, of "everyone is doing it."

- Parent in community. Don't be the first to buy your child a phone (unless there is a specific reason) because your child will often be considered "fast." And don't be the last because then they will often buck the system. Have a close network of other parents with similar values and decide together when your children will have phones, text messaging, and other privileges. Then the "everyone else has one" myth falls flat.

- Do your homework. Before you buy a phone, make sure you hear and understand its capabilities. Brush up on the features and turn any features off you believe your child is not ready for. For example, many phones can be connected to a computer so that instant messages go directly to your child's computer and phone.

- Start with a tricycle. Our friend, teen culture expert and author Vicki Courtney, advocates a "training wheels" approach to technology.[7] Start small in terms of phone capabilities and time allowed. There are phones for children in which they can only receive calls from their parents or preprogrammed adults. Also, phone services can turn service or texting off during certain hours. Prepaid plans can help. Limit their time to talk and text so that they have to interact in a three-dimensional world, big limits with little ones and small limits as they get bigger. By the time your children reach eighteen and move out, you want them to have learned to monitor themselves rather than simply operate under your rules. They are not given opportunities to do so if the training wheels never come off.
- Make limits clear. Help children know at the beginning of phone ownership what the rules and expectations are. And the phone itself will provide one of the best logical consequences for its misuse. A few examples of rules are:
  - You will be respectful of others and yourself on the phone. This involves when you talk (like not while you are eating a meal with someone, for example), where you talk (it can be rude in public places), and what you talk about.
  - Only answer phone calls from people you know. Children can receive calls from scammers, bullies, and predators on their cell phones without you ever knowing it.
  - You will never drive and talk or drive and text.
  - You will not delete text messages. I can check from bills and find out if you have done so and will assume you've deleted them for a reason.
  - You will use your phone only in the times allowed. (Many parents we talk to have a cell phone basket that all the phones go in during mealtime, family time, and bedtime).
  - You will *always* answer the phone when a parent calls.
  - If you go over on your minutes or texts, you are responsible for the costs.

○ We are buying your first phone. If you lose it, you will buy your next.

- Talk about sexting with your child, age appropriately. If children are old enough to have phones, they are old enough to know that inappropriate messages can come their way (or be sent by them). Let them know the dangers in their worlds and consequences inside your homes.

- Stay relevant. Learn to text or whatever the next thing is they're doing. It is always important that we speak their language, even if it seems foreign to us.

Gaming

A Different World

We've come a long way since Space Invaders and Frogger . . . or even Mario jumping into blocks overhead. Today's games have more adventure, more complex plots, and much more blood. They can also have sexual themes or even highly sexualized characters. A forthright friend told her teenage sons, who spent many hours in front of their gaming systems, "I just want you to know that women don't really have chests that are perfectly pointy. What you are seeing is not real."

It is most definitely not real. But technology has come up with a way for the game experience to look and now even feel almost as real as real life. We swing the controller and hit the tennis ball. We jab and stab someone in the television. We stand on another type of controller that measures our balance, weight, and body mass index.

In a study by Harris Interactive, the average eight- to twelve-year-old plays thirteen hours of video games per week. The average thirteen- to eighteen-year-old, fourteen hours. Tween boys average sixteen hours, and teen boys, eighteen hours. For girls, tweens average ten hours per week and teen girls eight hours.[8]

A search on Amazon reveals today's top-selling video games. The first is a combat-type game where you drop into the "dark, abandoned" streets of Africa to fight off an invasion. The rating is "mature," signifying mild language, violence, and blood and gore. (Where's Frogger when you need him?) Number two on the list is a colorful, much more childlike race game in which the player holds a steering wheel to compete against fellow drivers, who may be either inside or outside your home. Three is an interactive game where you can play Ping-Pong, ride a WaveRunner, or throw a Frisbee to your dog. The fourth most popular boasts of the main character as "a shady character with an even shadier past." It now even has technology that allows you to use your gun vertically, while climbing. And the list goes on.

A Deeper Look

Games are a world that our children and teens enter where they can test their skills, conquer their fears, and compete against a host of colorful or dark and shady characters. And with today's technology these characters can be their siblings in the same room or another teen playing the same game in another country.

Gaming does have benefits. In a study by Yahoo! Shine, more than 70 percent of mothers of tweens and teens say they believe video games have helped their child's problem-solving skills.[9] Other research supports this as well. In June 2009 the Sesame Workshop presented a report on how video games can enhance children's lives: expanding their vocabulary, teaching them problem-solving skills, improving hand-eye coordination, enhancing their creativity, and even teaching them to think systematically, where one decision affects the whole.[10] They gave examples of games to help children manage diseases like The Asthma Files and Sesame Street's Color Me Hungry, which helps children learn healthy eating, and even Dance, Dance Revolution, which requires kids to memorize and act out a sequence of dance steps to promote more activity.

In addition, kids tell us that they feel a sense of accomplishment playing games and advancing to new levels. I (Melissa) am working with a thirteen-year-old highly skilled in game play but, because of a developmental problem, lacking many of the skills to make and maintain relationships with her peers. The most success she feels in a given day is on her PlayStation3. Playing games, in effect, does help her feel more confidence in and control over her life.

Now for the drawbacks. A British article in *The Observer* in 2001 states that "computer games are creating a dumbed-down generation of children far more disposed to violence than their parents, according to a new controversial study."[11] It goes on to explain that it's not just the content of the game that causes the problem. It is the effects of gaming itself. A Japanese study found that the only areas of the brain that were stimulated in computer games were those associated with vision and movement. Arithmetic, on the other hand, stimulates the frontal lobe in both hemispheres. The frontal lobe has a great deal to do with self-control. The study asserts that children need activities that will further strengthen the frontal lobe, rather than ignore it. If only our children loved math like they love Zelda.

Another danger in the gaming world, as in the other arenas of technology, is that children learn to function and relate in a virtual world rather than a real one. Courage and valor in Halo doesn't necessarily translate to courage when a bully tries to intimidate your child's friend. But it's often much more appealing. How much easier is it to attack a foe with a bow and arrow sitting on the comforts of your couch than ask a girl out on a date? Video games can help children and teens learn qualities such as courage and problem-solving skills. When they bleed over into reality, they are helpful. When they only use that knowledge in the virtual world, it can create an ever-increasing need to remain in that virtual world.

Statistics are pointing toward a problem with game addiction. The Harris Interactive study in 2007 found that 8.5 percent of eight- to eighteen-year-olds who played video games regularly were "addicted."[12] This definition of addiction does not involve significant amounts of time spent playing games as much as it does an inability to go without games. Children and teens who are addicted to games incur damage to their family lives, school lives, and even psychological functioning. The symptoms are much like an individual addicted to gambling.

The reality is that our children are going to play video games, and they're going to want to play them much more than they're going to want to do math and problem-solving exercises. As our friend and frequent video game character, Yoda, would say, playing video games can be used for good or for evil. The research suggests that the games chosen and time spent playing may be the two most determining factors. And those are ultimately up to us as parents.

What's a Modern Parent to Do?

- Our friends and authors of the book *Wild Things*, Stephen James and David Thomas, talk about the importance of kids having more time in the real world than in the virtual world.[13] Make sure your child is playing outside and engaging in activities that foster relationships and growth, even if it's something as simple as kick the can or skipping rocks with friends.
- Set a timer. Video games are a chronological black hole. Kids lose track of time. Timers can help.
- Read the ratings. Allow only those games in your home with ratings you approve.
- Research the games. Buy games for your child or teen that are more problem solving in nature than reflex-driven.
- Keep the game system in a common area.
- Play with your children. It's the best way to understand not only what they're doing but also how it's affecting them. You might even have a little fun.

The Internet

Even writing those words, I feel like there should be some type of accompanying, ominous background music with lots of bass notes and low, rumbling drums. The Internet is a scary place for our children and teenagers. It's a scary place for adults. But it, too, has the potential for great good or great evil. Your child will use the Internet to play games and learn responsibility with sites such as Webkinz.com. They will use it to do research for school projects. They will take practice tests for the ACT, apply for colleges, and potentially even find a roommate on Facebook. (We know kids who have done all of the above.) It will be a source of help in their growing-up years.

In this section we want to look at the Internet in general. Later we will look more closely at social networking sites, chatting/Skyping online, and even cyberbullying. But for now let's take a look at what in the world they're doing on this wide, wide Web . . . and why.

A Different World

We watched Mr. Rogers on television. Now he has a Web site where you can click on the trolley to make it go and even watch wonderfully pixelated video footage from the seventies. Virtually anything and everything is available on the Internet now. I recently downloaded a scene from Electra Woman and Dyna Girl (for those of you who remember the *Krofft Superstar Hour*) for a mother/daughter retreat. You can't buy the videos any longer, but they're right there for all to see online. It's all there if you just know where and how to look.

"How old are they when they start looking?" you may be asking. According to the Rochester Institute of Technology in 2008, 48 percent of students from kindergarten through first grade interact with people on Web sites. Half of those say they do so with their parents watching. (Poses the question . . . what about the other half?) And by the way 48 percent of those students say they saw something online that made them feel uncomfortable, with only three in four children telling an adult.[14]

As far as teenagers go, they spend an average of eleven hours and thirty-two minutes per month online, less than their adult counterparts who spend an average of twenty-nine hours and fifteen minutes. Much of this is due, however, to the fact that kids are in school and a host of other activities that don't allow them to access the Internet. The Nielsen study (2009) that found these statistics also reported that teens spend the majority of their time online either on social networking sites (we promise, we'll get there) or general portals (such as Comcast, Yahoo!, or iGoogle) or search engines (Google, Bing, Ask.com).

If you are reading this book, you are likely one of the parents who is doing your best to be on top of technology. You watch your elementary school student. You have the monitoring software. The computer is in the living room.

And yet, note these statistics:

- Thirty-two percent of teens clear their history so their parents can't see what they've been doing online.
- Sixty-three percent say they know how to hide what they've been doing online from their parents.
- Fifty-two percent have given out personal information (their description or photos) to someone they don't know online.
- Sixteen percent have created e-mail addresses or identities on social networking sites so their parents can't "find" them.
- Eleven percent have unlocked or disabled parental controls (Youth 2009).

Even when we're on top of it, they're often one step ahead. And the Internet (or the marketing brains behind it) sure doesn't seem to mind.

A Deeper Look

Let's look specifically at pornography and the Internet. These search engines they're investing so much time in—or on—make it all too easy. One teenage boy actually said, "I had questions. I didn't want to ask my mom. So I asked Google. Why wouldn't I? I ask it everything else." Makes perfect sense. As a matter of fact, any one of us would have likely done the same thing rather than having awkward conversations with our "out-of-date" parents. It's anonymous. It's easy. And it's right in their living rooms . . . or bedrooms, depending on the location and type of computer.

So they ask one question. The answer is more information than they want. Thirty-four percent of kids actually have unwanted exposure to online pornography.[15] Maybe they don't even ask. They just have a pop-up ad. Or something on the side of their MySpace page. Then they try to click out of it, and it takes them to a pornographic site. For boys, particularly, and an increasing number of girls, this "accidental" surfing can quickly become not so accidental. It can become addictive. According to the *Washington Post* in 2004, eleven million kids regularly viewed pornography online.[16] A little bit like courage in a video game, they develop a sexuality without an actual member of the opposite sex. And with it often comes other individually oriented sexual exploration such as masturbation. Or they feel much freer to ask someone to sext because their threshold has been lowered and tolerance has been raised to erotic ideas.

Pornography addictions aren't the only problem. Much like gaming, simple computer use can become addictive. ReSTART is one of the first treatment centers for online addiction in the U.S. We would guess it is the first of many. The Internet and pornography are and will be the drug of choice for many adolescents. It is "safe" in terms of risk-taking behavior. They are not "bad kids" if they use. They can be anyone they want to be at any time of day or night. Again an Internet addiction is different from heavy Internet use. An addiction interrupts a normal life by affecting the emotional and physical health of the user.

Enough of the scary information. How can you help? A million statistics could make you want to move to Amish country and never even look at a computer again. But computers connect kids to each other, to new opportunities for learning, and even to us when we're away. They are not even a necessary evil . . . unless we allow it to happen.

What's a Modern Parent to Do?

- Do your own research. One of the best ways to safeguard your children is to understand the Internet and the ways it works.
- Talk to your children. Don't be afraid to ask questions. Find out their favorite Web sites and why. Play the games or go to the sites with them and have a conversation related to each.
- Use that good old training-wheels approach. Start them off in small increments of time with little freedom and large adult eyes watching. Widen the boundaries as they earn your trust and become older and more mature.
- Keep a timer for online use, as in gaming. Cyberspace is just as much of a chronological black hole as video games.
- Make sure they know the boundaries on Internet use. A few examples:

- ○ Never trade personal photographs on a site where anyone can have access (Facebook, MySpace, and other sites where friends can see photos and can be negotiable when they're older).
- ○ Never give out personal information to anyone such as your address or description.
- ○ Never respond to anything threatening or inappropriate. Always tell a parent or trusted adult.
- ○ If your child has a new "friend" online, insist on being introduced to that friend, just as you would in real life.
- ○ No computer till homework is done.
- ○ Have a power-off time for your computer, depending on children's age and maturity.
- Keep the computer in a common room. Even if children have laptops, you can regulate use in the beginning to a common room (and have consequences for misuse).
- With younger children share an e-mail account to help them learn what is safe and unsafe, appropriate, and inappropriate.
- Bookmark your child's favorite sites for easy accessibility.
- Monitor your credit card and phone bills for suspicious activity (porn sites often require them).
- Find out what online protection is offered at your child's school and strongly suggest the school have some in place.
- Take your child seriously if they let you know of anything online that has made them uncomfortable.
- Forward any threatening or inappropriate messages to your Internet service provider.
- Watch for signs that your child is becoming addicted: if they become angry or emotional when you ask them to stop, increasing amounts of time spent on the Internet, lying to others about use, failed attempts (on your part or theirs) to control behavior.
- Get protective software. It can tell you where they've been, how long they've been on, and even who they have talked to.

- Get protective software. You can find more information at www. GetNetWise.com or www.InternetSafety.org. Make sure your software includes a filter as well.
- If your child has a phone with Internet access, make sure you have protective software on it.

Social Networking Sites

Last spring several of the girls groups at Daystar talked about the purpose of Lent. Each of the girls came up with something that was a distraction for them from their faith that they wanted to give up until Easter, to remember Jesus' sacrifice. An overwhelming majority of seventh- through twelfth-graders had one answer in common—Facebook. One eighth-grader decided to give up Facebook and concentrate on her relationship with her mom. It only lasted a week. "I just couldn't do it. I couldn't not know or see what everybody was doing. I'll have to find something else that's not as big of a deal to me." Maybe not exactly the idea of Lent but a great picture of the power of social networking sites in the life of a teen.

A Different World

The first time I (Melissa) heard about a blog was from a young man who was angry with his friends. He started a blog (I remember thinking . . . what a strange word!) to talk about why he was angry and what he wanted to do about it. I couldn't imagine that he would put his thoughts and feelings out there for all the world to see and that others would take the time to read them. He did and they did. And now Sissy and I have a blog (with a great deal of forceful encouragement from our publishers). I still have a hard time believing that someone would want to read what we put out there.

This newest attempt at community has taken the world by storm. Whether it's Xanga, MySpace, blogging, Bebo, or Twitter, people are giving continual updates to the masses about where they've been, what they're doing, and even how they feel.

Pew Internet and American Life reports that 65 percent of teens are logged on to some type of social networking site.[17] The kids in our offices repeatedly say, "I don't check my e-mail. I'm on Facebook." For teens particularly, social networking sites have become their social arena. It's how they are invited to birthday parties. It's how they know if their friends are "in a relationship." It's how they share pictures of themselves. (Why would anyone need to carry cameras? One person takes a picture on a cell phone, uploads it to their Facebook page, tags a friend, and the rest of their friends can see who's in it and save it to their own hard drives . . . all in about five minutes).

Our experience is that Facebook is the most popular social networking site with kids. MySpace is a little edgier with often racy ads or videos that pop up on a welcome screen. We don't hear as many kids talk about Bebo or Xanga these days. And statistically at the time we are writing this, only 11 percent of teens are using Twitter.[18] They don't really need to. They just update their Facebook status and have the same immediate effect. It's on their twelve hundred "friends'" newsfeed immediately. And twelve hundred is no exaggeration. As we're writing this, we did a poll of the number of friends our Facebook friends have (high school students) who averaged twelve hundred. Can you even imagine that your son or daughter knows twelve hundred people?

A Deeper Look

The benefits to Facebook are simple. It is how kids connect today. In many ways keeping children off of Facebook is to prevent them from opportunities to connect with and get to know other friends in a non-threatening way. Or at least nonthreatening to them.

In my office I (Sissy) talk to kids every day—boys and girls—who struggle in relationships. They worry about how to make and keep friends. One of the biggest questions is how to move from simply a "hanging out at school" friendship to a "hanging out outside of school" relationship. When we were growing up, we would play at recess or eat lunch with a new friend and then invite them over. For today's child or teen this sounds terribly intimidating.

As we talk about in our book *Raising Girls*, the middle-school and teen years are riddled with self-consciousness for kids. They are embarrassed to stand out. They are afraid of being rejected . . . noticed, even, at times. And so they shrink back many times if they're girls. And they often overcompensate if they're boys, becoming sarcastic and larger than life in their sense of humor. They are afraid to step out and make a genuine friend. In our group counseling sessions, we even help kids on basics such as questions to ask a peer to get a conversation started.

Facebook simplifies all of this. You see a status of one of your friends and give it a thumbs-up. He notices that you've made a gesture and "pokes" you (Facebook language). Or your friend puts up pictures of her spring break, and you comment on how cute a picture is. You can even do something as simple as message a new friend about homework without the frightening actual voices on a phone line. It's a good first step. But it shouldn't be the only step.

Let's jump to those concerns about social networking. One is that your child will have an active, comfortable social life that exists only on Facebook. Social networking sites are a great place to connect but, as you already know, not to develop deep, genuine relationships.

Another risk is that Facebook pages broadcast more information than your child necessarily needs to know. I (Melissa) meet with a sophomore in high school who struggles with her confidence. She recently gave herself a break from Facebook because she thought it was regularly affecting her self-esteem. Because of pictures and status updates, she knew whenever her friends did something without her or she wasn't invited to a party. It can make girls or boys feel either rejected or that they have to keep up with what those twelve hundred friends are doing.

Another concern is precisely those twelve hundred friends. The reality is that your child probably does not know twelve hundred individuals. They are friends of friends, or maybe even people who saw your child's picture and wanted to connect. And they are not necessarily the types of friends you would want your child developing a genuine relationship with.

What's a Modern Parent to Do?

- As soon as your child asks to join a social networking site, ask for their password and log-in information. Check this often in the beginning or if you are suspicious.
- Back to the training wheels, you can check less regularly as your child earns your trust.
- Join the site and ask to be your child's friend (with the requirement that your child says yes). It will help you know more about what your children are doing and who their friends are. It does not, however, give you the access that having their log-in information does.
- Don't panic and don't react. You will see comments and pictures, at times, that will make you want to take your child off of the social networking sites and every other social outlet he or she has ever had access to. You will hear inappropriate words from their friends and see many inappropriate pictures. With these sites you are privy to the very internal lives of teens. Think about your teen years. Don't allow one misstep or two to turn you against their friends. We all had them in one way or another in our growing up years. Use the information to help you grow closer to your teen rather than cause a wedge between you.
- Set out strong guidelines at the beginning. If you see inappropriate language or pictures from your child, let the privilege of having a cell phone work for you. It is a highly motivating consequence. Help your child understand your concerns. Also, it is possible to delete comments after they have been posted.
- Make sure they only accept friend requests from actual people they know. In the beginning check to make sure. Assert and reassert that it's not that you don't trust them; it's the rest of the world that you don't trust.
- Parent in community on this one, as well. Allow your child to join a social networking site in a moderate time range—not as

the first child in their class but with a group of other kids whose parents you trust and respect.

- Check their privacy settings. Your child can set up their page to make it accessible to anyone or just to their friends. This is done under privacy settings on the profile link. Privacy settings can also control who sees their contact information, if their page comes up in search engines, and who is allowed to see their pictures. Familiarize yourself with the workings of this feature, and then teach your child.

iChat/Facebook Chat/Google Talk/Skype/ Immediate, Online, Conversational Gratification

"My sister has taken 'being with her friends' to a whole new level. Every time I see her, her computer is open, and she is on Skype with several of her friends. She walks around the house carrying her laptop with it open and her friends' faces on it. The other day I kept trying to ask her a question, and she wouldn't get off. So finally I walked in and said something to her about something we were supposed to do. She yelled at me and I yelled back. Then she turned to her friends (on her computer) and said, 'Can you believe she treats me like that?' I mean, with Skype, she talks to her friends ALL THE TIME. When she's not with them at school, they're all sitting on their computers talking to each other."

At first, it was iChat. When Facebook swelled in popularity, they developed Facebook chat. Gmail has now come up with their own version of Google Chat. And, now, there's Skype. They are not just talking to each other constantly on the phone, writing messages back and forth "chatting." Now they're talking with the cameras embedded in their computers. Skype makes the video phone system we all imagined growing up a reality. And it is a fun, convenient reality for kids in today's technological culture.

A Different World

A young man came into Daystar last week having been grounded from not only his computer but his entire social life. It seems that he had a Facebook chat session with a young girl in which he told her that he "really liked her boobs and her butt." Fortunately his parents had that whole software protection thing down and were alerted to the conversation within a few hours. And then, according to him, his life changed pretty drastically.

The reality is that kids have instant, continual access to each other twenty-four hours a day, seven days a week, with their computers (and cell phones). And because much of this communication is anonymous, they feel the freedom to be a little braver, a little more grandiose, and often a lot more stupid.

According to the Center for Media Research in August 2009 the following statistics are true of kids *and parents* today:

- Parents believe that 10 percent of their children have pretended to be someone else while talking online; 26 percent actually have.
- Parents believe that 18 percent of their children have made fun of someone online; 37 percent actually have.
- Parents believe 20 percent of their children have said something they later regretted online; 39 percent have.
- Parents believe 16 percent of their kids have said something online that they wouldn't normally share in public; 28 percent actually have.
- Parents believe that 2 percent of their children have sent naked or semi-naked photos or videos to someone else; 13 percent have, and 24 percent have sent pictures they're not sure they would want shared.[19]

A Deeper Look

Chatting can be innocent in itself. It is one of the primary ways middle- and high-schoolers today communicate. A FOX News Report in November of 2007 said that nearly half of teens aged thirteen to eighteen use instant messaging.[20] The numbers have only gone up from there. However, according to the kids we talk to, much of this dies down once teens have cars and can see their friends in person rather than just through their computer screens. But for a time this type of online communication is what takes up a significant portion of their free time if we'll allow it.

The benefits of iChat, Skype, and similar ways of online social networking is that it can help your child build in-school relationships out of school. They can strengthen their connections with each other and develop closer friendships. With opposite sex relationships, although there are definitely inherent risks, many early (as in middle school) relationships exist only online, with the average length of "going out" being a whopping forty-eight hours. Better that way, you may say.

IMs are also convenient when conversations are a little more difficult to have . . . say when you need to break up with your long-term, forty-eight-hour girlfriend. The same FOX News Report stated that 43 percent of teens use instant messaging for conversations they wouldn't want to have in person. Twenty-two percent use it to ask people out or to accept someone else's invitation. And 13 percent use IM to break up.

IM and other programs like it, however, aren't just for those awkward relational moments. Cyberbullying has become such a significant issue that as we write this chapter, two bills are currently in the house judiciary committee attempting to regulate this growing, tragic phenomenon. Just last week a mother of a teenage girl told me (Sissy) that two girls had set up a Facebook for her daughter. They used her pictures but created an identity that had a little bit of truth and an awful lot of exaggeration of every one of this unsuspecting girl's insecurities. It was cruel, but the girl was afraid to do anything about it because she didn't want to upset her peers.

This story is one of countless we have heard where the cruelty of girls goes unchecked because of their "anonymity." Girls have been mean since our grandmothers were in school (and probably their grandmothers, too). But there was a little more accountability when they had to face the actual faces—and possibly even the teachers, parents, or principals—of those girls they had hurt. Today they can bully without the other girl even knowing who did it. Or, in the bullies' minds, it has the same effect. Because the words are typed and not spoken, they won't get caught.

Much of the same is true for online "stalking." The kids we work with will jokingly say, "I'm a Facebook stalker," because they can spend hours and hours looking at what their friends have been doing without their friends knowing. But the real stalkers are out there. And they are finding our sons and daughters, befriending them online, and then iChatting/Skyping/Gchatting with them, as well.

In 2006, 54 percent of teens reported to frequent, private conversations with online strangers through IM; 10 percent of tweens; 27 percent have talked with an online stranger about sex.[21] A twelve-year-old in our office recently found out that the "sixteen-year-old she was in love with" was a forty-five-year-old with a daughter her age. Thankfully her father found out after she had given him their phone number but just before she gave him their address. There are countless similar stories out there. And those statistics are just for IM on the various Web sites. Skype presents a whole host of other problems.

The difference in Skype and other Web-based chat programs is that Skype is established on a peer-to-peer network rather than a Web-based server. A typical server like Yahoo! has moderators watching for suspicious activity or inappropriate content. Although they aren't able to catch everything, users can often push panic buttons to report activity as well as frequent posts giving warnings against inappropriate content. Because Skype is peer to peer, users speak directly to each other without even registering with any type of server. To use Skype, users create a profile with optional personal information such as age and then place themselves online. Then users from around the world can send messages and call. The London *Sunday Times* in 2007 called Skype a "magnet for paedophiles and sexual predators."[22] The problem is that this very magnet is also becoming the next big thing, according to the teenagers we see in our offices.

What's a Modern Parent to Do?

Fifty-one percent of parents do not know if they have monitoring software on their computers, according to the National Center for

Missing & Exploited Children and Cox Communications Parental Internet Monitoring Survey in 2005. Forty-two percent of parents don't know what their teenagers are communicating in chat rooms or on IM.[23] The first thing a modern parent can do is MAKE SURE YOU HAVE MONITORING SOFTWARE.

- Have software and filters in place. Software and filters. Software and filters. Get software and filters.
- Have conversations with your child around the importance of talking to you about any type of problem that comes up online, whether it involves cyberbullying, inappropriate content, or even conflict with a friend.
- Set some ground rules for IM/Skype/or any manner in which your children are talking over the Internet. Vicki Courtney suggests a written contract to have your child sign with rules you both agree on. For example:
  - You are only allowed to talk to people you know.
  - "Friends of friends" are not people you know. Don't add them to your buddy list.
  - Don't click on links you receive from others. My (Sissy's) sister had just started working as the assistant director of Development at Daystar Counseling Ministries. Her first week she clicked on a link that appeared to be harmless that someone had posted on her Facebook page. It immediately sent a message to all of her friends, many of whom were contributors to our ministry saying, "I found some naughty pictures of you I thought you'd want to see." To this day we have no idea where it came from or how it got there. But, as you can imagine, she was humiliated and had to spend several hours her first week of work explaining how she knew nothing about naughty pictures!
  - No public chatrooms.
  - Never type anything you wouldn't say face-to-face.

- Talk about the importance of relationships and conversations in the "real world." Online conversations can help deepen relationships at times, but kids need to understand the importance of face-to-face connections, as well.
- Watch for warning signs that your child may have gotten in over his/her head. If he spends increasing hours online in conversation with the same person, logs off whenever you come in the room, or has trouble making friends, it may be a good idea to restrict computer time and do a little more investigating yourself.
- Log on and learn about any server or online communication tool your children are using. To help and protect them, you will need to understand the workings of the site yourself.
- Learn a foreign language: IM. POS means parents over shoulder. P911 means parent alert. PAW means parents are watching. These statements and many more like them are important for us to recognize, understand, and address in the instant conversations of our children.
- Stay aware of everyone on your child's buddy list. Learn how to block unwanted conversation yourself and teach this important skill to your children.
- Periodically Google search your child's name to see if there are any instances where they have been bullied or the target of some type of public embarrassment.
- Keep the computer in a common room for as long as you can. (The prevalence of laptops makes this difficult.)
- Know that technology is the way of today's world—and especially today's teen.

"I just don't feel good about this new girl he's talking about," a sixteen-year-old's mother told his father. "He doesn't even know her, and they're talking like they're in love with each other. They've gotten romantically involved without even spending time together or even really hearing each other's voices. How can they think this is a real relationship?"

This conversation could have taken place yesterday in countless homes all over the world . . . or in your home. But rather than the parents standing next to their microwave and stainless appliances, imagine things a little more rustic. She stirs a pot in a wood-burning stove. He scratches his beard as the Pony Express rider brings in the most recent stack of mail. These parents could have been talking today . . . or in 1861.

Parents back then must have been concerned, too. Their children had to go on supervised outings to spend time with each other. All conversations took place face-to-face. And then, all of a sudden, the mail service began. Letters were carried from town to town on horseback. A guy could date girls he had never laid eyes on. She could be caught up in the romantic words of a young man she knew nothing about. Doesn't sound quite so different, does it?

Today, however, technology, rather than horses, carries messages from one child or teen to another. And it happens both instantly and often anonymously. Our children are learning a new language and a new way of communicating that language. More than anything, they need us, as modern parents, to do the same things parents have done for ages: love them with both awareness and intentionality. They need us to keep up, to be in the world of technology with them. And then at times they need us to remove them, to give them time to stretch their legs and their brains in ways that require a little more creativity and a little less battery power.

A Sunday Drive

A Few Nontechnological Suggestions

1. Bake a cake together for an elderly neighbor.
2. Build a birdhouse and place it in the backyard.
3. Pick seasonal berries and make jam or jelly together.
4. Have a chess or checkers tournament.

5. Plant a garden. Let your child choose a favorite fruit or vegetable to plant and take care of.

6. Start an ongoing monopoly game that relates to your family's life or interests . . . Hog-Opoly, for example, for Sissy or Lighthouse-Opoly for Melissa.

7. If you live by the lake, build sailboats with your children. Take them to the lake and have a family race.

8. Go fishing.

9. Go on a bike ride to lunch, a park, or a destination of some kind.

10. Pack a picnic basket on a Saturday or Sunday afternoon and have lunch outside.

11. Volunteer at the neighborhood animal shelter to walk their dogs or play with kittens.

12. Rake the leaves of a neighbor or family member who has been sick or is elderly.

13. Put these ideas and some like them in a basket and have your child draw one out for a surprise adventure!

A World of Warning

*Henrietta had an anxious and affectionate disposition and
the impossibility of keeping all the people she loved always
safely together under her eye was a trial to her.*

—Elizabeth Goudge, *The Blue Hills*[24]

*H*ow do I teach my son about safety without completely freaking him out?" We hear this question, or one like it, at almost every parenting seminar we offer. It is a question of our time and our culture. We are living in a post–9/11 world with terror threats staying in the yellow and orange ranges. One in four girls and one in six boys are sexually abused by their eighteenth birthday.[25] In one year 797,500 children (under the age of eighteen) were reported missing, making an average of 2,185 children reported missing daily.[26] It is a world of danger . . . and a world very different from when we grew up.

I (Sissy) remember waking up on Saturday mornings with cartoons that were as inappropriate as the coyote bullying the roadrunner and as scary as Casper the Friendly Ghost. I would eat breakfast, tell my parents good-bye, and head off on my bike for the day. That banana-seated, streamers-on-the-handlebars, purple wonder would carry me off into a world of adventure. I would spend a few hours playing in the creek with my best friend, Ryan. We would race our bikes to the edge of the neighborhood a couple of miles away and land at one of our other friend's houses for lunch. The afternoon would involve a host of other activities that involved no technology and no fear, on my part or that of my parents.

I (Melissa) grew up a few years before that. I was babysitting when I still needed a babysitter. My mom came and checked on me, but the most imminent danger was coming from inside the house with my lack of control over the kids rather than outside from a stranger. I walked home from school every day in grade school by myself. We played kick the can every night until bedtime. The kids in our neighborhood took blankets and laid on them in the backyard to watch movies on the drive-in theater behind our house. We would explore old houses, search for forsaken treasures in junk piles, and build secret hideouts in the trees. One of our college-aged interns recently said to me, "Melissa, I don't have stories like you do from my childhood. We lived in a pretty safe neighborhood, but my parents still worried. Your childhood sounds like such an adventure."

It was. And the "pretty" safe neighborhoods of today make many of those adventures a moot point. We just don't feel comfortable with our children taking off for the day on their bikes. We are nervous for them even to play for too long in the front yard. Not when we hear story after story of abduction, abuse, and exploitation. It's everywhere, which begs the question: How do I teach my child about safety without freaking her out?

Safety First

"Rather than teaching children to fear strangers, which is at best, woefully inadequate, we need to use positive messages. Children need to learn skills and confidence, not fear and avoidance," says Dr. Daniel Broughton, a pediatrician at the Mayo Clinic.[27] We couldn't agree more, so we've come up with a few suggestions to instill safety skills and confidence in your child. And we'll come back to the "freaking out" portion of the question a little later.

- Teach your child his name, address, and phone number (with area code). Children should know their address and your cell phone number.
- Help them learn your cell number by pairing it with a song they love. It can be anything from the ABCs to "Jingle Bells."
- Remain calm when you are talking to your son or daughter (we'll talk more about this later).
- Be aware of the "Stranger Danger" idea. It has been known to create more anxiety in children than resourcefulness. Help her or him come up with specific examples of people he knows well and those he doesn't. Teach them that strangers can be kind, but the best rule is to check with you before he talks to anyone he doesn't know. Explain to her that she doesn't have to worry about strangers if she follows your safety rules. Although we don't want to instill fear, children need to know to keep their distance from people they don't know—not to speak to them, go anywhere with them, or take something from them without you being there. If a stranger does approach them, they need to let you or a trusted adult know.
- Tell your child not to get into a car with a stranger, friend, or even a family member if you have not given permission or let them know about it ahead of time, or if they feel uncomfortable. Dr. Broughton says that the majority of children reported missing are either runaways or were taken by noncustodial parents.
- Make sure they tell you or an adult anytime they see something that looks or feels strange like a car they don't know circling the block or slowing down in front of your house.
- Come up with a lost plan when you're in a public place outside the home, such as in a large store or business. Have her go to the checkout counter, find a store clerk, or other adult in authority in that location.

- Use the buddy system. If your children are away from home, make sure they are with friends.
- If your children walk somewhere, teach them places to avoid such as parks and vacant lots. Don't let them walk alone.
- Listen to your children and respect their feelings. Children are intuitive, and if they feel uncomfortable, they often have a reason.
- Tell your child always to tell an adult where he or she is going.
- Help older children find someone they can confide in besides you if there is an issue they are uncomfortable talking to you about.
- Teach them the anatomical names of their body parts. If they are using slang, you may not notice what they are trying to tell you or are telling someone else as much as if you heard the correct words.
- Ask your children to tell you if someone asks them to keep a secret, whether it is an adult or another child. Make sure they know they won't get in trouble for telling mom or dad.
- Don't force children to give affection if they don't want to. They need to understand "body boundaries" and that they can always say no, even if it makes you a little uncomfortable socially from time to time.
- Keep a high quality photo of your child on hand at all times, in case anything were to happen. Promptly report a missing child. The Amber Plan recovered more than 130 children in its first two years of operation.
- Your child should be reminded always to think first and to know how to get help.
- Practice different scenarios with role playing either strangers or familiar people where your child can try out your new rules and his or her new voice!

Your Rules, Their Awareness

According to the U.S. Departments of Justice, most victims of non-family abductions were age twelve or older.[28] Therefore it is extremely important that our preteen and teenagers continue to learn about safety and develop their own awareness of dangerous situations. This is where it gets a little tricky. Try to remember the last time you laid down a hard and fast rule for your twelve-, fourteen-, or even sixteen-year-old. Probably didn't go over so well. Three words in, there were eyes either rolling or glazed over, or your words of wisdom were cut off with the proverbial "MOOOOMMMM" or "DAADDD." When we lay down the law, they often either don't listen at all or do their best to break it . . . just because we are the ones who laid it down.

Adolescence is a time of independence, intimacy (with anyone but us), impulsivity, and invincibility. Isn't it ironic how all of these words start with an *i*, which also describes their typical frame of mind during these years. In our book *Raising Girls* we devote a considerable amount of time to describing normal development for a teenager, which we refer to as the "narcissistic" years.[29]

All of these characteristics ARE a natural part of their development. They are clamoring for independence from you. They want to become their own people and, because you have been the ones closest to them, they have to push off of you the hardest in order to do so. They long for intimacy with both same and opposite sexes so many of their decisions will be based on this deep need to feel connected. They are impulsive in their decision-making and feel that they are invincible. "It will never happen to me," is the invincibility slogan for teens. The combination of these characteristics? A recipe for risk, which is also something their adolescent egos are craving.

"What's a modern parent to do?" you may ask. We want our safety rules to become their instinctive awareness. At the same time we can't talk instincts into them. They have to learn for themselves. And, if we continue to teach directly, they often either rebel or become so dependent on our voice telling them what to do that they don't develop their own awareness. This dependence can cause them to make even more risky decisions when we're not there or they haven't heard us speak to a specific issue. How many times have you heard your preteen or teenager say, "I just wasn't thinking"? The bottom line is that we want to teach them to think.

We know, we know . . . we haven't answered your modern parent question. We would advocate an approach that we wrote about in our book *The Back Door to Your Teen's Heart*. The first line of the book is, "To the degree that kids can predict you, they will dismiss you."[30] In these years they are quick on the draw to dismiss. How do we communicate safety to them in a way that they'll both hear and think? A front-door approach is more of what we talked about in the last section, one of direct teaching. We've already done that. And they are confident they've heard it all. So now our teaching necessitates more of a back-door, unpredictable approach. What does that look like? Here are a few suggestions we think might help give you options and a springboard for further backdoor ideas:

- Take a self-defense class together, such as some type of martial arts.
- If you are a member of your neighborhood YMCA or another gym, take Tae Bo or kickboxing rather than an aerobics class. Workout together in ways that are healthy and empowering. If they are feeling especially independent and won't go with you, offer to pay for a friend to go with them.
- If your teen calls someone a "creeper" (which is one of their most common descriptors these days) or you get a sense that someone has made them uncomfortable, find out why. Ask them questions that can help develop their own intuition and then encourage them for their intuitiveness.
- Read a book out loud together with adolescent risk-taking behavior like S. E. Hinton's *The Outsiders*. Ask questions about how your son or daughter feels and what he/she thinks about decisions the characters have made.

- Find other voices to reinforce safety and good decision-making skills. Find out what programs they're doing in school to increase awareness, and then have your child tell you about the program in his or her own words. Call and ask the youth director to devote a lesson and small group time to safety and awareness.
- If you know an older teen or group of teens you trust, have them speak to younger teens. This can take place in the youth group, at school, or in any arena where kids gather and can have a positive impact on each other.
- If a situation has come up on the news where a teen has been abducted or gotten in trouble, tell your child about it. Ask him or her what he thinks he could have done to prevent the situation.
- Be aware of your child's being approached by an "agent" for modeling, acting, or other appealing-to-their-narcissism type of career. Adults hanging around malls approach kids under the guise of setting up a job interview. Make sure to verify who they are and their credentials before making further contact, and accompany your child to any appointments.
- If your child makes an unwise decision and faces natural consequences at school or even legally, be cautious to step in and save them from the consequences. Those consequences can be other voices to reinforce the lessons you are teaching. And, again, if you rescue them every time, they may come to expect your rescue.
- Give your children opportunities to make mistakes at home, within reason. Don't overprotect them to the point that they never take risks. Often the consequences carry more weight than our words. But they have to have the freedom to make the choice. And we would much rather them experience consequences under our roof.

- In the mist of developing their intuition and making their own mistakes, they still need your boundaries. Set boundaries in community. Find a group of parents you trust and decide together when you will let them start to go to the mall in packs, group date, etc. The portion of their brains that controls impulsivity is not fully developed yet, so they need your widening boundaries to match their maturing instincts.

Their Safety, Your Anxiety

The two of us were recently in Texas speaking at a mother/daughter event. As is always the case when we travel that direction, we landed and quickly sought out the best Mexican food nearby. After a fiesta-filled dinner, we were making our way back to our rental car in the parking lot. Standing near our car were a woman and her precious four-year-old daughter. Feeling extra connected to mothers and daughters that weekend, we turned to them and said "Hi, how are you?" The mother's immediate response was to snatch her daughter by the arm and scream (we're really not exaggerating) "DON'T YOU DARE TALK TO STRANGERS! THEY'LL TAKE YOU FROM YOUR MOMMY, AND YOU'LL NEVER SEE ME AGAIN!" Talk about stranger danger, . . . and we're not sure if she felt more danger or we did!

According to psychologist and author Tamar E. Chansky, Ph.D., anxiety is the number one mental-health problem in young people today.[31] Based on the children and adolescents that come to Daystar for counseling, we would have to concur. The numbers of kids we see on a daily basis who are facing debilitating anxiety is staggering. Girls who are so afraid of going to school that they throw up every morning. Boys who have such high degrees of social anxiety that they either freeze in certain situations or become explosive because of a lack of control. We see them in all shapes, sizes, and ages in our offices. (We'll talk a little more about anxiety and kids in chapter 6.)

One of the biggest contributors to anxiety in children is . . . you guessed it, anxiety in parents. And of course you're anxious. Just reading the statistics in these first two chapters is enough to make a nonanxious

parent anxious. Statistics have proven that your child can meet a preda-
tor at school, in church, at summer camp, or in the safety of your own
home through the marvels of the Internet. They're everywhere. And all
you really want to do is protect your child.

But sometimes the news gets to be too much. It's just too many stories that hit too close to home. And so you panic . . . a little. Your words
of warning come out stronger than you intended. You keep them home
from playing in the neighborhood. You decide that summer camp just
may not be right for your child.

Unfortunately even a little panic leaks. When we teach parenting
seminars, we tell parents over and over that their stuff spills over into the
lives of their kids. We keep thinking someone in the audience is going to
throw something at us, . . . but they don't. Maybe because they remember
something their parents did that spilled over onto them . . . even that
little bit of panic.

In an article by Rick Nauert for *PsychCentral*, Golda Ginsburg,
Ph.D., a child psychologist at Johns Hopkins School of Medicine, says
that up to 65 percent of children living with an anxious parent meet
criteria for an anxiety *disorder*.[32] One of the most common responses
for anxious parents is to hover. Foster Cline and Jim Fay, our favorite
experts in the world of discipline, call these parents "helicopter parents"
in their book *Parenting with Love and Logic*. "They hover over and then
rescue their children whenever trouble arises. They're forever running
lunches, permission slips, band instruments, and homework assignments
to school. They're always pulling their children out of jams. Not a day
goes by when they're not protecting little junior from something—
usually from a growing experience—he needs or deserves."[33] These parents prevent rather than protect. Their children are not free to take the
risks necessary to develop independence. Helicopter parents scoop up
their toddlers before they skin their knee and don't allow their teenagers to begin to forge their own way in the world. Why would they? The
world is not safe.

In his book, *Freeing Your Child from Anxiety*, Chansky outlines a few
parenting behaviors that are associated with anxiety in children:

- Parental Overcontrol: Instrusive parenting, exerting control in conversation, limiting of autonomy and independence in conversation.
- Overprotection: Excessive caution and protective behaviors without cause.
- Modeling of Anxious Interpretation: Agreeing with child's distortion of the risk in a situation, reinforcing the idea that normal things in the world are too scary to approach.
- Tolerance or Encouragement of Avoidance Behavior: Suggesting or agreeing with not trying something difficult.
- Rejection or Criticism: Disapproving, judgmental, dismissive, or critical behavior.
- Conflict: Two out of five studies found fighting, arguing, and disharmony in family associated with high levels of anxiety.[34]

When children are overprotected, they don't learn survival skills. They don't learn how to handle real-life dangers in ways that will protect them when they truly need protection. And they will also miss out on many of the adventures that our childhoods were full of.

Their Need for Adventure

What are some of your favorite childhood memories? We would guess that a few of them might include summer nights catching fireflies or playing kick the can in the neighborhood, learning to ride a bike, or playing in a tree house. Think back on the feelings you associate with those memories: again, we're guessing, but how about contentment? Fun? Freedom? Confidence? Were you ever a pirate or a princess traveling in a faraway land? How about a fireman or a superhero? Those activities and ideas are riddled with adventure. Childhood is made for such adventures. And what adventure is to childhood, risk is to adolescence. Both adventure and an appropriate level of adolescent risk are foundational to raising kids with confidence. As we allow them to explore the world safely, we communicate our belief in their competence as explorers. And that competence mixes together with all of the skinned knees and speeding tickets to create kids who are confident in themselves and enjoying the adventure of their growing up years.

Your Need for Trust

Let's go back to the original question. How do I teach my children safety without freaking them out? It all starts with where you start. How do YOU teach your children safety without freaking them out? How do you feel safe when your child is out exploring in this world of warning?

It is easy to answer that question with a blanket statement like, "Trust God with your children." But that blanket statement often doesn't do much to quell our anxiety. It leaves us a little flat. Anxiety makes it hard to trust.

We'll say it anyway. *Trust God with your children.* We'll say it because for more than sixty combined years of working with kids, we have seen them hurt, rejected, abused, betrayed, left, and a host of other atrocities none of us would want our children to face. But they do. And year after year we are both more convinced that we serve a God who allows pain but redeems it. Maybe he knows the secret, too. Strength comes from struggle. Strength comes in struggle . . . his strength, not ours. His strength comes for us, and his strength comes for them. The blanket statement is true. God loves your children more than you could ever imagine—more than you could ever love them. He wants good for them, the best for them, and he will bring it to completion.

Fear paralyzes us and keeps us from being free to enjoy and have relationships, with our children or with God. But the Bible uses that blanket statement and uses it often. Sixty-seven times Scripture tells us to "fear not."

We would venture to say that the opposite of fear is not a lack of fear but trust. Somewhere deep down all of us know we're powerless to change things or truly protect our children the way we long to. But we don't want to parent out of fear. When we do, the emphasis is more on preventing than on encouraging. It becomes more about control than it does relationship. It centers on what is wrong in the world rather than who you and your child can be in the midst of it.

Trust God. Fear not. Studying God's Word can help hide these words inside your heart. They are words to learn on—words to bring his peace, confidence, and our trust to fruition.

- For God did not give us a spirit of timidity, but a spirit of power, of love and of self-discipline. (2 Tim. 1:7)
- GOD's strong name is our help, the same GOD who made heaven and earth. (Ps. 124:8 *The Message*)
- So do not fear, for I am with you; do not be dismayed, for I am your God. I will strengthen you and help you; I will uphold you with my righteous right hand. (Isa. 41:10)
- The LORD is my light and my salvation—whom shall I fear? The LORD is the stronghold of my life—of whom shall I be afraid? When evil men advance against me to devour my flesh, when my enemies and my foes attack me, they will stumble and fall. Though an army besiege me, my heart will not fear; though war break out against me, even then will I be confident. (Ps. 27:1–3)
- The LORD is my shepherd, I shall not be in want. He makes me lie down in green pastures, he leads me beside quiet waters, he restores my soul. He guides me in paths of righteousness for his name's sake. Even though I walk through the valley of the shadow of death, I will fear no evil, for you are with me; your rod and your staff, they comfort me. You prepare a table before me in the presence of my enemies. You anoint my head with oil; my cup overflows. Surely goodness and love will follow me all the days of my life, and I will dwell in the house of the LORD forever. (Ps. 23)
- Who shall separate us from the love of Christ? Shall trouble or hardship or persecution or famine or nakedness or danger or sword? As it is written: "For your sake we face death all day long; we are considered as sheep to be slaughtered." No, in all these things we are more than conquerors through him who loved us. For I am convinced that neither death nor life, neither

angels nor demons, neither the present nor the future, nor
any powers, neither height nor depth, nor anything else in all
creation, will be able to separate us from the love of God that is
in Christ Jesus our Lord. (Rom. 8:35–39)

This truth gives us confidence. He is our reason not to fear. He gives
us the ability and grace to teach our children safety without freaking
them out—without freaking us out. Instead of parenting out of fear, we
can echo for our children the prayer Paul prayed for those who were like
his children:

> And this is my prayer: that your love may abound
> more and more in knowledge and depth of insight, so
> that you may be able to discern what is best and may
> be pure and blameless until the day of Christ, filled
> with the fruit of righteousness that comes through
> Jesus Christ—to the glory and praise of God.
> (Phil. 1:9–11)

A Sunday Drive

For Children

1. *The Glasses Game.* Get two pairs of silly glasses/sunglasses. Name
one pair "danger glasses" and one "safety glasses." Parent puts on one
pair and child puts on the other. The parent, with the safety glasses, says,
"I see someone coming to the front door." The child responds through
the "danger glasses" with "I see _____." The parent helps the child
see the same scenario through safe eyes. Trade glasses. Repeat the game
with different scenarios and different family members wearing different
glasses.

2. *The "What If" Game.* Write out several scenarios on pieces of paper and put them in a container. The scenarios would be things like: "What if you lose your mom in the grocery store?" "What if your dad is in the shower and someone comes to the door?" Any time the child gives a safe, appropriate answer, reward points. The parents can play, too. Whoever has the most points, wins the game.

3. *Safety Charades.* Play charades with different safety scenarios that teams can guess such as a child calling 9-1-1, a child confronted by a stranger, a child walking through a park, etc.

For Teens

1. Have your teenager and their friends make two movies. One would be safety dos and the other safety don'ts. This can be something they show their younger siblings.

2. Have your teenager (and friends) create a board game for younger kids about safety.

3. Have your teen (and friends) offer a class on safety for younger children in the neighborhood (with your approval for content). Not only will younger kids love learning from the older ones, but this can also be a great incentive as a money-making project.

4. Have dinner with your teen, one of their friends, and that friend's parent. Talk about real-life safety situations that have happened with other teens. Because they have an audience, they are often more likely to listen.

The Issue of Entitlement

There was meaning in pain; it taught you how to survive with a modicum of grace when you did not get what you wanted.

—Anne Lamott, *Grace Eventually*[35]

*L*ast month my daughter spent more than two thousand dollars on clothing without my permission. I think we've got a problem." (Let's come back to this word *we*.) The teenage daughter, however, didn't believe she had any part in the problem. "I don't know what the big deal is. We have the money and I like clothes. My parents know I never wear the same dress twice, so they shouldn't blame me for spending money." (Let's come back to this word *blame*.) The mother brought her daughter into counseling for help. "I need you to teach her the value of money," is what she wanted, to be exact (Let's come back to this word *you*.) When I (Melissa) asked her what she had done in terms of consequences for her daughter's excessive spending, she said, "Oh, nothing. I don't want to damage her fragile self-esteem."

We have a problem, is right. Our culture has a problem. And that is the problem of a generation of kids who say, "They shouldn't blame me." These kids are entitled. Entitlement is the sense that we deserve all that we get and more. Entitled children are demanding, narcissistic, and believe the blame lies with anyone but them. And we, as adults, are afraid to damage their self-esteem. We're afraid they'll feel hurt or rejected. We're afraid they'll believe we don't love them, which they will most likely tell us if we don't give them what they want (and want right then). The real problem is that our fear of creating insecurity in our children often guarantees it.

The Origins of Entitlement

Every child wants. I (Sissy) remember how exciting the day was every year when the Sears Wish Book arrived in the mail. I would spend hours pouring over the toy section, turning down the pages of dolls that walked and stuffed animals that looked especially cuddly. What about you? Do you remember Saturday mornings, not just the cartoons but the commercials? In my memory the colors were extra bright, the music was extra loud, and the children were oh so happy playing with the newest and latest board game or action figure. Do you remember how intensely you wanted everything that caught your eye? Of course, you did. You were a child. Children want. They wish. They hope. They don't have an innate sense of limits on much of anything. A child has to be taught the word *no*, and their first and most powerful teacher is you.

The Parental Part

The mother in my (Melissa's) office wanted me to teach her daughter the value of money. She wanted to be the good guy. She didn't want to be the one setting limits. And neither do we at times. We understand not wanting to damage our daughter's self-esteem. We want to ensure our son's love for us, even when he is spending the weekend with his dad. We feel like our child's life is hard in so many other ways, at least we can give them _____. (Fill in the blank with whatever they want right now.)

They want, and we have the ability to fulfill that want, to make them happy, at least in this small way. And the next small way. And the next. Sooner or later the wanting on their part winds its desperate way into demanding, and we have a child with a strong sense of entitlement.

With almost every child we see in our offices who we would characterize as demanding, we can look back and find at least one parent who has been afraid or uncomfortable setting limits or simply would rather not be the bad guy. Suffice it to say that your children will expect their friends, their future spouses, their employers, and the world to treat them in the manner to which they've become accustomed—which may not be a manner that reality supports.

The Role of Culture

So, what does reality support? It depends on whether you're talking about the reality they often live in (the reality exists inside their books and television shows for tweens and teens) or the reality that you and I have come to know. One reality feeds off words like *whatever* and *as if*, while those words in the other world would cause us to lose our jobs or at least put some serious tension between us and the one to whom we were so condescendingly speaking.

Since I (Sissy) spend so much time talking to adolescent girls, I do my best to stay culturally relevant. I recently watched a television show that is all the rage these days. It featured a set of teenage girls and guys living in New York. The background for many of their get-togethers was a swanky, upscale bar in Manhattan where they would gossip over cosmopolitans and mojitos. As if . . .

One family at Daystar wrestles with allowing their son to watch a very "mild" show for tweens featuring precious children who are really disrespectful to their parents and get away with it. All characters also have their own iPods, iPhones, and i-anything else they might want. These parents believe there is a statistically significant correlation between their son's attitude and his time spent watching the show. He turns off the television set with a serious sense of entitlement.

In a parenting class we teach with our friend and colleague David Thomas, we talk about living in a culture that is at war against character. We would take that a step further to say that we live in a culture that advocates entitlement. So, what can we do? Do we simply throw out the televisions and turn off the iPods? Let's start by what our friends at LifeWay call "taking off the tiaras."

The Royal Syndrome

During a recent parenting seminar on *Raising Girls*, the children's minister followed us to our car at the end of a session to ask, "Can you please speak to these parents about this whole 'princess thing'?" Lest we be hypocritical here, we do have to admit that our *Raising Girls* book has a cute cover with a girl's photo from the forehead up wearing a tiara. We chose not to remind the children's minister about that.

On our last trip to Disney World (and we do go often), they had opened up a portion of Cinderella's castle for makeovers and costumes for little princesses. The girls were precious wandering up and down Frontierland in their ball gowns and tiaras. They are precious at five but not so precious at fifteen. Actually, the girls in costume would still look precious; it's their attitudes that start to tarnish the crowns.

Our friend, the children's minister, wasn't saying that girls aren't little princesses. What she was saying is that the problem occurs when the little princesses start to see us as their royal subjects. And let's not let the boys off the hook. The royal rubs off on them, as well.

My (Sissy's) mom recently bought our three-year-old friend Afton a bat for his birthday from a toy store. It was a soft bat, if you're thinking about the last chapter on safety, that came with a soft ball. The really cool part of the bat, especially for Afton, was that whenever it made contact, the sounds of a cheering crowd emanated from some type of internal speaker. As you can imagine, Afton loved it. He banged that bat on everything from the coffee table to his puppy dog's head. In SAT (the college entrance exam) terms, what crowns are to little girls, cheering crowds are to little boys. The toy was a wonderful gift in itself, but we don't want Afton, or any other little boy, to expect us to be a constant part of his cheering throng.

We want our children to feel loved, valued, celebrated, honored even. But we don't want them to expect to be treated that way at all times. If it's all we ever reflect to them of who they are, the honor and accolades can quickly become not only their expectation of the way we should treat them but another feather in their crown of entitlement.

The Faces of Entitlement

Money Makes the World . . .

Typically, when we think of entitlement, we think of the young girl in the beginning of this chapter. She, however, is not even close to the only one. I (Melissa) recently met a precocious, engaging, entitled ten-year-old girl by the name of Allison. I went to Allison's home for a meeting one evening, and Allison met me at the door. "I've heard so much about you. Everyone says such lovely things," Allison enthusiastically remarked. (I taught Allison's mom when she was in high school.) "My mom is so happy that you are here. Before we see her, would you like a tour?" Allison promptly took me through her house, which included a suite on the fourth floor just for Allison and her little brother. The suite included a flat-screen television, microwave, mini-fridge, Wii console, and bedroom for each child, which included a closet that was larger than my bedroom at home. Talk about the manner to which you've become accustomed—Allison had it all, including Seven jeans, a Juicy top and a Coach bag that she hung on her arm like a fur wrap. Allison was charming. Her manners were impeccable. She smiled and truly did her best to make me feel both welcome and important.

My guess is that, behind closed doors, Allison can be quite demanding. If she doesn't have the latest purse, coolest gadget, or trendiest clothes, she begins to feel insecure. And even when she is keeping up, once she gets whatever is the latest, she realizes that it doesn't fulfill like she thought it would.

"I have to be careful where I go to college," a senior in high school said in one of my (Sissy's) girls groups recently. "I get so sucked in to materialism, and I just don't want to go there. It's this revolving door of insecurity for me. I think the next thing is going to make me happy, and so I get it, and it doesn't. I end up feeling worse about myself." This young woman is doing her best to avoid the trappings of entitlement. She knows her susceptibility, as do her parents. And they are both committed to her security being found in who she is rather than what she has.

If you are financially able to provide all that your daughter wants (rather than what she truly needs), think about your motives for doing so. Are you trying to make or keep her happy with possessions? Are you trying to help her socially by making sure she has all of the things the popular girls have? Do you see things becoming a place where she finds confidence or draws security? Girls easily fall into this category, as do some boys, although often more in terms of toys, tennis shoes, and technology than clothes.

Luke 12:34 says, "Where your treasure is, there your heart will be also." Where is your treasure? Or, to put it more specifically, what do you treasure? We know a financially blessed family with a large home that houses a small movie theater because they want their home to be a gathering place for kids. Their treasure is investing in the lives of others. We know another family with significant means who are taking their children to Africa for the summer to work in an orphanage where they sponsor several children. Their treasure is in making a difference. We also know many families who live modestly and give generously, who are committed to teaching their children that their confidence comes from Jesus and who he has created them to be. Where is your treasure? What are you teaching your children to treasure? Because that very treasure will be the place they find their heart's joy and security.

The Search for Status

Josh was a starter on the football and basketball teams. He was president of his senior class and in the running for valedictorian. His principal frequently asked him to speak to the lower school about a variety of topics. He was winsome, winning, and won basically everything. He didn't know how not to win. He wanted people to see him as humble because that's the kind of guy he was, but underneath it all he believed he deserved all the honors that came his way. In his mind he not only deserved them; he expected them.

Boys can often fall victim to an entitlement that involves status, such as status on their particular team. We meet boys of all ages and all versions of sporting frustration who don't feel like they've been given their "fair" chance. And *fair* is often the operative word in this situation. "It's not fair. I kick, run, throw, (fill in the blank) better than all of the guys out there."

Girls aren't exempt from this type of entitlement either. I (Melissa) counseled a thirteen-year-old who was quite the track star in middle school. The varsity coach asked her to run with his team often and seemed to be grooming her at a championship level. For her eighth-grade year, however, the middle-school team hired a new coach. This coach didn't "realize how talented she was." In other words this coach made her work just as hard as all of the other members of the team. After a few months of "being treated this way," she quit track entirely.

Your children may be talented. They may be natural leaders, gifted artistically, academically, or athletically. Things that are hard for other people just seem to come easy for them.

We know a young boy with just this kind of talent. He came to our summer camp last year. One afternoon the boys all went to play baseball. Tommy happened to be on a team with another little boy we'll call Jeremy. Jeremy had a few physical challenges that in school would usually make him the last boy picked for a team. But at Daystar the boys are taught to treat each other differently. In the beginning Jeremy's team was happy to have him until he started dropping balls and striking out every time he went to the plate. Halfway through the game, Jeremy walked up to the plate and hit the ball—very low and very softly—but he hit it. Tommy hustled to the ball, picked it up, and dropped it. Tommy's teammates were furious. "What are you doing? Did you drop that on purpose?" On Jeremy's next hit Tommy did the same thing. He just couldn't seem to hold on to the ball whenever Jeremy hit it.

In terms of treasure, Tommy's treasure was more in kindness to Jeremy than it was in winning. We know Tommy's parents and feel pretty sure where that idea came from. They are an athletic, achieving, fiercely competitive family. But they value relationship and compassion over competition and have taught their children the same kinds of ideals.

Emotional Tyranny

I (Sissy) learned my lesson about emotional entitlement in my first few years of counseling. I met with a girl regularly who struggled with friends. For reasons I just couldn't understand, the other kids in school rejected her again and again and again. And so I decided that I would help her see all that they missed. I told her often how compassionate she was, how intelligent, how kind and wise and deep, and how shortsighted those other girls were. In reality she was all of those things. She had more maturity at twelve than most girls have at twenty. But in my telling and retelling her that she deserved something different, she quietly but definitely became arrogant. She was better than the girls who rejected her. In fact, she was better than most everyone in her grade. Her mom, teachers, and every other adult she knew agreed.

A junior in high school came to Camp Hopetown because of several learning disabilities that caused him to struggle academically. His parents were worried about his self-esteem. This young man walked into camp like he owned the place. In fact, rather than sleeping on a bunk in the cabin with the other boys, he slept on the couch in the main house (not really with our permission). He was smug, sarcastic, and talked down to the other guys at camp. Things had been hard for him, after all, so he should have a few perks along the way.

Her mother died of cancer her sophomore year. When her father brought her in for counseling, we immediately put her in a group. We wanted her to have the support of friends her age—friends who had been through hard things, too, and knew how to walk alongside her. And walk with her they did, beautifully, for girls of any age. They prayed for her, asked her deep questions, were available for her any time she needed them. Slowly she started to pull away from her other friends. "They just don't know how to love me like you all do," was her response to the girls in the group. When she went to college a few years later, she just couldn't seem to plug in. "I feel like no one here knows how to ask me questions. It's like they're all so consumed with themselves."

The way children are treated becomes how they expect to be treated. Wanting, when met every time, can lead to expectation, which, in turn, can lead to demand.

"Everyone should treat me better than this. I deserve more."

"My life has been hard. Give me a break and let me do what I want."

"People don't know how to love me the way they should."

All of our children will feel all of these ways at different times. We will, too. We deserve more. Our lives have been hard. We're not loved the way we want to be. We often feel these things on a weekly, or even daily, basis. But when our children feel them, it's something else entirely. If your child struggles with any kind of limitation, you know. If your child has been through a tragedy, you get it. You would do anything you could to make life easier. You just want your child to have a little happiness, after all.

We get it, too. We see kids in these situations every day in our offices. We see kids whose parents are going through a divorce so they ease up on discipline for a time "because they've got so much going on already." We see boys with attention issues whose parents allow them to rage around their homes "because they're put down so often at school."

Children need boundaries even in the midst of pain. Of course you want to shield your children. Of course you want to protect and take care of and defend them. The problem is that, if we only defend them, not only will they come to expect that everyone else will do the same; they will also come to believe that they are always the ones in need of defense. They will see themselves as victims, which is another by-product of entitlement. And victims end up with that same old insecurity we talked about earlier. Their treasure becomes an elusive sense of being protected, cared for, loved enough. And the idea of what it looks like to love someone else fades into the far-reaching background.

Breaking the Chains of Entitlement

Entitlement is undoubtedly a force to be reckoned with in today's culture. Whether it's emotionally, status, or financially driven, children expect more today than ever before. They expect that their North Face jacket will be replaced when it disappears, even after the third time. They expect that we will drive them to and from practice, to school when they forget their books, and to a friend's house thirty minutes away to spend the night on a school night. They expect our time, our attention, our pocketbooks, and every available resource we have to ensure their comfortable lifestyle. So, what do we do? How do we combat this "deserving" culture? We have included a few suggestions to keep your child both grounded and grateful.

- Help your children distinguish between wants and needs. They may want something, but do they really need it? Teach them these words as a part of their vocabulary. Let them look forward to Christmas, birthdays, special occasions, and every-so-often special days for the things they want.
- Let them participate in fund-raising. My (Sissy's) only gift that I remember giving my mom for Christmas growing up was one I saved for. I gave her gifts every year, but none meant as much to me, or probably to her, either. Match funds they earn for bicycles, cars, or other major purchases.
- Model gratitude. Take time at meals not to just say grace but to talk about the things you are thankful for in a given day. Be aware of how you speak of presents you've received (and didn't necessarily want) or things people have done for you. They will learn as much by example as by teaching.
- Give as a family. We have friends who spend time every Thanksgiving at their local soup kitchen. Obviously not every family can do this. But consider what you can do together— sponsor a family for Christmas, go on family mission trips, train your dog to be a pet therapist and take him to nursing homes.
- Teach your children to ask questions. Have conversations

together, real two-way conversations. If someone asks your son a question about his day, help him know how to ask one back. If family members ask your daughter about school, help her ask them about their life. If you have teenagers, encourage them to ask questions back, rather than just give one-word answers. Your children will not only feel more confident in conversations, but they will see that they can make a difference to someone else with something as simple as a question.

- If you have a child or teenager who continually feels like a victim, even when that's true, ask them what they could have done to help the situation. You can have compassion and empower your child at the same time.
- Have financial boundaries, such as an allowance for even young children. If they spend their given amount before their next allowance, they will learn how far a dollar will go and also have a chance to model resourcefulness.
- Allow your children to experience the consequences of good and poor decisions financially. If they have saved up a certain amount of money, allow them to buy something they really want, even if you consider it frivolous. If they have spent their gas money for the month, let them have the opportunity to be creative in finding rides.
- Give them consequences for overspending. Have them pay the cell phone bill or the credit card charges, even if it means they have to do extra chores to raise the money.
- If your children want to buy something, give them opportunities to earn money by doing extra work around the house. Anything earned by hard work and struggle is more valuable for the effort given. I (Melissa) still remember earning money to buy a transistor radio and a bicycle when I was a child.
- Give children jobs at home, or chores, as a part of their role as a responsible family member. Children are not guests in your home and can learn to take better care of things for which they feel some degree of ownership.

- Spend time with other families who are like-minded. You don't want every family around you to be the Joneses—setting the bar for the lifestyle you and your children have to chase.
- Don't allow your child to quit when things get tough. Struggle can break through the arrogance of entitlement and build compassion in kids of all ages (including us!).

From Entitlement to Gratitude

> Now Naaman was commander of the army of the king of Aram. He was a great man in the sight of his master and highly regarded, because through him the LORD had given victory to Aram. He was a valiant soldier, but he had leprosy.
>
> Now bands from Aram had gone out and had taken captive a young girl from Israel, and she served Naaman's wife. She said to her mistress, "If only my master would see the prophet who is in Samaria! He would cure him of his leprosy."
>
> Naaman went to his master and told him what the girl from Israel had said. "By all means, go," the king of Aram replied. "I will send a letter to the king of Israel." So Naaman left, taking with him ten talents of silver, six thousand shekels of gold and ten sets of clothing. The letter that he took to the king of Israel read: "With this letter I am sending my servant Naaman to you so that you may cure him of his leprosy."
>
> As soon as the king of Israel read the letter, he tore his robes and said, "Am I God? Can I kill and bring back to life? Why does this fellow send someone to me to be cured of his leprosy? See how he is trying to pick a quarrel with me!"
>
> When Elisha the man of God heard that the king of Israel had torn his robes, he sent him this message:

"Why have you torn your robes? Have the man come to me and he will know that there is a prophet in Israel." So Naaman went with his horses and chariots and stopped at the door of Elisha's house. Elisha sent a messenger to say to him, "Go, wash yourself seven times in the Jordan, and your flesh will be restored and you will be cleansed."

But Naaman went away angry and said, "I thought that he would surely come out to me and stand and call on the name of the LORD his God, wave his hand over the spot and cure me of my leprosy. Are not Abana and Pharpar, the rivers of Damascus, better than any of the waters of Israel? Couldn't I wash in them and be cleansed?" So he turned and went off in a rage.

Naaman's servants went to him and said, "My father, if the prophet had told you to do some great thing, would you not have done it? How much more, then, when he tells you, 'Wash and be cleansed'!" So he went down and dipped himself in the Jordan seven times, as the man of God had told him, and his flesh was restored and became clean like that of a young boy.

Then Naaman and all his attendants went back to the man of God. He stood before him and said, "Now I know that there is no God in all the world except in Israel. Please accept now a gift from your servant." (2 Kings 5:1–15)

Let's sum up the story: Naaman was a great man. He was courageous, important, highly regarded, a valiant soldier; and he had leprosy. Naaman's wife's servant came to him, told him there was a prophet named Elisha who could heal him, and Naaman went to his master. The master saddled him up with lots of material credibility and sent him not to the prophet but to the king. When the king had no idea what to do,

Elisha came to him and said he'd take care of it. So Naaman pulled his chariots and intimidating entourage up to a prophet's humble house. When Elisha's servant came to tell him how to be healed, Naaman was furious. Naaman, with all of his expectations and entitlement, was angry that Elisha delivered his news by lowly messenger and the news involved immersing himself in a dirty river. He surely deserved more than that.

Once again the servants shared the truth. They caught up to Naaman after he "stomped off, mad as a hornet" according to *The Message*. (Sound familiar?) They appealed to his arrogance by saying that surely Naaman would have done whatever the prophet asked if it was something courageous. Surprisingly, the great man dipped himself seven times in the dirty river. And not only his skin but his spirit came out clean. Naaman's response was, "Now I know." He walked away with a sense of gratitude. He walked away from that river wanting to give back to the one who had healed him of both a skin disease and a sense of entitlement.

Maybe our role is that of the servants. We are the agents of humility in this culture of entitlement. We remind our children that there is and can be healing. We take them back, again and again, to that river of humility. The first servant reminded Naaman that he needed cleansing. The second servant creatively showed him the way.

Our children are not just great boys and girls. They are made in the image of a wise, wonderful God. But they don't "deserve" to ride up in their chariots and order us or anyone else around. They can't expect that every want they have will be met and met right now. Their demands will cause them more insecurity. Our children are great. They are courageous and valiant and they need healing. They need healing from their struggles, from their entitlement, . . . from their sin. They are dignity and depravity. And, as they come to know both—as they learn what it means to bow their entitled knees to a God who can and does heal them—they will know the power of grace. They will walk away with a sense of gratitude saying, with Naaman, "Now I know."

A Sunday Drive

1. Send shoes. A church in our community recently taught on the affluence of our society. At the end of the service, the pastor challenged each person in the church to take off their shoes and place them in boxes at the front of the sanctuary to send to children and families in Africa. As a family, it might be difficult to pull this off without lots of eye rolling and "oh, pleases." But it might be especially effective to have a larger institution, like a church or school, challenge you together, and your child wouldn't necessarily have to know that you were the one who initiated the challenge.

2. Create a "denim for dollars" day or something like it. You can also strategically place a phone call to your child's school or youth group with a similarly mission-minded idea. A uniform-wearing school in Nashville has a day once a month where the kids can wear jeans if they bring a dollar for a certain charity. The kids are able to nominate and vote together on the charities chosen.

3. Once every few months your family can have an official "Missions Day," where you choose as a family or even let your children choose the organization you will serve. Go together on that day for a few hours to do whatever the ministry needs and give your children an opportunity to feel that they've directly made a difference.

4. On one night, or several nights a year, pick an impoverished country. Have your kids help determine how much money you save by eating a typical meal that families are eating in that country, prepare it together, and send the money directly to a relief organization that can help.

5. Watch a movie together like *Patch Adams* or most any superhero movie. Have them write a story about their own adversity and how God is using it for good, either for them or for others whose lives they touch.

6. Give your children money, as part of their Christmas gift, that they can choose to give to any ministry or nonprofit they choose. Then arrange with the organization for your child or teenager to have an opportunity to visit the site and give that money directly to see a visible response to their generosity.

7. Help your kids participate in a fund-raiser of some type for a cause they believe in once a year . . . whether it's a local ministry or the local animal shelter. They can run a lemonade stand, hold a garage sale, sell things from the garden, etc.

8. Allow your children to be around other people with adversity, whether it's financial, physical, or emotional. It is a great thing for children and adolescents to experience the "and I thought I had it bad" phenomenon. This can be in a volunteer or a small-group setting.

9. Have your child interview their grandparents or older family friends about what life was like when they were growing up (all that walking-to-school-uphill-both-ways, barefoot-in-the-snow kind of thing). Video- or audiotape it, so that they can have it as a keepsake.

A Lack of Respect

*If you want to be respected by others the great thing is
to respect yourself. Only by that, only by self-respect will
you compel others to respect you.*

—Fyodor Dostoyevsky, *The Insulted and the Injured*[36]

I love my parents. They're good parents, and they really try to do the best they can for me. I respect them, but I'm going to have to run away." A teenage boy said these words to me (Melissa) in a counseling session a few years ago. "I respect my parents, but I'm going to have to run away." Somewhere along the way, respect has gotten a little, well . . . disrespected. It is one of the subjects parents ask us about the most:

- "How do I get my child to respect me?"
- "What do I do when my daughter rolls her eyes at me?"
- "My son talks back constantly. What do I do?"
- "My teenagers act like I'm running a hotel. They talk to me when they want money or rides. And, even then, they're telling me what they're doing instead of asking if they can."
- "If I talked to my parents the way my son talks to me, they would've worn me out."

Do any of these scenarios sound familiar? Is respect an issue around your house . . . or, more likely, a lack of respect? If it hasn't already been one, at some point in the life of your child, it will. They will roll their eyes, sigh dramatically, talk back, draw out "Mom" or "Dad" in as many syllables as possible, and potentially use words like "whatever," "shut up," or "hate."

We recently spoke with a friend of ours whose eleven-year-old son used these and a few other choice words on a recent road trip with his family.

> I can't really remember how it started. He yelled at his sister or was bothering her when she asked him to stop . . . one of those daily occurrences in the car. So my husband took his DS away, and he had a meltdown. He started screaming, "You give me my DS or else!" When my husband looked at him and said, "Now, do you really think that's going to work?" things went from bad to worse. He continued ranting until we pulled over to McDonald's for lunch. When we got out of the car, he continued screaming in the parking lot. My husband grabbed him by the shoulders and said firmly, "You will NOT talk to me like that any longer." Before we could get inside, a police car pulled up. Someone inside called the police because they evidently thought my husband was hurting him. When the policeman came over and asked what was going on, my son said, "I hate my dad so much I want to kill him." Thankfully, the policeman's response was quick, strong, and compassionate . . . more to us than our son. "Son, do you have a home? Is it heated? Do your parents feed you? Do you think they love you?" When he answered these questions with a humbled yes, the officer said, "Then you've got a lot more than many of the boys your age I see. Now you respect your father, and I don't want to see you ever again."

Respect is more of an issue—problem, even—with kids today than ever before. They do talk to us in ways we could never have imagined speaking to our parents. We wouldn't have imagined it—mostly, because if we did, they wouldn't have stood for it. They would've gotten out the switch, or the spoon or the paddle or simply grounded us for even a fraction of the disrespect children today throw at parents. Maybe, for us, the motivation was as much fear as it was respect. In either case the motivation for kids today seems gone.

So, as a modern parent, what do you do? How do you not only teach but expect respect in your home? William Glasser, a psychiatrist, author, and noted theorist, has outlined the primary means by which we learn:

- 10 percent of what we read
- 20 percent of what we hear
- 30 percent of what we see
- 50 percent of what we see and hear
- 70 percent of what is discussed with others
- 80 percent of what is experienced personally
- 95 percent of what we teach to someone else

This list challenges many of the typical ways we approach teaching, especially teaching our children. If you'll notice, some of our more prolific parenting approaches like nagging, scolding, and criticizing aren't on the list. Basically, according to Glasser, we teach directly, we model, we help them experience, and even give them opportunities to teach others. In this chapter we'll break it down into four basic categories and talk about what each category looks like in the life of a child versus a teen: teaching, earning, modeling, and requiring respect.

Teach It

For Children

According to Glasser, only 20 percent of learning takes place from what children hear directly. But, at least in their early years, that 20 percent is crucial. You can model respect and discuss it with others all you want, but your son may still open a Christmas present from his grandparents and say loudly (and whiningly), "Awww. This isn't the one I wanted." He needs to be taught directly. Or your daughter, who has watched you countless times make eye contact and say, "It's nice to meet you," may be unwilling to speak to or even look at another adult who has greeted her. She needs your help in respecting someone else.

In their younger years, children need to be taught directly. They need our words telling them what to do with their actions. "Find Mrs. Smith's eyes when she's talking to you," or, "I would love to tie your shoes if you'll say 'please.'" As a parent, you are not only their first but also their most influential teacher in all things, including respect.

When we were starting this chapter, we had dinner with a friend who is in the early stages of this parenting journey with two sons under the age of three. We asked her what she would want to read in a parenting book about respect. Her answer was simple but foundational: "How do I get my sons to respect me?" Teaching directly, especially in those early years, is a pivotal piece of that answer. So how does she . . . how do you teach your children to respect you?

- Start with the basics. Give them polite words to use such as "please," "thank you," and "yes" instead of "yeah." Have them call adults by their titles such as Mr. and Mrs. If you live in a culture like we do (the South) and don't find these offensive, "Sir " and "Ma'am" can also act as a one-word way to teach your child to show respect to adults.
- Stick with the basics. Together as parents, decide on the major rules of respect you want to reinforce, such as eye contact, please and thank you, and asking rather than commanding. Having a limited number of concepts to focus on helps children remember those concepts and not feel as though you are "always" instructing or they are "always" in trouble.
- Reinforce these words with both repetition and response. Saying things like "I am much more willing to do things for you when you say please" can be a respectful way for you to teach that same idea.

- Stay consistent inside and outside your home. Sometimes we do a better job of teaching children to respect family members and even strangers than we do teaching them to respect us, as parents. As they move closer to adolescence, you will be the first place they start to test the limits of their respect. Start with a good foundation inside your home so that you will have a foundation laid before the teenage turbulence hits.

- Help them find expressive words. Your children will often sound disrespectful simply because they don't know how else to express how they feel. They will grunt, roll their eyes, or sound really angry for lack of a better or kinder option. You can help them put respectful words to their feelings. "I know you must be frustrated with me right now. You can be frustrated, but you can't be disrespectful." Or you can simply say, "Would you like to say that again a little kinder?" and even "try again" until they learn to say what they feel with respect.

- Don't overreact to their overreacting. Emotion begets more emotion. If their emotions are escalated and you give them an angry response, they will often just become angrier and more disrespectful. Instead, you can say with a calm and firm voice, "We don't talk to each other that way in this home."

- Exit disrespect. Allow them one chance to say something differently, and then, if the disrespect continues, either send them out or leave the room yourself. Don't reinforce their disrespect with your time and attention. Cline and Fay advocate giving them choices in these situations. "You can either go to your room or sit in the dining room until you can talk about this respectfully," leaves them some choice in the situation while you are in ultimate control.

For Teens

By the time they reach adolescence, most teens feel that they have heard everything that you have to say. You get three words out, and they cut you off with "Mom, I know" or "I heard you when you said that before." You may still have great words to say; they have just shut off their ears to hear. So, what do we do? How do you teach teenagers respect, especially if your earlier lessons don't really seem to have stuck?

- Expect disagreement. Preteens and teenagers are in the business of asserting their independence. They are trying to find themselves. They are also low on patience and long on grandiosity. The combination of these three ideas makes them want and often feel compelled to disagree with you. In these years it really is healthy for them to find and assert their own voice. It is possible, however, for them to express their independence and even disagreement with kindness. Know that disagreements will come and that you can honor them with conversation when they are respectful. Sentences such as "I'd really like to know what you think but not when you tell me like that," and, "Try again" are especially handy with teenagers.
- Choose your battles. If you point out every time your teens roll their eyes or sigh with great meaning, you will be in a constant war. Value relationship over control, letting some of the smaller infractions go.
- Don't allow yourself to become the object of their venting. By this age your children have most likely learned how to push your buttons. They will often pick a fight when they have been hurt by a friend at school or are angry at a teacher. Watch for signs that something else is going on with your child. Exit the situation if it escalates, or send them to have some time to reflect. Then, when things have settled, go for a walk or another neutral activity, and ask them what's going on . . . if anything else could have been fueling their anger.
- It's never too late to start. If your child has a problem with respect, you can model a tremendous amount of respect for them by taking ownership for their behavior. "I've noticed that you seem to have a problem with respect. I think we didn't do a great job of teaching you that when you were younger. It

is important enough to me that you learn that we're going to start now." Such an attempt models humility and respects them enough to communicate that you believe they're capable of more.

- Follow through with follow-through. Consequences often communicate more to teens than words. We talk to many parents in our offices who threaten but don't follow up. I (Sissy) was in a family counseling session just last week with one of the most disrespectful teenage girls I have met in seventeen years of counseling. In a moment of vulnerability, she turned to her mom and dad and said, "I'll never learn to stop if you don't stop me." Her parents threaten often but don't give her the consequences she is actually craving. Consequences help children feel that we care enough to help them become all they're really capable of being.

- Don't believe the "I don't care" line. When you take your son's car, your daughter's cell phone, or make them stay home from a birthday party they've been looking forward to, their first answer will often be, "I don't care." Don't fall for it. They not only care, but they care enough that they're working hard to fool you into letting them off the hook.

- Consistency is key. We often meet with frustrated parents for the first time who say, "Nothing works. I ground my child, take things away, give her chores. She doesn't change." Sometimes she doesn't change because they haven't been consistent. They try grounding once . . . taking her cell phone once . . . making her clean the bathroom once (or twice). None of it worked because she had their number and knew that if she threw a fit eventually they would give up. Some parents are consistent with their love and logic, and their children still don't change. The bottom line is that *we* cannot change the heart of a child, even with the best parenting we can offer. God can and does but sometimes not on our timetable. Consequences and consistency are important no matter what. You may need to change your tactics from time to time, to keep some of that backdoor unpredictability. But he or she still needs to know what is unacceptable behavior, and your consequences communicate that, even in light of your child's refusal to change.

Earn It

It may sound strange to talk about earning the respect of your children. Kids should respect their parents naturally, you might think. You might think that, but what do you see reflected in your home? What about in the way they speak to you? What about in the way you speak to them?

Fifteen-year-old Rachel has divorced parents. When her dad lost his job several years ago, the only one he could find was in Florida. Since then, he remarried a woman with three children. Rachel and her sisters spend one weekend a month with their dad and his new family. Out of all of her siblings and step-siblings, Rachel is the most like her dad. They are both strong willed and hotheaded. They both really love each other and want to make their limited time together count. On her last trip Rachel and her dad were trying to decide where to have dinner. She wanted Mexican food. He wanted Italian. Neither would give, and so the conversation quickly escalated. "Why don't you ever listen to what I want?" Rachel said, with her tone somewhere on the line between whine and demand. "This is ridiculous. It's just a restaurant. Why do you always have to get your way?" her dad tried to say calmly. "I don't, and I think you're being ridiculous," she shot back. Something in her dad snapped. "Just shut up, Rachel. I don't want to hear it anymore, and I want you to SHUT UP!" Before Rachel had time to think, she screamed, "WHY DON'T YOU JUST SHUT UP YOURSELF?"

Rachel was undoubtedly out of line. Children should respect their parents. Period. But parents should also respect their children. And the two are inextricably linked.

For Children

Erik Erikson, a psychologist and one of the pre-eminent developmental theorists, called the first stage in a child's development "trust versus mistrust."[37] As a parent, you are the first person your child learns to trust. Your children trust you to meet their basic needs, to love and nurture them. As they learn to trust you and know you will take care of them, they learn to believe that others are trustworthy, as well. In other words, their trust in you affects their level of trust with the outside world. In the early stages of a child's life, it also earns you the beginnings of respect.

Okay, so what from there? Most parents—definitely most parents who read a parenting book—are providing those basic tenets of trust and respect for their children. What else builds trust in your children? How else do you earn their respect?

- Be fair. Listen to and consider your children's perspective even when you know they're in the wrong.
- Be trustworthy. If your child tells you something and asks you not to tell anyone else, don't. Even if it is something that involves a friend's child, value your relationship as a parent first.
- Be reliable. Help them know that you will keep your word and your promises.
- Be a good listener. So often we tell our children to make eye contact, but we don't stop what we're doing long enough to look and listen to them.
- Be honest. Whatever you're going through, if your children ask a question, tell them the truth age-appropriately.
- Be enjoyable. Children have a hard time respecting someone who is constantly critical and demeaning.
- Be bigger than they are. Children clamor for power, but they really don't want it. They will push your buttons to get you to respond with anger or with hurt. If your child feels that he or she is stronger than you emotionally, he will feel too powerful. And, for kids, too much power actually creates insecurity. They feel safe when they know you are stronger. And, even though they may push up against you at any age, they are pushing to make sure that you're strong enough to hold.

For Teens

All of the above, plus:

- Be conservative with your history. When your adolescent starts to find out that other kids are experimenting or even wants to experiment herself, she may ask you what you were like as a teenager. Did you have sex? Did you drink? Did you take drugs? What she is really asking for, in most cases, is not information but license. What kids will say to us is, "My mom did it and she turned out great," or "My dad did it and he's really successful and a strong Christian now." If they're asking because they've really messed up and are in a repentant place, that's one thing. But if they're asking out of curiosity, that kind of curiosity didn't necessarily kill the cat, but it sure gave the kittens license to lose respect. This doesn't mean you shouldn't be honest or forthcoming if you feel like they're asking from a genuine place, but you should be careful and thoughtful, making sure to present any mistakes from your past in the context of your repentance, the grace of God, and yet the consequences experienced.

- Point out the positives. You will feel, at times, like if you dealt with everything that came up, you would be correcting your teenager all of the time. Your children need to know that you still believe in who they can be, even when you know you're not so crazy about who they are right then. Much of a teenager's disrespect for you really comes from disrespect for themselves. Help them see that they still have so much to offer in spite of their adolescent angst. Tell them whenever you see them treat other people with respect and show admirable characteristics. It will make a difference in how they see themselves and how they treat you.

- Be aware that they are growing up. "My parents still talk to me like I'm ten." On a daily basis we hear teenagers say these words. Adolescents want your respect. They want to know that you see that they are growing up. You can show that you are aware of their growing maturity both in the ways you speak to them and the freedom you give them. In *Raising Girls*, we advocate an idea of increasing by increments. With every growing year of your son or daughter's life, he or she needs a few more privileges and a few more responsibilities. For example, children should have a little later bedtime and curfew with each passing year, as well as a few more chores added to the list. When you give children more freedoms and responsibility, they think you believe they are up to the task. They feel trusted and respected and, in turn, often rise to the level of maturity needed for new responsibilities.

Model It

If earning respect has to do with the way you respect your children, modeling it has to do with the way you respect others and yourself. According to the previous Glasser study, they learn much more by what we model than by what we teach directly (even though we still believe the former is really important). So, what do you model? How do you talk to your friends in front of your child? Your parents in front of your teenager? The waitress at dinner? How do you talk about yourself and your body? Would you want the way you treat others and yourself to be the bar your child strives to live up to?

The Way You Treat Others

The plan was to spend four days over Christmas with her parents. This mother of four, ranging from age seven to fifteen came in to our offices for help with the holidays. "The last time we were home for Christmas, the wheels came off for our entire family—starting with me. I really think that, when I'm home, I revert back to the last age I was when I lived there. It's like I become a teenager myself, with every bit of the moodiness and defensiveness of those years. And my husband jumps right in there with me. My mom likes to tell me what she thinks I could do to be a better parent. The problem is that she tells me in front of my children, and she doesn't really tell me anything else. It's constant. On day three, my husband had had it. He walked in the room where my mother was lecturing me yet again, and started yelling. 'Stop it, just stop it. Don't you think she knows how to raise our children? We are their parents, not you.' My mom stomped off in tears, and we left town the next morning. How do I act like a grown-up, even if my parents are treating me like a child?"

We could probably write another entire book on this subject. Many of us relate to the "home for the holidays" syndrome. It's understandable, especially in light of how this woman's mother was treating her. And in some ways it's noble that her husband came to her defense. But just because her husband's behavior was understandable or noble does not mean he was being a good role model for his kids. He wants them to learn respect for their elders. He wants them to know how to resolve conflict with strength and kindness. But what he modeled was disrespect for his mother-in-law.

Whether with your parents, your siblings, friends, or strangers, your behavior will model your children the way to treat others. They hear what you say and watch what you do. And then often do that very thing themselves. Model respect. Teach them by your words and your actions.

The Way You Treat Yourself

> Like the appearance of a rainbow in the clouds on
> a rainy day, so was the radiance around him. This
> was the appearance of the likeness of the glory of the
> LORD. When I saw it, I fell facedown, and I heard
> the voice of one speaking. He said to me, "Son of
> man, stand up on your feet and I will speak to you."
> As he spoke, the Spirit came into me and raised me to
> my feet, and I heard him speaking to me.
> (Ezek. 1:28–2:2)

Two parents come to mind in reading this chapter in Ezekiel. We'll call the first Carol. Carol was a single mom of two girls. She had a poor opinion of herself. She didn't believe she was capable of much of anything. Although she was gifted with creativity and many skills, she didn't even apply for jobs that would suit her because she didn't believe she would be hired. As a parent, she felt like a total failure. She didn't know how to handle her daughters or even what to say to them half the time. The oldest was arrogant, feeling stronger in her mom's weakness, while the youngest clamored about literally asking for consequences. Carol needed to stand.

The other parent we'll call Bill. Bill grew up feeling like he never measured up. Although Bill was now a successful businessman and father of three, sometimes those old familiar voices of insecurity called out to him. They called out to him when he couldn't be the best, and they called out to him when his children weren't their best. His wife knew his constant criticism of their children was creating the same type of insecurity in them that their father knew all too well. Bill needed to stand not with the strength of his success but because of his God-given sense of dignity.

That's what happened with Ezekiel. In light of his vision of God's majesty, Ezekiel fell to his knees. He knew he was unworthy to stand in God's presence . . . as are we. We are unworthy. We don't parent right. We don't love right. We don't live right. But God said to Ezekiel, "Stand up." Ezekiel could easily have come right back at God with a list of the reasons he just couldn't stand. "I'm not successful enough. I'm not thin enough. I don't have the right answers. My child isn't as _____ as all of the other kids." It doesn't matter. God says, "Stand up on your feet and I will speak to you."

If you are Carol or Bill or somewhere in between, God wants you to stand up. Parenting from your knees (other than in prayer) creates a situation in which your child feels stronger than you are. Parenting by standing in your own strength often creates a criticalness of yourself that can't help but spill over to your children. God wants you to parent from a place of dignity. Self-respect really is a proper sense of one's own dignity—his dignity. He says, "Stand up because I have something to say to you." He has called you and redeemed you; you are his. Stand up because he wants to tell you something. If you don't, you might miss all you need to be a good parent. You may not feel like you know how, but he does.

Require It

"There has to be a bottom line." Bruce was a seasoned marriage counselor who shared office space with us several years ago and was working with a couple who had just separated. "There has to be a bottom line of trust, or a marriage simply won't work." As counselors who work with kids and families, we would say what trust is to a marriage, respect is to a parent/child relationship. Without a bottom line of respect, often the whole thing crumbles to the ground. And that goes for any age child.

As we said before, a lack of respect is one of the main reasons parents bring their children of all ages in for counseling. These kids are acting up, talking back, lashing out, and simply being rude to their parents, teachers, grandparents, siblings, even the family pets. What we believe these kids need is a foundational requirement of respect in their households.

Great, you may be thinking. *I don't even know what that means, let alone how to accomplish it.* First of all, we suggest starting with what respect does mean. At every age (or developmental level), kids need a clear understanding of what kind of respect is a requirement for your family. They need you to define it. We'll give some suggestions for this in the Sunday Drive section of this chapter. For now let's sum it up by saying how they are to treat others needs to be clear for kids—you, their parents, grandparents, servers at a restaurant, other adults, authority figures, people who are different. And they need to know the consequences when their behavior falls short of your definition.

Another important principle to remember in terms of respect is that we often confuse the feeling of respect with respectful behavior. Just as we can't change the heart of a child, we can't create a warm feeling of admiration inside of them for us or anyone else. What we can focus on, however, is their behavior. And much of the way we do this is through those same ideas of teaching, modeling, earning respect, and giving good ole consistent consequences when they miss the mark.

You may remember the name Captain Richard Phillips. In April 2009 Captain Phillips was sailing a vessel with twenty crew members toward Mombasa, Kenya, when four pirates boarded and hijacked his ship. The captain offered himself as a hostage to free his men and was taken by the pirates in a small lifeboat for four days before the navy was able to rescue him. When commended for his heroic efforts, Captain Phillips simple response was, "That's just what I was trained to do."

It would be nice for our children always to speak with kindness, never to roll their eyes, and to say "please" and "thank you" when appropriate. And, then, when other people compliment their behavior, they would smile and simply say, "That just what I was raised to do." Chances are, they won't . . . at least until they're adults and have children of their own. But what they might say is, "My mom will get mad at me if I talk back," or, "I don't want to get in trouble with my dad." That is an age-appropriate response that still reflects respectful behavior.

Don't get distracted by the emotion, either their emotional outbursts or your fears that you have raised a child with no understanding of respect. No matter how old your child is, respect can still be something that you teach, model, earn, and require. God respects you as he calls you to stand up. As you stand by his grace, he will speak truth to you as a parent . . . truth that will free you to parent with more love, more dignity, and more respect than you ever imagined.

A Sunday Drive

In this section we wanted to include a few practical suggestions to prompt respectful behavior in your children at any age. The next section of the book has a chapter on manners, so this list is specifically geared toward the relational part of respect.

- Help them learn respectful responses when other kids are unkind. Role play different ideas and scenarios depending on their age.
- In areas of competition, teach them to win and lose showing respect to their rivals, saying things like "good game," or pointing out when the competitor did well.
- Role play different types of humor. Be aware of your own sarcasm, which is often disrespectful, and help them learn to have a sense of humor that remains respectful of others. We see many Christian kids who use sarcasm as a way to cut down others even though they're "just joking." It is good for kids of any age to know the hurt that sarcasm can cause.
- When you watch other children showing respect or disrespect, use this opportunity as a teachable moment to talk about what happened.
- If you walk into a room and are greeted without respect by your children, walk out and repeat the scenario until they use respect.
- Take any opportunity to make learning fun and experiential. If your child is a teen, try to make it as unpredictable as possible, also. For example, role play with your teenager without saying what you're doing. Just break into adolescent lingo spontaneously. Catch them off guard, using humor to point out how they're acting, rather than just telling them directly.

Risky Business

*Our addictions are our own worst enemies. They enslave us with
chains that are of our own making and yet that, paradoxically, are
virtually beyond our control. Addiction also makes idolators of us
all, because it forces us to worship these objects of attachment, thereby
preventing us from truly, freely loving God and one another*

—Gerald May, *Addiction and Grace*[38]

*F*or several weeks eight out of every ten teenage girls I (Sissy) met with
talked about the same guy. No, it wasn't Edward Cullen, although
he did create quite a stir whenever one of his movies came out (or Jacob
Black's movies, depending on the perspective of the girl we're referring
to). This guy's name was Charlie. And they were all talking about Charlie
for the same reason. He was having a party. Charlie evidently has four
parties per year, each around certain holidays. They're citywide, if only
you're "lucky" enough to be invited. The way to get invited is to talk to,
text, Facebook, or e-mail Charlie and tell him you want to come. He then
sends you several tickets in the mail, for you and your chosen friends for
a minimal fee of five dollars each. Charlie's parties average around four
hundred kids. He has a valet service, a caterer, a DJ, and even police to

help with traffic flow. One of the girls was telling me about Charlie the week before the party.

> "Charlie is such a nice guy. He has these huge par-
> ties and is really giving with the money he makes.
> Everyone loves him." *I'm sure they do*, I thought.
> "Does he pick some charity to donate the money to?"
> I naively asked. "No. He uses it to buy even better
> lights or something like that for the next party."

Charlie was not only beloved but very smart, in a Ferris Bueller type of way. And, so, the days marched on till Charlie's big shindig with much anticipation and Charlie-directed admiration from many girls in middle Tennessee. The week after Charlie's party was another matter entirely. It started with not-so-respectable pictures popping up on Facebook. Next came the not-quite-so-look-you-in-the-eye looks from the previously buoyant girls. Then the tears.

One girl, who has been very conservative with boys and broke up with her last boyfriend because he wasn't a Christian, made out with two different guys. Another girl who has fought a hard battle to stand up to her peers in terms of alcohol was drinking and "all over" her boyfriend. Another whom I was a little worried about already arrived at the party drunk and alternated kissing her boyfriend and her girlfriends all night long.

Charlie's party sounds like a twenty-first-century version of one of those eighties Brat Pack movies to me. The kids don't look different on the outside. They definitely don't feel any different on the inside—insecure, awkward, longing for relationship and purpose. But the options to escape those feelings have definitely ramped up in intensity. That intensity is what this chapter is about.

We see the trends in our offices on a daily basis. One year kids are selling Ritalin at school. The next, cocaine is the hip drug of choice. Girls are chasing each other to the bathroom to see if their friends are throwing up. Boys are wearing sweatbands on their wrists to cover up marks they've made with knives. And the alcohol continues to flow freely . . . just at younger ages. In this chapter we'd like to explore those risky behaviors that kids are all too familiar with today. The problem is that we're the ones who aren't sometimes. So these next few pages will be a crash course in addictions . . . or idolatry, as psychiatrist and author Gerald May called it. We will look at the choices kids are making today: what's happening, why it's happening, and what you can do about it.

Alcohol

What's Happening

According to the Center for Disease Control, alcohol is the most common drug of choice for kids today. Eleven percent of all alcohol consumed in the United States is by kids twelve to twenty years of age.[39] In 2007 the Youth Risk Behavior Survey found that among high school students in a thirty-day period,

- 45 percent drank some amount of alcohol
- 25 percent binge drank
- 11 percent drove after drinking
- 29 percent rode with someone who had been drinking[40]

A Century Council study found that 39 percent of eighth-graders and 72 percent of twelfth-graders had experimented with alcohol.[41] Kids who start drinking before age fifteen are five times more likely to develop an alcohol addiction in later life than those who start at or after age twenty-one.[42] Children and teens who drink under age are also statistically more likely to have academic issues, social problems, legal problems, illnesses, unwanted sexual activity, disruption of normal development, higher risk for suicide and violence, alcohol-related auto accidents; abuse other drugs; and have long-term effects on brain development.

For teens alcohol is not only accessible but often the most socially acceptable drug of today, as well. Many kids who tell us they would "never" use drugs drink every weekend on average. In their minds they can drink and not be labeled a "druggie" or even "wild." Alcohol really does fall into the normal category for today's teens . . . not just those at Charlie's party.

Unfortunately many parents are contributing to the normalcy of alcohol with today's kids. I (Melissa) met with a teenage boy several years ago who had been suspended from his school for attending a school dance while intoxicated. As a matter of fact, he was so drunk that his friends (who had also been drinking) were worried enough about him that they took him to the emergency room where he had his stomach pumped for alcohol poisoning. When the school mandated that he come to counseling, his mom came in and met with me first.

"His dad and I really feel that the school is overreacting. Every teenager drinks and our son is no exception. He promises me he'll keep it under control and won't drink at any school events again. I don't think it's any big deal."

When the boy came in my office, he told me it was, in fact, not even close to his first time and that he was a little concerned himself about that night and how little he remembered of it. He told me he had been drinking to keep himself from feeling sad about things that were bothering him, including his recently exed ex-girlfriend. He told me that he would really like someone to talk to so that he didn't have to drink to feel better and would even like help learning how to say no to his friends. He left with a promise to talk to his parents about his alcohol use and come back to see me that next week. His parents haven't brought him in since.

Why It's Happening

Recently exed exes, loneliness, the betrayal of friends, family problems, sadness, stress, anger, and a million other emotions that bombard teenagers on a daily basis are just a few of the reasons kids today turn to alcohol to make themselves feel better. They simply feel so much. We see a multitude of kids in our offices every day suffering from depression, anxiety, and what feels like debilitating insecurity. In fact, it is difficult to diagnose preteens or teenagers with depression because normal brain development causes so many ups and downs in those years that their emotions truly mimic clinical depression. Add all of that teenage angst to potential genetic predisposition to alcoholism. Stir in a group of friends where everyone drinks but your child. Mix with scenes of jet-setting, high-fashion teenagers gathered in a bar having conversations over cosmos on the hot TV show for teens. Put all of this in the family bar that is conveniently located away from the parents' bedroom who are either fast asleep or not at home when friends are over, and you've got a recipe for alcohol use and abuse.

Teenagers are vulnerable. They are driven by acceptance from their peers and sometimes rebellion from your rules. Alcohol is an easy answer for many teens who want to escape or live on the edge just a little. But the easy answer, as we know, has painful ramifications.

What You Can Do

If your child has been experimenting or even abusing alcohol, there will be signs. You may not want to watch for them because you want to believe your child wouldn't be the one to drink. We would suggest you watch anyway. We see entirely too many parents who fall into the "my child would never . . ." category while their children are sneaking themselves into destructive behavior. These are just a few signs to watch for, actually for either alcohol or drug use:

- A change of friends, especially toward older teens or young adults
- A lack of interest in activities at home
- Rumors that friends are drinking or using drugs
- Diminished interest in activities he or she used to enjoy such as sports or hobbies
- Changes in eating or sleeping patterns
- Lack of concern for personal appearance
- Irritability, impatience, and overreacting with family
- Change in values
- Extreme mood swings
- Secretive phone or Internet use
- Lying
- Drop in grades or missing school
- Any legal trouble such as shoplifting, etc.

- Glassy, dilated, or red eyes or runny nose with no physical reason
- Family history of alcoholism or drug use
- Cigarette smoking
- Actually finding beer cans or drug paraphernalia in his or her room

If you start to notice these signs or discover that your son or daughter has been drinking:

1. Trust your instincts more than their excuses, especially if there is hard evidence. You would not believe the number of parents who find vodka bottles "that my friend asked me to keep so he wouldn't get in trouble," or bags of pot "that someone gave me but I didn't know what to do with."

2. Pray that your child will be caught. As silly as it sounds, we talk to so many parents who have prayed this prayer regularly and just happen to call at the right time to find out that their daughter isn't really spending the night at Courtney's house at all or is the one who is caught by the school or even police.

3. Don't accuse your children until you catch them or have a strong leaning that they have used alcohol or drugs. Kids who feel accused often say to us, "My parents already think I do. I might as well."

4. Allow them to face logical consequences if those are in place. If not, create your own. When the school puts your child on probation or mandates counseling, follow through. If you are the one to catch your child with alcohol, restrict activities, freedoms, or phone use (something important to them). As basic as it sounds, if they are not given consequences, the behavior will continue.

5. If the behavior is repetitive, seek professional help. An emotional reason may be driving their destructive behavior. Find someone they can talk to about those emotions and help them find other ways to cope.

6. Give your child opportunities and places to talk about all of the adolescent emotions. Every child needs adults and a group of kids they can talk to where they will feel safe and accepted. Be parents who offer

this, but help them find other adults they can confide in, as well. You remember how difficult it was to talk to your parents about certain topics. Even if you are a completely different parent than yours were to you, you are still your child's parent. Children today need other mentors in these years, too.

7. Create positive peer pressure. Help your child find a group of kids you can trust to speak positively into their lives. The older they get, children often hear each other's voices more loudly than ours. Make sure at least a few of those voices are speaking truth into the life of your child.

8. Keep some type of spiritual influence in the life of your child. The older a child gets (especially in terms of their teenage years), it becomes increasingly important that they develop their own faith, not just your faith as their parents. We definitely believe in older teens having some choices in terms of spiritual influence, but make sure they choose something, be it youth group, Young Life, FCA, etc.

We believe there are three primary reasons preteens and teenagers don't participate in the risky business of substance abuse: they have their own sense of faith that drives them, they have friends that are making good choices, or they are terrified of being punished. If you can have all three of these ideas in place, the better your chances are that your child will make good decisions.

Drugs

What's Happening

As we started writing this section of the chapter, we did a lot of research. We researched which drugs were most popular today and which drugs had declined in use. One article reported that while illegal drug use had steadily increased in the 1990s, the good news is the first decade of the 2000s had been one of steady decrease among youth.[43] Great news! The next article said that heroin was gaining in popularity, particularly in the northeast section of the U.S.[44] Oh. Most articles (and most kids) tell us that marijuana continues to be the illegal drug of choice. And many, many articles talked about the widespread prevalence of over-the-counter and prescription drugs among kids today.

We could tell you story after story of kids we have seen over the years with serious addictions to "nonaddictive" (according to them but not researchers) pot. But you know the drill. It is addictive. It often leads to other drug use. And it leads to a host of other problems with the rest of their social, academic, and emotional worlds. The bottom line is that kids are continuing to smoke pot. In fact, 20 percent of eighth-graders have tried marijuana. In addition, more than 60 percent of teens said drugs were sold, used, or kept at their schools.[45]

We could fill your head and these pages with statistics on crystal meth, cocaine, crack, and heroin. But the likelihood in today's culture is that those drugs are not the drugs that are being used or kept at your child's school. If drug dogs walked in today, they would be much more likely to find some marijuana, several bottles of over-the-counter medicines like cough syrup and cold remedies, and even more vials containing prescription drugs such as pain killers and stimulants.

In our counseling groups kids don't typically talk freely about wanting to share each other's stash of pot. But I (Sissy) have heard several conversations among "good" girls, rather innocently and naively, who want to borrow a few pills of Ritalin from each other to help concentrate around finals. Stories abound about kids having "pharming" parties, where they raid the pain killers, antidepressants, and stimulants from their home medicine cabinets to trade, share, and mix with alcohol for a little added high.

Bidis are also a drug-related item on the rise. They are flavored cigarettes, imported from India, hand rolled and exotically packaged. They are highly addictive and dangerous, with twice the amount of nicotine and five times the amount of tar as regular cigarettes. The attorney general's office conducted an undercover operation where children as young as nine were able to purchase bidis, some even from a toll-free number on a Web site. As of 2009, 13 percent of high school students are reported to have tried bidis.[46]

Today pot, bidis, and OxyContin. Tomorrow there's no telling (although pot does seem to have serious staying power). Regardless of the drug name or its position on or over the drug store counter, it is serious.

Every drug is addictive and dangerous. And a majority of your children will be exposed to one drug or another. Let's get to the much more important information of why and what you can do to prevent it.

Speaking of tomorrow, things have changed again since the "today" we wrote about just a few short months ago. I (Sissy) read an article on a Tuesday about a drug called K2 or spice that is similar to a legalized form of marijuana. On Thursday a girl in one of my groups said that her brother had been using K2. Immediately another girl in the group turned to her and said, "Oh, K2? That's what everyone is talking about these days."

So here's the lowdown on K2. It's a type of herbal incense, sold online or at smoke shops around the country. It is sprayed, however, with a synthetic compound similar to THC, which is used in marijuana. It's referred to as "fake pot." It mimics many of the effects of marijuana use but has also been known to cause elevated heart rates, agitation, and blood pressure. States are banning it as we speak. But for now it can be ordered as easily as a click of the button. Most likely any of these drugs can.

Things really do change quickly. By the time this book is printed, another drug will have jumped in line to compete for the attention and addiction of teenagers. All the more reason we need to move beyond the whats to the whys and what we can do to help.

Why It's Happening

The majority of statistics show that brain development does not stop until the mid-twenties, although drugs and alcohol can end that growth prematurely. What does this mean for your son or daughter? It means he is impulsive. It means she is insecure. It means his emotions are all over the place. It means she has a limited, sometimes very limited, awareness of long-term consequences. It means he grossly overestimates his power and grossly underestimates your wisdom.

One of the main regions of the brain that is not fully developed in teens is called the frontal cortex. The cortex is made of lobes that grow from the back to the front so the frontal lobe is last to develop.

The frontal lobe is responsible for reasoning, planning, and judgment. According to an article in *Harvard Magazine*, this region is not fully developed until somewhere between twenty-five and thirty.[47]

Without the reasonable, logical portions of thinking fully developed, teens are often overcome by their emotions and impulses. These emotions and impulses only add fuel to the hormonal fire that is constantly stirring in your teen. And that's only what's happening on the inside. On the outside they've got the voices of their peers, media that glamorize drug use, and that age-old need to live life on the edge.

What You Can Do

So what is a modern parent to do? Does your voice have any impact amid the cacophony of voices tempting your child? According to the Teen Drug Abuse Web site, the answer is a resounding yes. Teens whose parents talk to them about the dangers of drug use are 42 percent less likely to use drugs than teens whose parents don't.[48] So talk, talk, talk. Ask, ask, ask. And even help them think through rational responses they can give in the moment.

David K. Urion, an associate professor of neurology at Harvard Medical School, advocates that helping kids find practical strategies for making in-the-moment decisions serves teens much better than lecturing them about the dangers of drugs.[49] We would advocate both. And actually we would suggest helping them understand the way their brains have yet to develop, as well as the consequences drugs and alcohol have on those fledgling brains. We'll list some resources in the Sunday Drive section of the chapter.

In the meantime, if you have younger children, help them understand, age-appropriately, what drugs are and the effects they have. If you have family members who have suffered from an addiction, don't hide that information from your child (again, within age-appropriate reason). We know many kids who have grown up worried about a family member and are determined to turn out differently. Teach them about genetic predispositions toward addictions.

If you have a teenager, you can continue to have those kinds of conversations with them. And you can also get to know your child all over again, as a teenager rather than a child. Ask questions . . . not as a detective but as a person who is showing love. Find out what the culture is like at school and even at your church. It might be different from what you would expect. Have your child's friends over and get to know them. It helps you to stay a little more "in the know" and builds a little more accountability into relationships. Equip them with how to say no. Role play different scenarios that could come up. Make sure they know that you will always be willing to be the bad guy. "My dad would kill me" or "My mom would ground me for the rest of my life" really can be great excuses when they feel pressure.

Sex

What They're Doing

"Our seventeen-year-old son was supposed to be staying at his aunt's house. We were on a family vacation, but he plays football and couldn't miss the big game. So we let him stay, trusting him to do what he was supposed to do and be where he was supposed to be. Late one night he called my sister and told her he was spending the night at his friend John's. He came home the next day in time for lunch and said that he and John had a great time watching movies and Facebooking friends. Two days later my sister ran into John's mother. My son had never even been to their house that weekend. After some investigating, I found out that my son's new girlfriend just happens to have a lake house forty-five minutes away. She and my son evidently had a getaway at the lake, unbeknown to and absolutely unpermitted by us. When I confronted him, I'm afraid I lost it a little. I think I screamed the question, 'Did you have sex with her?' He promised me that he didn't. They slept in the same bed but didn't have sex. And I really think I believe him."

- Forty-six percent of all fifteen- to nineteen-year-olds in the United States have had sex at least once.
- By age fifteen, only 13 percent of teens had been sexually active.
- By age nineteen, 70 percent of teens had been sexually active.

- The average age for most teens to have sex for the first time is seventeen.
- Teens are waiting longer to have sex, with 19 to 21 percent (females to males) before the age of fifteen in 1995 and 13 to 15 percent (females to males) in 2002.[50]
- Slightly more than half of all teens age fifteen to nineteen have had oral sex.
- Seventy percent of eighteen- and nineteen-year-olds have had oral sex.[51]

And that's what kids today are doing as far as sex goes—oral sex, at least some of the kids. According to the *Washington Post* in 2005, oral sex has become a "societal norm" for kids. It has for many of the kids we talk to, as well.

But we don't want you to panic completely. We still see a smattering of kids who don't even kiss until they are in college because they don't want to get sidetracked during high school (although it's also sometimes for lack of appealing options). We see a few kids who believe dating is silly as teenagers because they probably won't end up marrying the other person. We know girls and boys who date like we did in the old days, where the boy calls the girl (with actual voices, not text), picks her up by walking to the door and speaking to her dad, and pays for a real date. We also know parents who require this.

We know other kids, too. We know a lot of kids who believe that "people just don't go on dates anymore. They meet up at the movies or the mall" if they're in middle school. "They meet up at a friend's house or a party" in high school. And this meeting up often leads to "hooking up" (making out, in our vintage terms). They are often not dating or even in a relationship with the person. Kisses have become commonplace, and sexualized relationships have become "easy access" between technology, media, and "friends with benefits" driving what many of our kids believe is right, or at least the norm.

Why It's Happening

Obviously peer pressure plays a major role in many teens' decisions to have sex. For many of them, it is the norm. Subsequently guys and girls feel "stupid" if they're the only one in their group of friends who hasn't. In addition, their hormones are pushing them toward sexual experiences. As they move into older adolescence, they also develop a hunger for deeper connection. Girls talk frequently about wanting to "belong" to someone. Guys enjoy being able to talk to girls and have close relationships without the ribbing that boys often do with each other when any vulnerability is displayed. As a result, everything physically, emotionally, and socially is pointing toward a longing for intimacy for many teenagers.

What in the World Can You Do?

A dad we know had a long conversation with a boy who wanted to take out his teenage daughter, Michelle, before they went on a first date. He explained exactly how he required that his daughter be treated and what would happen if the boy did not follow through—or followed through in other, nonapproved ways. The conversation must have taken because several months later this boy hurt Michelle's feelings pretty badly. When she confronted him, he apologized not only to her but to her father, as well. Chivalry does still exist in today's world. (As a side note, this dad included Michelle's brother in the conversation with her boyfriend to be. He wanted him to hear the conversation in case his future dates' fathers didn't explain expectations to him.)

I (Sissy) was counseling Michelle and heard the story from her. I was, of course, curious about her beaux, Sam. (We'll use the word my grand-mother would have used because he was sure acting like a vintage type of guy). When I asked why she thought he had called her dad, Michelle gave some of the credit to her dad and their conversation—and some of the credit to his dad. "Sam's dad has taught him a lot about what it means to be a gentleman. They talk about it and have even practiced on Sam's mom." Sam was also the kind of guy who was committed with Michelle to staying pure (from any kind of sex) until they were married.

One of the things you *can* do is talk to your child about expectations, like the dads of both of these mature teens. Another is to talk to their potential dates about expectations, assuming they actually bring them home. And you don't have to be a dad to do it. It doesn't matter if you're their mom, grandparent, aunt, or uncle. They need to hear from you—not just what you expect but what you value, as well.

But, before you ever get to that point, you can start educating your children about sex at a young age. Build a bridge that makes conversation easy and as comfortable as possible for you both, regardless of how uncomfortable you may feel in the beginning. Let your children know that they can ask you anything about the opposite sex or sexual activity of any kind. Way too many kids that we meet have never had a conversation with their parents about sex or even puberty. Your children need to hear from you and what you believe God has designed male-female relationships and sexual intimacy to be. They also need to know the why's behind that design. Many kids know they are not supposed to have sex, but they have no idea that God has made sex to exist in marriage for our protection. He not only is trying to protect us from physical harm like disease but the kind of harm that we end up counseling girls and boys about with tragic frequency: the emotional devastation that occurs when a girl and guy have sex and then break up. Educate your children about the spiritual, emotional, and physical repercussions of sex.

Don't forget to include oral sex. Many teens mistakenly believe that oral sex is "safe." They believe it's not considered sex from a spiritual standpoint and that diseases are not transmitted that way. Unfortunately HIV is transmitted through oral sex as well as vaginal, as are STDs.

Help your child find a group of kids who are making good choices in this department, as well. Youth groups have ceremonies where purity rings are given. Parents do, as well, for that matter. Small groups read great books such as *Every Young Woman's [and Young Man's] Battle* together. Find a group where your children are positively influenced by their peers. Every little bit helps fight those statistics.

If you do find out that your children are sexually active, have them talk to someone about it. It may be that they are struggling under the weight of a lot of guilt. It may even be that they want out of the relationship and don't know how to get there. But it often helps to have a third party to talk to in that situation. A youth director, counselor at school, a professional counselor, or even an aunt or adult friend they respect can be another voice echoing the values that you want for your child.

Sexual activity and even relationships can easily move from risky business to an out-and-out addiction. We see many kids in both situations and know how much they benefit from communicative, supportive relationships with their parents and the trusted voice of another adult.

Eating Disorders
What's Happening

I (Sissy) recently sat with a group of girls who were all talking about concern over their weight. (These girls ranged in size from 0s to 10s.) They admitted that they thought the easiest way to lose weight was simply to throw up or stop eating. And therein lies the problem. These methods are often less work than the rigors of a prescribed diet. The problem is that, from my perspective as a counselor, eating disorders are one of the most difficult addictions of all to overcome.

I believe (Melissa) that eating disorders are often a "good girl or boy's" way to rebel. They're typically kids who are high functioning, bright, put lots of pressure on themselves, and feel lots of pressure from others. Kids who recover from eating disorders make highly successful adults. We just want them to recover. And to recover from an addiction to food is extremely difficult. You can stay away from alcohol or drugs, but eating is a daily part of life.

And by "all of us," we don't mean just girls. Statistically, one-fourth of eating disorders occur in men or boys.[52] Specifically, eating disorders among boys are on the rise with a preoccupation with thinness spilling over to boys in today's culture. In addition, boys feel pressure to maintain certain weight levels for competitive sports. As younger children, boys also tend to berate each other for being overweight and can struggle with low self-esteem as a result. For years boys who suffered from eating disorders did so in secret with it being considered more of a "girl's" disease.

Thankfully, public opinion is changing, awareness of eating disorders as a multigender issue has finally broadened, and boys are getting the help they need.

Statistically children as young as five are concerned and even obsessed with their weight. Obesity is considered the primary health risk among today's kids with one in five children considered medically over-weight.[53] In our offices we hear kindergartners who feel like they look fat. Our experience, however, is that most of the kids who talk about looking fat don't fall within the overweight category from a medical standpoint; and the ones who are externally struggling with their weight often feel shame talking about it.

The National Association of Anorexia Nervosa and Associated Eating Disorders calls eating disorders an epidemic in the United States. Seven to ten million women and one million men suffer from some type of eating disorder. Of those reported, 86 percent said their eating disorder began by the age of twenty, 33 percent by the age of fifteen, and 10 percent by the tender age of ten years old.[54]

Whether anorexia (starving oneself), bulimia (binging and purging), or compulsive eating, eating disorders are all too rampant among the young people in our culture. Girls skip lunch by going to the library and then skip dinner because of "too much homework." Boys make themselves throw up before being weighed for wrestling. We have talked with kids who plot all day long how much they can eat and how they can find enough privacy to throw up. The Internet has pro-ana (promoting anorexia) and pro-mia (promoting bulimia) Web sites where kids swap stories and ideas to encourage each other in their eating disorders. It is an epidemic and one that ravages not just the bodies but the minds of girls and boys.

Why It's Happening

In our book *Raising Girls*, we quoted an adolescent girl who told us she felt she had "given herself over to this god of thinness."[55] It is a god . . . not just in her mind, but in our culture. We are all too familiar with the air-brushed photos of models and celebrities. Some companies and ads are beginning to promote a more balanced representation of beauty, but the wheels of progress are painfully slow, especially to reach the eyes of our kids.

What they see are the girls on television and movies who look emaciated and the boys who have rippling muscles with every turn of their unclothed torsos. They're too young to remember the tragic loss of Karen Carpenter. Instead they hear stories of celebrities in and out of rehab for eating disorders and every other addiction under the sun who bounce back with even greater success the next round on the red carpet.

I (Sissy) am currently counseling a high school student with bulimia. We'll call her Ashley. Ashley is precious, inside and out. Just as Melissa said, she makes wonderful grades, is a leader in her school, one of the more responsible teens I have met, and cares deeply for her family. And, on the subject of her family, they are struggling pretty badly. In fact, I would say that her eating disorder is an outward manifestation of the chaos and turmoil that is going on within the walls of her home. Her mom is an alcoholic. She drives the kids regularly while intoxicated. Her dad is angry, yells a lot, but is too afraid of what would happen to his already empty marriage if he really put his foot down. So Ashley, who feels no control in her home life, is taking control of the one area she feels she can—her food. And, Ashley, by the way, is maybe a size 4 on her biggest days.

Self-hatred and a need for control are the defining motivators for eating disorders. Girls and boys who struggle with them don't like themselves. They often don't like who they are or believe they have anything to offer, but it is often easier to focus on what you look like than who you really are. So they feel fat even though many of them look anything but.

These girls and guys feel a lack of control in their lives, for one reason or another. So food, just like for Ashley, becomes something they can control. The problem is that it begins to control them. They become consumed with what they can eat, what they can't eat, when they can throw up, how much they've eaten in the past few days, how much (or little) they will eat in the next few days.

What You Can Do

I (Sissy) was recently teaching a parenting class at a church in what we could call a comfortable community. In this population I often try to talk the strongest about eating disorders because eating disorders often run most rampant in perfectionistic places. So I was on my soapbox saying something along the lines of:

> Eat healthy as a family. Teach your children about healthy choices in food, but don't make food an issue in your family. If you feel like your children are overweight, take them to the doctor. Let them get advice from a nutritionist. Get them in to see a counselor if the problem seems serious. But, if you try to control their eating or weight, they will fight you that much harder for control. It's a control issue so the harder you fight, the more control they'll feel the need to take. And PLEASE don't tell your children you feel they have a weight problem. I have never met a girl or boy who has received that information from a parent and said, "Gee, Mom/Dad, let me get right on that. I'd really like to lose weight now." It often has an adverse reaction and makes them feel worse about themselves, plunging them into wanting to eat more simply for the sake of comfort . . . or even out of rebellion toward you. If you feel that your child is struggling, get outside help and let your voice be one of support and encouragement.

After I finished my rant, a mom who I am sure was well meaning came up to me and said, "Yes, but what do you do if your daughter is fat?" We cannot say it strongly enough. Do not tell her that. Do not tell him that. Let the doctor say if your children fall within the medically diagnosable category of overweight. If they don't, and you're more concerned about their weight than they are, then the issue really may be more yours than theirs. You would benefit by having someone to talk to on this, as well.

If your child does ask for help, get a nutritionist and a counselor on board. There are always emotional reasons for any type of food addiction and simply treating the behavior doesn't cure the cause. And please help your child at every age learn that real men and women have curves. Beauty has much more to do with who you are than what you look like. They need to hear these messages and even know the specifics of the beauty you see in them. They can't hear it too much. And probably neither can we.

Cutting/Self-Harm

What's Happening

Every time we teach a parenting class and this subject comes up, parents start to panic. It is a scary subject. It is also a common occurrence in today's culture to see kids who are hurting themselves. They cut themselves with scissors. They pull at scabs or wounds that haven't quite healed. They bruise themselves or pull their hair. They scratch themselves with fingernails or paper clips. Some actually brand themselves with irons. We knew one high school girl who cut her breasts with a knife. The trend as we are writing this is for kids to embed needles, pins, and other objects into their skin.

Statistics on self-harm are difficult to find, as it is often a hidden behavior. According to an article in the *Los Angeles Times* in December 2008, 15 to 22 percent of teens and young adults have purposefully injured themselves at least once in their lifetimes.[56] These statistics are similar to what we see in our counseling offices. And much of what is scary about cutting or self-harm is that we, as adults, often don't understand. That's what comes up during our parenting classes. "Why in the world do kids hurt themselves intentionally? I just don't get it."

Why It's Happening

The reasons behind self-injurious behavior are actually the same reasons behind any other type of addictive behavior, especially for preteens and teens. Kids, however, have been reported to self-harm as young as seven years old. The main reasons kids hurt themselves, in their own words, is that they'd rather "feel themselves hurt physically than emotionally." Physical pain deadens emotional pain . . . quite literally. The way God designed our bodies is that when we are injured, endorphins rush to the site of the injury to dull the pain. This happens in intentional injuries just as much as those that are accidental. So, in effect, cutting/embedding/scratching produces a degree of "high" for the cutter. They actually feel better, which is why self-harm can easily become addictive. It works, or at least works temporarily, like its addictive relatives.

Teens are specifically vulnerable to the allure of self-harm because of the emotions we've been talking about through this chapter. They just feel so much hurt, betrayal, sorrow, grief, pain, loss, abandonment. And many kids who injure themselves on purpose have been through some type of specific pain from which they are seeking relief, such as family problems or social struggles.

The other issue is that cutting has been "cool" in some circles. Just as you'll find pro-eating disorder Web sites, you'll also find Web sites devoted to teaching and encouraging self-injurious behavior. Thankfully, wonderful resources are available to encourage kids toward healthy behavior as well. But the reality is that most every teen knows peers who have hurt themselves on purpose. Word spreads and the drama of someone who is "having a hard time" is often alluring. Maybe the friends who have been leaving them out will pay more attention. Maybe the girl he likes will finally talk to him, if she can tell he's hurting.

What You Can Do

Regardless of the reason children are hurting themselves, if they are, they need help. They need someone to talk to about their emotional pain, and someone who can help them find healthier coping strategies than injuring themselves. If you suspect children may be harming themselves to get attention, they may need to talk to someone about their desperate need for approval and validation. In either case counseling can greatly benefit a child who self-harms.

If you are suspicious that your child or teen might be hurting himself, watch for these signs: unexplained injuries, making excuses for injuries repeatedly, long sleeves in the summer or sweatbands worn daily that could be hiding an injury, secrecy, a history of visiting Web sites involved with any type of self-injurious behavior. Talk to your child. Don't be afraid to ask if you have noticed some of these signs in your teen, but be aware of not sounding judgmental or harsh. Listen, be supportive, and get help.

As we know, an ounce of prevention is worth a pound of cure. So let's talk about prevention. As your child is growing up, teach positive coping strategies for stress. Help children find healthy ways to deal with sadness and grief. Any addiction comes from a variety of stressors but also a lack of available alternatives. In the Sunday Drive section, we'll focus on alternatives that are much more healthy and fulfilling than the behaviors mentioned in this chapter and not nearly as risky.

A Coping Strategy for Parents

I (Melissa) was walking on the beach with my puppy today. Sounds really nice, doesn't it, especially after reading this chapter? The sun was shining, a breeze was blowing, dolphins were jumping in the distance. But it wasn't really so nice. Part of the reason is because my puppy is a seven-month-old English sheepdog, known for stubborn will and sheer strength. Our walk was more like a trot for me, trailing behind her shaggy self, yelling "Wait, Blueberry! Stop! Slow down!" I didn't even see the dolphins.

And then I remembered. I heard the voice of my dog trainer in my head. "When Blueberry pulls, Melissa, stop, turn around, and start again." I did it. Actually, I think I probably did it thirty-seven times in the span of a forty-five-minute walk. But it worked. A few minutes later it stopped working, and I had to do it again. But, over and over, as I stopped and turned around, I started to feel more in control. I think she even began to enjoy the walk.

As we were turning our way back home, I thought about you. I thought about parenting and how so much of it feels like you are being pulled behind shouting, "Wait, Ben! Stop, Caroline! Slow down!" It's exhausting, and children end up driving themselves into behavior that is maddening for you and destructive for them.

So let me be the voice of your child trainer in your head. Stop. Turn around. What does that mean when it comes to a fourteen-year-old who has just been exposed to alcohol or drugs for the first time? Don't chase her in a panic screaming, for starters. Stop. Turn around. Ask her questions about how she felt when it happened. Assure her that she can call you any time she gets into a situation that scares her. And help her find friends, such as in the youth group, who are making good choices.

What about when your son comes home drunk for the first time? Stop. Turn around. Give him consequences. Help him find an outlet where he feels like he is able to take some risks without their being addiction producing. Let him pick between hang-gliding lessons and rock climbing or some such life-on-the-edge type of activity.

What about when you find vomit on the toilet for the third time in your teenage daughter's bathroom? Stop. Turn around. Remember that she feels bad about herself and longs for some type of purpose. Give her opportunities to make a difference without feeling pressure to perform. Research volunteer opportunities with her and help her get connected to something she feels passionate about.

"Taste and see that the LORD is good," says Psalm 34:8. Your children and teens are longing for a taste of purpose, of risk, of security, of comfort, and of hope. What better taste is there than that of knowing Jesus and his love for us. As you stop chasing them, as you turn and point them toward something different, you can help them know not only a deeper purpose but also a taste of the glorious good God has prepared for them (and us).

A Sunday Drive

A New Kind of Business: Healthy Alternatives to Help Your Child Learn to Destress and Grow at the Same Time

To Relieve Stress

- Painting/drawing
- Listening to music
- Playing a musical instrument
- Dancing
- Writing in a journal
- Writing a song or poetry
- Exercising
- Taking a bath
- Yoga
- Rock climbing
- Going for a walk
- Talking to a friend or adult they trust

To Find Purpose

- Learning martial arts
- Volunteering with underprivileged kids
- Helping build a Habitat house
- Going on a mission trip
- Helping coach a children's athletic team
- Teaching Sunday school
- Visit a nursing home or learn some type of activity, such as cooking with grandparents

Resources

Books

Every Young Woman's Battle, Shannon Ethridge and Stephen Arterburn

Preparing Your Son for Every Young Man's Battle, Stephen Arterburn

Preparing Your Daughter for Every Young Woman's Battle, Shannon Ethridge

Wild Things, Stephen James and David Thomas

Addiction and Grace, Gerald May

The Wounded Healer, Henri Nouwen

Life without Ed, Jenni Schaefer and Thom Rutledge

Every Young Man's Battle, Stephen Arterburn, Fred Stoeker, and Mike Yorkey

Raising Girls, Melissa Trevathan and Sissy Goff

Mirrors and Maps, Melissa Trevathan and Sissy Goff

Growing Up Without Getting Lost, Melissa Trevathan and Sissy Goff

Web Sites

AbovetheInfluence.com

Theantidrug.com

ANAD.org (eating disorders)

Eatingdisorderscoalition.org

ToWriteLoveonHerArms.com (self-harm)

Oceans of Emotions

I have heard there are troubles of more than one kind.
Some come from ahead and some come from behind.
But I've bought a big bat. I'm all ready you see.
Now my troubles are going to have troubles with me!

— Dr. Seuss, *I Had Trouble in Getting to Solla Sollew*[57]

As a senior in high school, Hannah still sucks her thumb at night. She worries almost constantly about everything. She makes great grades but panics over every test. She has a sweet, supportive group of friends, but fears most days that one of them might be mad at her. She has a boyfriend of four months, whom she worries secretly likes her best friend. Her family doesn't want her to go away to college because they don't think she's capable of driving in a town she doesn't know. In a year of her life that is supposed to be full of friends, freedom, and the confidence that she can go away and do anything, Hannah feels trapped. And no one who knows her would have any idea, except for her family. Hannah is anxious.

Ten-year-old Michael has a hard time tying his shoes. Whenever he starts to, his hands shake, and he just can't seem to loop them the right ways. His grades are not good. He can't concentrate on his homework; and, when home, he sticks mostly to his mom's side. He doesn't speak to people he doesn't know. They think he's shy, but really he is very sad. His father has a problem with anger . . . anger that is directed mostly at Michael. Michael is struggling with depression.

We have the privilege of spending every day with Hannahs and Michaels—kids who are struggling with their emotions, be it emotions of sadness, anger, worry, fear. Their parents bring them in because they want help for their children and they want help for themselves.

Kids feel. They feel a lot, even on a daily basis. They literally do have oceans of emotions that flood over them with wave upon wave. Some of the feelings are external, because of things that have happened. Some are internal because of the changes going on in their bodies and brains. Some are genuine, and some may have a little bit of a dramatic flair. It depends largely on the age, the child, and the circumstances.

We don't know your child. We wish we did. We wish we could sit and talk to you about your child's emotions and yours. Do you wonder about why he is sad sometimes? Does she worry a lot? Does he tend toward explosiveness with his anger? The reason we ask is because, as counselors who have worked with kids for quite a few years, we believe that not just the addictive issues but also emotions have ramped up in intensity for our kids. Today in our offices we are seeing more kids with anxiety, depression, low self-esteem, and a host of other emotional struggles than ever before.

You may be asking why. We wish we knew. Maybe it's the familiarity with which we and even they have with these ideas. We see teenagers who diagnose themselves with depression or obsessive-compulsive disorder. Maybe it's the pace in which we live in our culture. Maybe it's the lack of stability in families. Maybe it's the pressure we put on ourselves and inadvertently put on our children. We simply don't know why it's changed, but we know that it has. And that change is affecting the daily lives and emotions of today's kids.

So, what can you do? How do you know what is typical and when to be concerned? Why is this a struggle for your child, and what can you do? This chapter will deal with these issues—or, actually, these emotions. We would like to give an exhaustive report of each one, the various kinds of anxiety/depression, etc., all of the things that might cause them, exactly how to get help. But we can't, at least in one chapter in one book. The well is simply too deep. What we can do, however, is give you an overview: a definition of the problem, what to watch for, where it might be coming from, and how you can help your child who might be struggling.

Anxiety

Anxiety Defined

"Anxiety is a psychological and physiological state characterized by cognitive, somatic, emotional, and behavioral components. These components combine to create an unpleasant feeling that is typically associated with uneasiness, fear, or worry."[58] The main difference between anxiety and fear is that fear has a trigger; anxiety does not. It is more of a general feeling or mood. As we stated before, anxiety is the number one mental health problem in America with 13 percent of children and adolescents suffering from an anxiety disorder.[59]

So, what does anxiety really look like in a child? It can be one who cries before school every morning. It can be one who worries incessantly whenever you are away: where you're going, when you'll be home, who you're going with, when you'll be home. It can be one who is debilitatingly afraid to speak in front of the class or swings alone on the same swing every day at recess.

In adolescents it looks a little different. It can be teens who worry about washing their hands, obsess over college and every grade that might potentially have an effect on that decision, feel that nothing they do is ever good enough. Anxiety can look like withdrawal, sadness, obsessive fears, or even anger in an adolescent or child.

A Potential Problem

All children worry. It's part of their and our normal, daily emotional lives. Infants are often fearful of strangers and cry when held by someone they don't know. Young children are afraid of creepy crawlies and things that go bump in the night. Their imaginations drive much of their fears of what could be, whether it's in the dark, behind Mickey Mouse's mask, or even what happens to you when you leave their sight. School-aged children develop normal real-life types of fears such as fires, burglaries, diseases, and even social and academic fears. Much of teens' typical fears center around their social lives, how they see themselves fitting in and succeeding or failing. These fears are a normal and often healthy part of a child's growing up. They have to do with learning what is real, who they are, and how they interact with others and the world at large.

Typically worry in children or teenagers arises from a certain situation. They are worried about a friend who didn't invite them to their birthday party. The SAT has them in their room studying frantically for several weeks. But when those anxieties don't subside, when you notice that your child lives with a constant, low or even high-grade level of anxiety, then it may be time to do a little of your own worrying.

As a parent, whatever age your child is, you will be often the first to notice signs of anxiety. These are a few signals that your child could be struggling with anxiety, rather than just an anxious situation:

- The worry doesn't go away after the situation resolves itself.
- The worry affects other areas of life, such as grades, concentration, enjoyment of typically pleasurable activities.
- Events that would normally cause a little worry are devastating to your child.
- Reassurance doesn't help calm them.
- Live in a constant state of tension.
- Ask constant "what if" types of questions.
- Have frequent headaches or stomach aches when participating in a certain activity.
- Engage in overly pleasing behavior.
- Are highly perfectionistic and overly critical of themselves.
- Lack of ability to sleep or frequent nightmares.
- Significant distress over normal occurrences such as fixing hair, getting ready for school.

- Inability to leave home for fun events such as parties or going to a friend's house.
- Fixation on a certain idea, such as cheating or winning.

The Root of the Problem

The experts break the causes of anxiety down into three types: genetic, learning/modeling, and environmental. Genetic has to do with anxiety that runs in the family. If family members struggle significantly with anxiety, your child can have a higher level of anxiety or even lower tolerance of stressful situations. We talked about learning and modeling in chapter 2 on fear. A parent who lives in a constant state of anxiety often inadvertently (or even purposefully) teaches the child that the world is a threat.

Environmentally speaking, because anxiety is a more generalized state, it typically does not have one triggering event. A loss or tragedy can cause a child to fear that same loss being repeated. In many cases children and teens develop anxiety in times of transition. For example, I (Sissy) am meeting with a senior in high school who is kind, compassionate, successful in her peer and family's eyes, well liked, and is struggling from an anxiety disorder known as obsessive-compulsive disorder. She has violent and sexual thoughts that she can't control and that are completely opposite from who she is or would ever want to be. These thoughts have made her call herself "crazy" repeatedly in my office. She feels horrible for them and thinks there must be something terribly wrong with her for thinking them. The reality is that she can't control them—at least until she gets some help.

How You Can Help

- Slow down, but don't change your expectations. Anxious children need to learn the same things other children do: going to school, being away from you, spending the night away. But they may not be able to learn them in the same time frame as the others. Role play fearful scenarios. Take it a step at a time and celebrate even the minor victories.

- Find something your child feels successful in and give him plenty of opportunities to live in that confidence. Try different lessons or things he or she might enjoy: sports, arts, academics, but find something where he can draw a little strength to carry him through the more anxious activities.
- Allow her to learn to do things herself. Don't always do the work for her. She can learn, in her own time. If you always do it for her, she won't feel that she is capable on her own.
- Help him verbalize his fears. Come up with a fear scale. Many kids are debilitated by small events. Help him realize that it's okay to be afraid. Reassure him that you won't be angry with him.
- If her anxiety causes her to act out, she still needs consequences. Let her know that you know she's afraid, but unacceptable behavior is still unacceptable.
- If older children are anxious, give them opportunities to talk. Point out that you've noticed something going on, and then let them talk. Make sure they know that nothing they say or worry about is going to upset you. Many anxious teens struggle with sexual and violent thoughts and are terrified for anyone to find out.
- Brainstorm with them on things they can do that help ease their worrying.
- Memorize verses together on fear that children of any age can repeat when they start to worry, such as Psalm 46:1–2; Isaiah 41:10, 13; 43:1–2; Romans 8:14–15; 2 Timothy 1:7.
- If they seem to be struggling with what to say or even recognizing that something is going on, they may benefit from talking to someone. Sometimes anxiety is so debilitating that medication is needed to help stabilize irrational fears enough to learn other ways to cope.

Depression

Depression Defined

Meredith's brother died a year ago, and she still can't seem to stop crying. Kyle doesn't feel like he's worth anything so he sets himself up to fail continually. Hillary's mother and grandmother were depressed when they were in high school. In the past few months she has had significantly more trouble with grades and less trouble staying in her bed so she doesn't have to face it. Kendrick has quit every activity he used to enjoy except for video games and food.

Depression is defined as an "all-encompassing low mood accompanied by low self-esteem, and loss of interest or pleasure in normally enjoyable activities."[60] All of us can relate to that kind of feeling. At a seminar I (Melissa) recently attended, the presenter described it much like a bad cold. You feel crummy but not so crummy that you can't do anything. You just don't care. That's normal depression. It becomes clinical depression when that feeling doesn't go away for a prolonged period of time.

Low self-esteem is a normal state of feeling for many children and teenagers. In fact, it's so normal that our next section will be entirely devoted to it. Sadness is a normal state of being for many children and teenagers. They are emotional, passionate, little creatures that feel the tides of even the smallest event often very deeply.

Expect that your child and your teenager will feel down often. When something difficult happens to your young son or daughter, they may cry huge cartoon-like tears for a few hours or even days. But then they will want to play again. They will come back around and feel more burdened by the fact that they haven't played soccer in a few days than whatever loss they just encountered. For toddler-age children those transitions typically cycle through the hours.

Particularly with teenagers, as we talked about in the last chapter, their normal emotional state mimics much of what clinical depression looks like. They are moody, temperamental, sad, frustrated, melancholy, and angry on a daily basis. Their hormones, brain chemistry, and often truly dramatic lives cause significant (to them) emotional turmoil. Girls and boys are fickle creatures and hurt each other continually—even the best of friends. So expect that your teen will be an emotional roller coaster. As long as they're rolling, they're most likely living as typical teens. When the rolling bottoms out and stays there, it's time to be truly concerned.

A Potential Problem

Let's talk about some signs of depression in children and teens. These symptoms need to be present every or nearly every day for at least a two-week period for a child to be considered depressed:

- Sadness or hopelessness
- Anger, irritability, or rage (especially in teens)
- Frequent crying or tearfulness
- Loss of interest in activities they used to enjoy
- Withdrawal from family (especially children) and friends (especially teens)
- Feelings of worthlessness and guilt
- Lack of energy
- Difficulty concentrating or declining grades
- Mention of suicide or not wanting to live
- Changes in eating or sleeping habits
- Unexplained aches and pains
- Extreme sensitivity to rejection, failure, or criticism

The Root of the Problem

Depression is often caused by either an imbalance of chemicals in the brain or a stressor that results in depression. The imbalance can be passed on genetically through families with either depression or bipolar depression. It can also be that a child or teen has a family history for depression, and it is not an issue until a specific event brings about the depressive cycle.

Kids will often talk about being "depressed." This does not necessarily mean they have a chemical imbalance. It can mean that either they are experiencing these symptoms and are concerned about themselves or they are dramatic and looking for a response. Sometimes both can be the case. But in either event sadness does not change brain chemistry unless it is drawn out over a period of time.

Kids feel depressed with everyday occurrences such as when they're rejected by someone they have a crush on. They're sad when a friend leaves them out or a teacher rebuffs them in front of a class. They're devastated when their parents divorce or a family member dies. They feel each of these things, no matter how daily the occurrence is, deeply.

Again, when the feelings don't go away, clinical depression can become a problem. In terms of the chemicals, this is the way a psychiatrist explained it to me (Sissy). It is a bare-bones, really simplistic explanation, but one that I use with kids and parents often. Our brains fire hormones across the synapses or gaps between nerve endings. When a child (or adult, for that matter) is sad for an extended period of time, the hormones stop firing. When that happens, no amount of talking or journaling can re-start the hormones. A pharmacological intervention is needed in that scenario, with medication acting as a jumper cable between nerve endings.

If depression goes unchecked in either a child or teen, it can lead to suicidal thoughts and even actions. If you suspect that your child may be depressed, please seek help—for their sake and for yours.

How You Can Help

- Watch for signs and symptoms of them communicating without doing so verbally: stomach aches, sleeping a lot, not wanting to participate.
- Talk to your child. Ask him or her about thoughts and feelings.
- Don't minimize what they feel. Whether it's related to a friend, family member, or even losing a pet, they feel whatever it is they're feeling deeply. Give them opportunities to talk through it and verbalize the emotions.
- If your children or teens seem angry over an event, give them time to calm down and then talk about it. Look deeper than the anger to see if something painful could be driving it.

- Talk in the car or on a walk. It is sometimes more difficult for kids to talk when they feel pressure. A shared activity can help relieve some of the tension and awkwardness for them.
- If your child is artistic, ask him to draw or paint what he feels. Have her write a song or poem.
- We have parents who will write in a journal back and forth with their children. This can be a positive way to find out what they're feeling without them having to say the words out loud.
- Seek help if you feel that your child is not bouncing back from whatever event precipitated the sadness. Take your child to your family doctor. Talk to a counselor. Try to find one that your child connects with and trusts. It may be that you need a psychiatrist, as well.

Low Self-Esteem

Defining Low Self-Esteem

I (Sissy) was driving a group of high school students up to our camp, Camp Hopetown. On the way there, Melissa, who lives at the camp in the summer, called to ask us how far away we were. She then had me ask the kids what they wanted to learn about during the week. They all—literally all fourteen in my car unanimously shouted, "Low self-esteem."

When I (Melissa) do assessments, or first-time appointments with kids, many parents cite low self-esteem as the reason they want counseling for their children. Many older kids, preteens and teenagers alike, tell me that they wanted counseling themselves because they have low self-esteem. Now low self-esteem is tricky. We all have it to some degree. But many of us live our lives believing that no one else does. We are the only ones thinking we're not smart enough, attractive enough, strong enough, or whatever enough we saddle ourselves with.

Kids start the saddling process at a young age. Five-year-olds talk about not being fast enough on the playground or as pretty or thin as their classmates. Lower school children don't feel funny enough or smart enough. Middle school kids say, "No one likes me," when in reality it's just the popular kids who don't. Everyone else thinks they're great. But those popular kids, at every age, do a lot to cause low self-esteem. In high school it's any number of factors—popularity, looks, grades, athletics, social status. Basically anything they can rate themselves on, they often rate themselves poorly. But teenagers would never want others to know. So some compensate by acting like they have terrific self-esteems. In their words, not so much.

Low self-esteem is not something Wikipedia tackles in terms of definitions. But we would define low self-esteem and particularly the low self-esteem we see in children and teens as a lack of belief in one's own worth, a persistent feeling that you have nothing to offer and little reason for anyone to like you.

A Potential Problem

Again, many kids, in fact many of *us*, have low self-esteem. We probably all do at one point or another, or in one or two areas of our lives. The problem comes when the low self-esteem is pervasive.

I (Melissa) was counseling a nine-year-old boy who had two best friends. Those friends would include him one day at recess and not the next . . . over and over and over. He didn't understand what he had done to change their minds about him. And, like anyone who struggled with low self-esteem, his next jump was to "What's wrong with me?" The progression of his thoughts went from "what's wrong with me" to "no one likes me" to "I hate myself" over the course of just a few months. His low self-esteem was concerning to his parents. His mom brought him in for counseling and eventually decided to leave the small private school he attended (with only seven in his class) and send him to the neighborhood public school where he had more opportunities for friendship. The next fall when I saw him, he was on cloud nine. His mom was, too. He finally had friends and more than just two.

Every child and every teen will suffer from low self-esteem at one point in their lives or another. We urge you to watch for the following:

- If children make repetitive, self-berating comments.

- If unwilling to try new sports, arts, or activities because they don't believe they would be "good" at it.
- If they continually make comments such as, "I'm never good enough," or, "I can't ever please you."
- If they come home from school every day in tears or dejected.
- If their friend choices reflect that they're only seeking out the kids that are most accepting—either because they make themselves outcast or are unaccepted.
- If your child is rejected repeatedly by peers.
- If they're hurting themselves or showing any other signs of addictive behavior.
- If they start to show signs of anxiety or depression.

The Root of the Problem

The root of the problem for low self-esteem is fairly self-explanatory. Your child feels bad about himself. This can happen, however, for a variety of reasons. One is the body and brain changes we've discussed before. Starting before puberty begins, your son and daughter will experience drops in their confidence. I (Sissy) remember one mom telling me her daughter would look in a mirror and say to her mom, "Mom, I'm really pretty. Wait, am I?" Children who feel confident about themselves will often turn into a preteen or teen who questions how other people feel about them. For girls, particularly, their brain growth surges in a manner that literally short-circuits their confidence, a phenomenon we discuss at length in our book *Raising Girls*. But boys experience this phenomenon, too, with their surging hormones and changing bodies.

In addition, many children and teens suffer from low self-esteem when they feel rejected by someone else. It can be a parent, friend, family member, or teacher. If that person doesn't like them or approve of their behavior, they will often turn on themselves with thoughts like *I'm a bad person* or *I don't deserve anything better*. It is easier to be disappointed in themselves than in someone else, especially a person they respect.

Low self-esteem also occurs when a child notices the areas where they're weak but not those in which they are strong. An artistic child may feel horrible about himself because he can't run a mile as fast as the other kids in class. An athletic child may feel stupid if she can't raise her chemistry grade.

Some who appear to have high self-esteem can actually have low self-esteem, as well. They have a grandiose idea of who they are and how other people will receive them. It may be because of a certain strength or talent. In other words, their self-esteem is tied to their success in one area of their image. Then, when either they fail or simply are not received as well as they imagined, their previously high self-esteem plummets.

Low self-esteem occurs for as many reasons as people who have low self-esteem. We feel bad about ourselves. We're critical of ourselves, and we often start early.

How You Can Help

If you suspect that your child has low self-esteem, here are a few suggestions of ways to help them find their true worth:

- Encourage them. If they've failed, don't ignore it. They already know they've messed up. But help them find the positives, as well. Point out strengths in your child and characteristics you respect.
- Be unpredictable in your encouragement. Write them notes or point things out when they don't expect it.
- Help your child find places and activities in which he or she can feel successful.
- Ask grandparents, aunts, uncles, and teachers to become cheerleaders for your child—not just in what they do but who they are.
- Give your child opportunities to feel a sense of purpose. If younger, that purpose can be helping you around the house. If older, help them find a place to give of themselves, something they feel passionate about. One of the best cures for low self-esteem is to see that you really can and do make a difference.
- Study Scripture together on their identity in Christ, such as Jeremiah 31:3; Zephaniah 3:17; Matthew 5:14; Luke 12:7;

John 14:14; 2 Corinthians 5:17; Ephesians 2:4–5; 5:1; Colossians 3:3; 1 Peter 2:9.

- If they are really struggling, take them to talk to someone like a counselor. It may be that you need another voice that can help them understand their feelings of inferiority and find their strengths.

High Stress

High Stress Defined

"I'm going to have to quit something." He was the forward on his basketball team, the quarterback in football; he led worship for his youth group and had straight A's. "The thing I would most like to quit is football. I know they feel like they need me, but I just don't enjoy it. I want to stop. But I'm afraid the coach and the other guys will be really mad at me." He wanted to stop something, and the reality was that he really needed to. He was at school seven hours a day and practice for one sport or another for an additional two to three hours most days. On Wednesdays church and rehearsal for church took three. His schedule was worse than a forty-year-old workaholic's. His family never saw him. His friends complained that he was too busy. And he was beginning randomly to have trouble breathing.

It's easy for us to think about life as a fifteen-year-old or even a ten-year-old and think they have it easy—no job responsibilities, no family responsibilities; they barely even have to take out the trash. But the reality is that kids today live under a tremendous amount of pressure. School is harder, athletics are more competitive, and the opportunities to excel or fail are more intense than ever before. I (Sissy) meet with a twelve-year-old with a multialbum record deal who can't attend traditional school because of her touring schedule. It sounds fun, but she wants to quit and have a "normal middle school life." And what is normal today? Gone are the days, for most kids, of coming home from school and playing outside for several hours before coming in for homework. Kids don't sit and color. They take art class. They don't kick around a soccer ball outside.

They play on a travel team with a practice schedule that rivals those of the professionals.

Don't get us wrong. Kids today have more opportunity than ever before to develop their gifts. We didn't have the options to compete, perform, advance, or even learn many of the skills kids today are learning. But we have to admit that with learning comes some degree of pressure. Some kids flourish under it. But some kids end up in our offices in tears or with shortness of breath. And, as their parent, you're often right there with them because you're the one driving them to all the practices and watching all of the games and recitals.

A Potential Problem

How many activities per week does your child participate in? How many nights per week are you able to sit down and have a family dinner? How many times do you refill your gas tank per week, simply from chauffeuring to and from practice? Are you burned out from all of their activities? If your answer is yes, then theirs very likely is, too.

Some kids will know their limits. We see children of all ages who talk about having too much stress. But some don't. Some have no idea that they are doing or performing or playing or practicing too much. You will often be the first to know. For many kids and teens, stress manifests itself physically. They'll feel fatigued, become irritable. A child with asthma will have attacks more frequently. A teen with allergies or stomach problems will have more frequent flare-ups. They will get teary more often or simply withdraw from social or family activities because they "don't have time." If your child is suffering from stress, either physically or emotionally, it may be time to take a deeper look.

The Root of the Problem

What is with all of the over-scheduling? Is your child driving the frenzy? Is it a coach or teacher? Is it you? We see kids living with a high level of stress from a variety of sources.

Some children and teens simply want to succeed. They want to participate in a lot of different activities and excel in each of those activities in which they're involved. A tenth-grader named Eli used to complain week after week about how hard it was to have a part-time job and keep up his grades. He "didn't have time to hang out with his friends or do the things other kids were doing." Every week his friends in group would give him helpful suggestions as to how he could rework his schedule for more time for his friends, his family, and himself. But Eli didn't do it. He didn't want to. Eli thrived under pressure and under a busy schedule. Eli was also trying to escape having to think about the problems at home— maybe even escape home in general. But Eli liked it that way.

The young man who opened our chapter was a talented athlete, student, and musician. But he was not a fan of the pace of his schedule. He wanted and needed to cut something out. What kept him from doing so had nothing to do with what he wanted. It was about his coach and friends. He was afraid to let them down. We know many guys and girls in similar situations. It could be an art teacher, a violin instructor, a track coach, or even a drama teacher. It could be friends on a team, in a play, or going to a certain camp. Children and adolescents want to please their friends. They want to live up to their teachers' and coaches' expectations, even when they act the opposite. Your child may be continuing in a high-stress situation just so he doesn't disappoint someone else. And he may need your help getting out of it.

I (Melissa) counseled a young woman who was considered a star on her middle school track team. She won state championships and was thinking about trying out for the junior Olympics. But she was one of those in tears most days after practice. Her grades were suffering, and she, too, "just wanted to live a normal life." But her mom saw her immense talent. "I just want to take a break," Lakisha told me privately in my office. "If she takes a break, she'll ruin her chances for the Olympics," her mother told me privately. "I don't care about the Olympics. I just want to have a life." It was as if Lakisha and her mother were in the same room. It was obvious that this conversation had played itself out many times. Lakisha was talented, but her mother cared more about her athletic advancement than she. That's when potential problems arise.

Your son may want to quit piano lessons, but you feel he needs to stick it out. Your daughter complains when she has to go to softball practice, but you know it's the right thing and that really she loves the activity. And sometimes you know they are playing or painting or acting because you want them to and they want to please you.

How You Can Help

- Talk to your children. Check in with them regularly about their schedule and stress level. Is it too much? Do they feel like they are having time to be a kid?
- Give them time to think. Kids of all ages need time to dream and to imagine. Even though they may whine to you about it, it is good for them to be bored. Creativity is often born out of boredom. They will also learn to be dependent on themselves for fun rather than the next activity you have planned or scheduled.
- Limit their time in front of the TV, computer, or video games. Build a tree house with your children. Ride bikes together. Get them outside where they can stretch their legs and experience a little of old-school, after-school freedom.
- Exercise as a family. Go for walks. Hike. Exercise relieves stress. If exercise or athletic practices are creating the stress, they may need more time at home playing Monopoly. But, if your child feels pressure in other areas, exercise can be a great way to relieve tension.
- Play together as a family weekly, if possible. Have a family game night. Eat together. Pick a television show or movie you can enjoy with each other. This will carve out time for you to stay connected as a family and limit the number of nightly activities.
- If your children are talking about too much stress or asking to quit a certain activity, listen to them and then talk to someone else about it before you make a decision. It may be an activity that they can continue for a period of time because you know they will ultimately enjoy it and grow from it, as well. Or maybe your need for them to continue is greater than theirs. Find a

trusted person who can help you figure it out before you go back to your child with an answer.

- Every child is different. You may have one child who can and truly enjoys four activities per week and another who is overwhelmed with more than one. Listen to and watch for signs of too much stress in each child.

- Be willing to be the bad guy. If children are afraid to quit an activity because they don't want to disappoint someone else, help them come up with ways to quit with kindness. Role play the conversation with them. Give them opportunities to do it on their own. The pressure, however, may just be too much, especially if it's with a respected adult. They may need you to step in and make the decision for them.

- Talk about failure as a family. When you mess up at work or fail in a friendship, mention it around your children. Help them know that failure is a normal and natural part of everyday life. If you're uncomfortable with your own sense of failure, they often will be as well. Teach them about God's grace and His unconditional love for us in all areas of our lives.

- Remind children often that their value is not in the skills they possess or the merits they achieve but in who they are and the people God has created them to be.

Anger

Anger Defined

Anger is the emotion we'd rather not talk about. It's much harder to feel compassion for an angry child. We get angry back. We take it personally and get hurt. We come up against it too much and get overwhelmed. Or all of the above. I (Melissa) recently spoke with a young mom with an angry son. He acts out constantly. He yells, throws things, and generally makes their home life pretty miserable. When she came to my office, she was just about at the end of her rope. "Some days when he goes to school, I literally think, *I'd be fine if he never came back. My life would be easier if he was killed in a car accident and went home to be with the Lord. I hate* myself for thinking that. I feel like a failure as a mom and as a Christian. I just have no idea what to do, and I'm so tired."

If you have a child who battles with anger, or more likely, battles with you because he's angry, you know some semblance of how she feels. You are exhausted. You're exhausted from her anger and exhausted with yourself for the way you feel in response.

Define anger? Not sure we need to. You know what it looks like. It looks like a six-year-old boy who kicks and throws punches every time he hears the word *no*. It looks like a ten-year-old girl teachers describe as a "delight" but who rages at you every night at bedtime. It looks like a fourteen-year-old girl who stomps rather than walks, screams, and slams her door with every opportunity. It looks like a seventeen-year-old boy who thinks everyone and everything is "stupid" and lives life in a constant state of disdain. Anger can be subtle or explosive. It can emerge in calculated cruelty or exaggerated outbursts.

A Potential Problem

The problem with anger does not lie so much in the feeling as it does the expression of that feeling. One of the most important things we can do for any child, not just an angry one, is to teach him healthy, appropriate ways to handle anger. He will feel anger. She will feel angry as part of those oceans of emotions. But the problem comes in what she does with it. We'll come back to that idea a little later.

The problem with anger is that it is not an isolated emotion. In fact, anger feeds off the emotions of others. When your child is angry, he wants to express it. He wants an emotional if not physical release from the tension that anger creates. But that release often comes at the expense of others. It may be you or her siblings. It may be his teacher or best friend. But often with kids, because they have not yet learned how to express their anger constructively, it becomes destructive.

If you suspect that your child may be struggling with anger, watch for the following:

- Isolation from other kids at school.

- Comments reflecting that he feels guilt over his anger such as "I'm a bad kid."
- Incidents at school or with other children where he or she hurts them physically such as pushing, hitting, or even biting.
- Frequent exaggerated, irritable responses from minor occurrences.
- Regular explosions at home with you or siblings.
- Continually defiant attitude with persons in authority.

The Root of the Problem

Almost all psychologists and counselors agree that anger is a secondary emotion. In other words it's coming from somewhere else. Underneath the anger lies sadness, fear, shame, or some other emotion. But anger makes them (or us) feel in control. Kids tell us it's easier to feel angry than anything else. It's less vulnerable. We know. We've been there ourselves a time or two.

The problem with anger as a secondary emotion is that it's often hard to get to what's underneath. You can't hear the hurt past the screaming. You can't get her to talk to you about why she's sad when you continually have to discipline her for hurting her sister. But, even with all of the yelling and screaming, the likelihood is that something else is going on.

Many of the kids we see in our offices who are angry have attention issues. These kids don't know how to get just a little bit angry. It's as if they can't put the brakes on their emotions. Everything is a "ten." They can't tie their shoes and they scream. Someone spills their drink, and they retaliate with a punch. The anger is really a symptom that something else is going on, an inability to focus and an impulsivity that makes them feel out of control.

An angry child can be one who is suffering from ADD. An angry teen, as we've said, could be suffering from depression or even an addiction. Angry children feel shame or helplessness. The anger can be stemming from any number of emotions. But, as parents, we've somehow got to learn how to both handle the anger and help the emotion that's underneath it.

How You Can Help

- Teach your child the principle of Ephesians 4:26, "In your anger do not sin." Talk to your children about the differences between feeling angry and acting out that anger. Role play with them. Give them opportunities to talk about their anger when it emerges.
- Give them appropriate options to express their anger such as a punching bag, Wii boxing, or a tennis racket to bang on their bed. Boys, particularly, need physical outlets for their aggressive feelings. Help them find options that can give them the physical release they may need for their anger.
- Teach them ways to express their anger verbally. Start sentences for them with phrases like, "It makes me really mad when . . ."
- If your child has an angry outburst or can't talk about their anger without acting on it, give consequences. Consequences help children learn what is appropriate and not appropriate as they learn to express their anger.
- Catch your child when he's acting appropriately, as well as inappropriately. Don't just point out negative, angry behavior. Try to stop him when he's being kind or compassionate, as well, and comment on those times. Help them learn what to do rather than just what not to do.
- Choose your battles. If you have a child who is always angry, you can find yourself reprimanding her constantly. Let the minor grievances go, so that she won't tune out the sound of your voice. Save it for the times that really matter.
- Watch what you model. What you do matters as much as, if not more than, what you say.

A Lesson from Two Football Players

David came to camp when he was in the fourth grade. He was funny, warm, and a natural leader. Kids flocked to him. We did, too, as a staff. David's heart was incredibly tender to the Lord. During worship or teaching, he would sit in front of the room with a thin layer of tears just inside his eyes. As a teenager David continued to feel intensely. He was sad and he was angry. He was passionate about his friends and passionate about his love for football, as well. Over spring break of his sophomore year in high school, David took his life. We know there had to be many reasons in his own mind for David's tragic and impulsive decision. But we think a lot of it had to do with the intense oceans of emotions crashing inside of him. He just couldn't or didn't know how to handle it.

At David's funeral the minister offered a powerful message directly to the many kids present: "Your anger is okay. Your fear is okay. It is okay to feel disappointment and hurt. It is okay to feel like life is hard and you don't know how to handle it. What David said that afternoon was that it wasn't okay. He said it was too much. But I'm here to tell you that it's not. You will feel disappointment. You will feel hurt and angry and even depressed at times in your life. But those feelings will come and go. You will also feel hope and happiness and joy. I just want to remind you of that truth that David had somehow lost."

Another football player must have been feeling several of those emotions just a few nights ago. It was the national championship for college football—the 2010 BCS Bowl, or Rose Bowl, as we called it in the vintage days. Number-one-ranked Alabama took on number-two Texas. The Texas quarterback, Colt McCoy, had been dubbed the winningest quarterback in NCAA history. This game was to be the biggest of Colt's career and one he worked toward all year long. It was also one of the shortest. In the first quarter he injured his shoulder with a pinched nerve and was out the rest of the game. He watched his backup quarterback, a freshman named Garrett Gilbert, bring the Longhorns back to a near victory after halftime.

After the game was over, McCoy's response was simple but one we would want our children and even ourselves to echo in times of trouble. "I always give God the glory. I never question why things happen the way they do. God is in control of my life. And I know that if nothing else, I'm standing on the Rock."[61]

David knew that Rock, too, in times of trouble. Maybe he just needed a little more reminding. Whether depression or low self-esteem, anger or anxiety, we all need to be reminded of who we are and exactly where we stand. Second Peter 1:12 says, "Therefore, I will always be ready to remind you of these things, even though you already know them, and have been established in the truth which is present with you" (NASB). You may have told your children these things time and time again. But that was Peter's point. We never cease to need to be reminded. Neither do our kids. In our minds that's the great big bat Dr. Seuss was talking about in the quote at the beginning of the chapter. God's Word is our reminder . . . of who we are, who our kids are, and his great, gracious love for us all. These verses serve as a little extra reminder:

- John 16:33
- John 14:27
- 2 Corinthians 7:5
- 1 Thessalonians 5:24
- 2 Thessalonians 3:3
- Matthew 28:20
- 2 Timothy 4:15–16
- Psalm 56:3–4
- Matthew 11:28
- Psalm 55:22

A Sunday Drive

Do you remember when your parents or even grandparents used to tell you stories? This Sunday Drive takes the form of a story—one that was told to your parents, their parents before them, and so on. And it's one that you can tell your children, as well . . . one that speaks to those oceans of emotions and God's response to us in the midst of them. This story is one for children but could be adapted to be a conversation with teens, as well.

In Numbers 13, God told Moses to choose a group of men to go scout out the promised land. These men were supposed to come back and report what the land was like: Was the food good? Are there trees? What were the towns like? What were the people like? Oh, and he wanted them to bring back some food while they were at it.

So the twelve spies set out. They went through deserts and valleys and brought back pomegranates, figs, and one branch of grapes that was so big it took two men to carry it. They were gone for forty days.

When the men came back, they told Moses that the land was flowing with milk and honey, just as God had said. (In other words, it was really great, beautiful, and had lots of wonderful things in it.) But it also had large, powerful people in it . . . giants, you might say. The men were scared—all of them, that was, except for two. Caleb and Joshua thought they could do it.

"Let's go up and take the land—now. We can do it," said Caleb.

When the rest of the guys heard this, they panicked. "Everybody we saw was huge." They went on to say that the giants were so huge they felt and looked the size of bugs next to them—grasshoppers, to be exact.

At times in your life, you will feel as small as a grasshopper. Perhaps one of your friends has left you out and made you feel really bad. Or your dad hurt your feelings, or you've made a bad grade in school. Maybe you're worried because someone you love is sick.

But do you know what happened to Caleb and Joshua and Moses? They went into the land and God blessed them. God took care of them. And God even said that Caleb had what he called a "different spirit." Caleb trusted God and God believed in Caleb.

God believes in you, too, and wants you to trust him. Sometimes you will feel sad and scared and hurt and disappointed. But that's okay. God knows that but also knows that he's going to take care of you. He loves you and knows that you can beat any giant that comes your way. (Excerpts taken from *The Message*.)

Resources

For Adults

Worrywisekids.org
Kidshealth.org
Cry of the Soul, Dan Allender
Freeing Your Child from Anxiety, Tamar Chansky
Monochrome Days, Cait Irwin
The Wonder of Boys, Michael Gurian
The Wonder of Girls, Michael Gurian

For More Mature Teens and Adults

Abba's Child, Brennan Manning
Life of the Beloved, Henri Nouwen
Captivating, John and Stasi Eldredge
Wild at Heart, John Eldredge
The Sacred Romance, Brent Curtis and John Eldredge
To Be Told, Dan Allender

For Kids

Wemberley Worried, Kevin Henkes
You Are Special, Max Lucado
Alexander and the Terrible, Horrible, No Good, Very Bad Day, Judith Viorst
The Way I Feel, Janan Cain
The Feelings Book: The Care and Keeping of Your Emotions, An American Girl Book
How to Take the GRRRR out of Anger, Elizabeth Verdick and Marjorie Lisovskis
My Many Colored Days, Dr. Seuss

Part 2

Vintage Values

The Value of Kindness

Be kind and compassionate to one another.

—Ephesians 4:32

A boy comes to Daystar named Caleb. Caleb has been a part of Daystar since he was a scrawny, precocious third-grader with glasses and red hair. In those days Melissa had a sheepdog named Molasses, and Sissy had a Maltese named Noel who were both part of our counseling staff. Besides knowing Caleb from Daystar, we also all go to the same church. For years, at the end of every church service, Caleb would race over to one or the other of us and excitedly greet us with "How's Noel?" or "What's Molasses doing today?"

Caleb was a kind kid. He was thoughtful, not just of our dogs but also of us. When Noel and Molasses both died this past year, Caleb was one of the most heartbroken kids at Daystar. His mom told us that he cried when he heard the news. Caleb is now a freshman in high school. Today, when Caleb walks into the office, he's a little more subdued. "Hello, Melissa," he will say. When I ask him how he is, he answers me thoughtfully and directly with, "Well, it hasn't been the best day," or, "It's been a fun one." He will then turn right back and say, "And, Melissa, how are you today?" It seems small. And that's the deal with kindness. It does often seem small, but it feels big when you stop to notice.

Defining Kindness

When we started working on this chapter, we had a hard time distinguishing kindness from compassion, which we talk about in the next chapter. What we landed on is that kindness is daily. It is humble, gentle, and quiet . . . much like Caleb. It is as much in the way we talk as in what we do. It is motivated not by a felt need but by an act of will.

Think about kindnesses offered to you in the past week. You really do have to think, don't you? More often than not, the things that come to mind are more acts of compassion than kindness. Someone brought you a meal when you were sick. Someone called when you were sad. While kind, those acts fall into the category of compassion. They are the result of your need, not someone's spontaneous decision to show kindness.

It's also easy to confuse those who are kind with those who are nice. Nice is someone who responds with politeness and appropriateness. A nice person can speak the same words as a kind person, but her motivation may be different. Sometimes we're nice simply to avoid conflict. We're nice primarily to gain someone's approval. But we're kind because we desire to do good to or for someone else.

Compassion motivates your high school son to go on a mission trip. Kindness motivates him to treat you with more respect when he gets home. Both are addressed in Paul's letter to the Ephesians. Both are important values for children and adolescents to learn. But often we major on compassion and miss opportunities to show kindness.

How many times have you taken dinner to someone who just had a baby? How many times have you taken dinner to someone who didn't have a need, but you or your children had a desire? Several years ago we rode bikes with our friend Mimi to Chili's for dinner. During the meal we noticed that a Daystar family was sitting several tables over. We had a quick conversation and then went back to our salsa and chips. When we asked the waitress for our bill, she said it had already been taken care of. This other family had bought our meal. It was a random act of kindness, as they say. It made us feel great, but we would guess it made them feel the same way. The twelve-year-old son and fourteen-year-old daughter were part of the process. We know these parents are ones who see and teach the value of compassion to their children. Their kids are part of their known generosity in the community when there is a need. But they were also a part of their kindness.

Kindness in Children

What Kindness Looks Like

Children are often naturally kind. Your four-year-old draws you pictures "just because she loves you." Your seven-year-old does his best to make you breakfast in bed, complete with runny eggs and burned bacon. They have the capacity for great kindness.

Several years ago second-grade Jennifer came to camp for the first time. Jennifer was adorable with curly hair and a grin that stretched all the way across her face and then some. Jennifer was also quite the little writer. Over the course of our five-day camp, Jennifer wrote not only every counselor but also every camper a note of encouragement. "I love you," "You're the best counselor I've ever met," "You make everyone happy" were just a few of the comments on the notes that would randomly turn up in people's cubbies.

But Jennifer's curls were reminiscent of another little girl that has been talked about since those good old vintage days. "There was a little girl with a little curl right in the middle of her forehead. When she was good, she was very, very good; and when she was bad, she was . . ." Do you remember? Jennifer had the capacity for equal parts kindness and equal parts horrid! She could turn with venom on the very child to whom she had just written a note of kindness.

Obstacles to Kindness

We talked earlier about the frontal cortex not being developed in children's brains until their mid-twenties. As you might remember, this frontal lobe helps manage emotions. In other words, it keeps our impulses from having complete control over us. For children, although they have increasing capacity for emotional control, they haven't quite arrived. They are often ruled by their impulses . . . or at least their emotions.

So, when your son feels like being kind, he will warm your heart in the way he speaks to you or his brother. But when your daughter is cross, she will have the ability to ruin not just your day but an entire vacation.

Children can be tenderhearted and incredibly loving in the way they treat others. But a moment later they can be cruel. We see it at home and on the playground. You have felt it in how he responds to you. You have seen it in how she treats her little sister. And you have heard it in the shouts coming from the backyard when his friends come over to play. Kids need to be taught kindness, kindness that stretches beyond their emotions to their actions.

A Few Tips to Instill Kindness in Children

- Let your child help you. If your son or daughter volunteers to help or do something for someone else in the family, give him a chance. Even if it means that he makes a mess in the kitchen, he needs opportunities to show kindness and a good response from you when he's done it.
- Make sure they know that you value kindness. Talk about it around your home. Point out when someone else is kind and how.
- Practice the positive. We all get caught up in the negative. If your daughter is kind to her sister, focus on her behavior. "Caroline, that was very kind when you picked up your sister's cup. Did you see the smile on her face? You made her happy, and you sure made this car ride much more enjoyable than it was before." Teach her the effects of kindness. It may sound hard, but we naturally do the same in the negative. "Caroline, that was rude. You really hurt your sister and made me angry." Sounds familiar, doesn't it?
- Treat him like he's kind. Give your child the benefit of the doubt. If you assume he wants to give and love others, he will learn to live up to those expectations.

- Model kindness. Be aware of how you talk and treat those you come in contact with, including your child. Little eyes watch and little ears listen more than we have any idea.
- Foster family teamwork rather than competition. Rather than "Who can clean up the kitchen fastest?" which can set up unkind attitudes, ask, "How fast do you all think we can clean up the kitchen together?"
- Teach your child to read facial expressions. One of the aspects of learning kindness has to do with seeing life from someone else's perspective. Help him learn how others feel through their expressions. Ask him how the grocery store clerk might have been feeling that day? Or his teacher when he gave her a present?
- Teach him that meanness can be as hurtful as hitting. It can help him hear the reality of how hurt feelings feel. He understands physical hurt better than emotional. Explain kindness and meanness and their effects in language he understands.
- Pull in other teachers, both real and fictional. Tell her teacher at school and Sunday school that you're working on kindness at home. Watch movies and read books that model kindness for your child and talk about them.
- Make kindness fun. Keep a family record book of who did or was the recipient of someone's kindness that day. Play charades and act out kindnesses, allowing family members to guess who did them. Engage in activities together that not only teach about but reinforce kindness in your children.

Kindness in Teenagers

If you're a parent of a teenager, you may be thinking, *I have no earthly idea what kindness looks like in my child*. You are probably not seeing a whole lot of it. In our book *The Back Door to Your Teen's Heart*, one of the primary words we used to describe teens was "narcissistic." The word comes from the story of the Greek hero Narcissus. Narcissus was famous for his beauty, but he was known for his cruelty and "disdain for those who love him," according to Wikipedia. His divine punishment was that, upon seeing his own reflection in a pool, he became so enraptured that he could not leave his own side until he died.

Teenagers, in our offices, talk constantly about "trying to figure out who I am" or "finding myself." Their sentences begin and end with a whole lot of I's and me's. Sounds a little like our friend Narcissus, along with his disdain for those who loved him. Unfortunately this narcissism is a normal part of their development. They are becoming their own people. When their focus shifts from who you are and what you think, it naturally lands on them. Who am I? What do I want? Who do I want to be? are questions that plague the minds of preteens and teenagers almost constantly. This self-preoccupation often makes kindness come in short supply for the twelve- through twenty-year-olds in our lives.

But they are capable. I (Sissy) meet with a seventeen-year-old named Emma who writes me thoughtful notes and even brings me flowers from her garden on occasion. I (Melissa) know a young man who works part time as a mechanic and brings me air filters for my 1970 Jeep CJ–7. (I'm not sure if his kindness has more to do with me or his infatuation with my Jeep.) These are just two examples of teens we know who also have the capacity for kindness.

If you see kindness arise in your adolescent, it will most often be directed toward his or her peers. Your daughter will make an elaborate Christmas gift for her best friend. Your son will wash his girlfriend's car . . . just because. As teens get older, their narcissism begins to fade. They gradually begin to see life from another's perspective. The ones they see first, however, are those their own age. As a parent, you will often be the last to see or experience the kindness of your own teenage child.

In Paul's letter to the Ephesians, he admonishes us to be kind to one another (and compassionate). In the Greek derivation of this use of the word, kindness doesn't refer as much to "being" kind as "becoming." *Becoming* is a terrific word to describe your teens. They are becoming. You have taught them great truths about kindness. Even though you may not see evidence of it today, those truths are still tucked away inside. They may just need your reminders, at times, to help the kindness emerge.

A Few Tips to Instill Kindness—Teenage Dos and Don'ts

- Don't lecture. They will tune you out as soon as you begin.
- Do ask questions when you notice kindness in someone else. What did they see? What did they think? How do they think the recipient and the giver of kindness felt?
- Don't pay more attention to their criticism than their kindness. Kids can be very critical. Rather than always reprimanding, point out when they're kind. Tell them how proud you are of them, even if they act awkward.
- Do give them opportunities to be kind. Give them chances to do something for their grandparents. At a young age, give them money to buy Christmas gifts rather than just purchasing for them.
- Do have other kind adult role models in their lives.
- Do continue to model kindness as they get older. Let them overhear conversations about others who are kind rather than just conversations about those who aren't.
- Even when they're at their most narcissistic, continue to show unexpected kindness to them in notes, comments, etc. In doing so, you are modeling that kindness is an act of will, not just an emotion.

A Valuable Reminder

Remember our verse on reminding? Second Peter 1:12 says, "Therefore, I will always be ready to remind you of these things, even though you already know them, and have been established in the truth which is present with you" (NASB). We want to remind you of a few things about your becoming . . . and your kindness in the process.

When you think about your own childhood, do you remember times you were kind? What about your teenage years? "It wasn't so long ago that we ourselves were stupid and stubborn, dupes of sin, ordered every which way by our glands, going around with a chip on our shoulder, hated and hating back. But when God, our kind and loving Savior God, stepped in, he saved us from all that. It was all his doing; we had nothing to do with it. He gave us a good bath, and we came out of it new people, washed inside and out by the Holy Spirit. Our Savior Jesus poured out new life so generously" (Titus 3:3–7 *The Message*).

In the words of Titus, it wasn't so long ago. Be patient in teaching your children. Give your teens a mixture of grace and truth. They are becoming. We once were, too. But our kind and loving God stepped in. Pray for his mercy toward your children. Pray that they will intimately know his kindness and love and that his kindness will be the ultimate motivator for theirs.

A Sunday Drive

Remember the movie *Pay It Forward*? It may or may not be one that is appropriate for your family to watch, based on the ages of your children. But it is a concept that can catch hold—not just of your family but of the communities in which you live.

At dinner one night, make a *Pay It Forward* announcement. "This night is going to be the first in the *Pay It Forward* week"—or month—or year . . . however long you decide to make it. Talk about kindness. Share the verses in Ephesians and Titus; talk to your children about kindness. Share examples of times people have been kind to you. Have them come up with examples of times others have been kind to them. Talk about God's kindness and what it means for us. Have them come up with ways his kindness affects their daily lives.

Give them an example of the idea of paying kindness forward. One person does a kind deed, often unknown. That person does another and so on. Have each family member make a card with the words "Pay It Forward" and a verse they choose about kindness on it. Each family member can also come up with one way to show kindness in their community . . . work, school, youth group. Every one of you can participate.

When you commit your act of kindness, leave or give the recipient the card.

As the week or time period goes on, talk about the effects of kindness. How did it make each family member feel? Do they know what has happened as a result of the card? Share stories. If it isn't carried on in one community, talk about why and what you could do to help. Paying it forward gives your child a taste not only of daily kindness offered but what it can mean to make a difference in their communities, as well.

The Value of Compassion

So, chosen by God for this new life of love, dress in the wardrobe
God picked out for you: compassion, kindness, humility,
quiet strength, discipline.

—Colossians 3:12 *The Message*

Neither one of us will ever forget a camp we had for fifth- and sixth-graders several years ago. The boys at this camp were not yet teen-agers but old enough to experience a deep connection with each other. On one particular night the kids came to the front one by one and talked about an area in their lives in which they really needed prayer. One boy talked about how badly he was made fun of on his fifth-grade football team because of his weight. Another talked about how his father left his mom for another woman. Both boys were tender and vulnerable in ways that most eleven- to twelve-year-old boys would only allow in the solitude of their own rooms. They sobbed.

The same thing happened in both situations. One boy moved as quickly as he could to the front of the room, put his arm around his friend, and started praying. Then another. And another. Until literally the entire camp of boys was surrounding the one in tears. No counselor prompted them. It wasn't the assignment of the night to pray for each other. It was simply compassion at its finest led by a group of tender-hearted, courageous boys.

Defining Compassion

Compassion is defined by *Merriam-Webster* as "a sympathetic consciousness of another's distress together with a desire to alleviate it."[62] The world involves both feeling and a desire, at least, for action.

I (Sissy) work with a group of high school girls who are intensely compassionate. We meet every Thursday night for them to have an opportunity to talk about their lives—where they struggle, what they hope for, and who they long to be. It is basically an opportunity for them to talk about what is, for many teens, their favorite subject . . . themselves. This group, however, is different. Led by the merciful heart of a fifteen-year-old named Laura, these girls spent an entire two hours one evening talking about the horrors of sex slavery among young women in Africa. Several of the girls were in tears as they described the terrible pain those young women must be feeling and what they could do to help. It was an emotion brought on by a tremendous need resulting in an intense desire to help.

Regardless of the precipitating cause, compassion plays itself out in similar circumstances. Need leads to feeling, which leads to a desire for action. It's the same for us as adults as it is for Laura and her group of tenderhearted friends. And in their little worlds it's even the same for our children.

Compassion in Children

What Compassion Looks Like

If you're reading this chapter as a parent of a kindergartner or even a fifth-grader, you may be thinking, *This is one value my child has down.* Young children have a natural bent toward compassion. When we were writing our book, *Raising Girls*, we heard story after story of young girls who felt and acted out of their awareness of others. One six-year-old literally went from pew to pew in her church speaking to anyone she noticed was alone before the service began. And boys are not too different. Our friends David and Stephen, in their book *Wild Things*, talk about the ages of five to eight as "The Lover" years in the lives of boys.[63] As children, boys can be rough and tumble, but they can also have a powerful compassion that flows from their love.

At camp last summer, the second- through fourth-grade boys went to play baseball one afternoon. They used a Whiffle Ball and a large plastic bat to level the playing field across all levels of athleticism . . . all levels, that is, except for Josh. Josh has a congenital disease that makes any athletic endeavor extremely difficult. He has trouble tubing, swimming, running, and playing most of the games the other kids played, including baseball.

Ben, on the other hand, is a naturally gifted athlete of all kinds. He can hit or kick or catch any ball thrown at him. Ben has other gifts, too, which emerged in this telling game of baseball. Josh stepped up to the plate, swung, and missed. He struck out his first time at bat. The second, he hit the ball on the first try. It slowly skipped its way across the field to Ben. Ben dove for the ball and unexpectedly missed. His teammates were furious and yelled. It didn't make a bit of difference to Ben. Every time Josh took a swing that afternoon and Ben had an opportunity to get Josh out, clumsiness took over. He dropped balls, missed catches, and ran much slower than usual. Ben was aware. He noticed and felt compassion for his friend Josh. And he acted on that compassion.

Children do that. They are aware of others' needs and naturally respond to those needs. Developmentally they have a freedom from self-consciousness that they'll lose in their adolescent years.

Obstacles to Compassion

Enjoy the compassion of your children. Give them opportunities to walk that compassion out, whether it's with a friend of theirs, a grandparent, or a hurt animal. One of the primary obstacles to the compassion of our children is us. They want to help a bird who has a broken wing, and we're in a hurry to finish our errands. They comment on the homeless man on the corner, and we keep driving with a lesson on "stranger danger." When we are motivated by compassion, we may allow them to help with our ideas. But often their attempts at compassion don't come at times or in situations that are necessarily convenient for us.

If your son sees someone at church that he thinks looks sad and comments, praise him for his awareness. If your daughter wants to do something for a person on the street, run to McDonald's and let her buy a hamburger for him. If your son is worried about his grandmother, take him to visit her. Let your daughter help make a cake if she wants to do something for your neighbor who has been in the hospital. Although it may not have been what or when you would have responded, your encouragement of their compassion helps. It lets them know that you value what they see and what they feel . . . even if they're not sure they value it themselves.

Another obstacle to compassion in children is often their passion in the situation. Children often don't understand what they feel. They are easily embarrassed by it if it feels strong or if it surfaces with tears, and their emotions are strong. Children are passionate little creatures and that passion often catches them by surprise. Your son doesn't want his friends to notice that he cried when Simba's dad was killed. Your daughter doesn't understand why she cried watching you cry. And then, because they are uncomfortable, they often try to dam up those powerful feelings.

Tips to Instill Compassion in Children

You are the model for young children—not only in what you teach and talk about but in the way you live. To facilitate compassion in young children, we would suggest three main ideas:

1. Have them talk about their feelings. Because your son and daughter will likely not understand the swell of feelings inside of them that truly is compassion, they need your help. Encourage them when you see their tears, whether a boy or girl. Our culture often tries to stop boys from showing tenderheartedness, which can easily make them feel like

compassion is not an appropriate emotion for a boy. Affirm your son *or* daughter's kindness toward a friend, a family member, or even an animal. Have them express the feelings inside of them.

2. Model compassion as a family. Allow your children to be a part of giving to families who are in need. Adopt an Angel Tree child together for Christmas. Let your young children help you make dinner for a friend who's had a baby. As you make compassion a priority in your home, they will grow up seeing it not just as a valuable characteristic but as a way of life.

3. Teach them about the abundant compassion of God and how our compassion not only pleases but makes us more like him (Ps. 103:8).

Compassion in Teenagers

If you are a parent of an adolescent, the phrase above may sound like an oxymoron. Teenagers don't seem to have the natural inclination toward compassion that children do. At times they don't seem to be aware of anyone other than themselves.

What Compassion Looks Like

When I (Sissy) think mostly about my teenage years, what I remember the most are my friends. I honestly don't remember noticing a lot of homeless people. I was not nearly as generous as Laura and her group. I had never tried to raise awareness or money for any cause I believed in other than my Christmas presents. But I do remember nights of desperation calling my mom to stay out later than my curfew with one or another of my friends who was really sad. I remember the anguish I felt with a friend whose parents were separating. And I remember that same compassion flowing right back to me from a group of girls who would have done just about anything for each other. But not necessarily for our parents. They didn't see our compassion. They saw our selfishness and sulkiness.

What compassion looks like in your teenage daughter will often be the way she talks to her closest friends on Facebook. With your son it will be the hours he spends with a friend playing basketball when he knows that friend is struggling.

Robert is an eighth-grader whose parents describe him as angry, reclusive, and rebellious. His friend, Will, would say just the opposite. Robert recently wrote Will a letter. Robert's parents divorced two years ago. Will's are divorcing now. Last week Will's mom saw a letter from Robert lying on his desk when he left for school.

> *Hey Will. I just wanted you to know that I heard about*
> *your mom and dad. I know how hard it was on me and*
> *wanted to tell you that if you ever need to talk, I'm here.*
> *God helped me get through this, and he'll help you, too.*
> *So will I.*
> *Your friend, Robert*

Will never mentioned the letter to either of his parents. Neither did Robert. Both boys would be hesitant for their parents to see or hear about that type of compassion coming from either of them. Adolescents live in fear of parental intimacy.

You will see glimpses of their compassion . . . often toward their friends, maybe toward their younger cousins, favorite dog, or even an elderly neighbor. You will see even fewer glimpses of it toward you. Hang on. Remember and cherish the glimpses you do get. And remember that the compassion is still there. It's just buried beneath a few adolescent obstacles.

Obstacles to Compassion

This lack of compassion is actually a natural part of their development. It's a part of the same narcissism that blocks their kindness. Their preoccupation with themselves and what others think about them is the beginning of discovering their own sense of self, apart from their parents. The problem with this burgeoning sense-of-self phase that we call adolescence is that, during it, kids become really awkward. They feel awkward inside themselves so that awkwardness often spills over into their actions. Their grandmother pays them a compliment, and they just stare. Something sad happens to someone they care about, and they giggle.

Teenagers are actually a lot like children with ADD. They miss social cues. They don't know how to read people, and if by some small chance they do, they don't know what to do with the information. And so they gawk. Or giggle. Or say something that is as random as it is embarrassing, both to them (although they've often missed that, too) and to us. Even when their hearts might feel compassion, they have difficulty showing it.

I (Melissa) remember sitting with a group of seventh- and eighth-graders several years ago. For Christmas they wanted to do something special for the second- through fourth-graders at Daystar. They had fifteen minutes to plan and thirty minutes to execute that plan. I decided to let them brainstorm ideas. One girl thought it would be a great idea to make individual pizzas for each of them and take them to see a movie (all in an hour and a half). A boy thought it would be fun to take them to the park and have a giant game of tag (in the twenty-degree, rainy weather). Another girl thought that they could have a sleepover with them in the Daystar office with all of the Daystar staff as chaperones (the week before Christmas). Right. I quickly dismissed their ideas, and we ended up taking the second- through fourth-graders candy canes while we sang one Christmas carol. My idea.

Another typical trait of teens is their grandiose ideas. In the last chapter we talked about their frontal lobes not being fully developed. The frontal lobe helps them think through ideas. It keeps them from being impulsive. It helps them match an activity with the time and resources it takes to complete that activity. How many times has your teenage son overestimated his ability and underestimated his time? "I can get all of my homework done in an hour so I can go to Tommy's house for the party." How often does your daughter end up at a friend's house for an elaborate project and then call you to bring her the materials she didn't realize she needed? This grandiosity spills over to their compassion, as well. They come up with elaborate schemes that they have neither the time or resources to complete. And, like me, you may throw out their ideas altogether just because "there is no way that will work."

The "there is no way" ideas exist in a lot of teens, as well. It just looks a little different. With all of the emotions and self-consciousness swirling inside of them, there is also often a lot of self-doubt. Their thoughts can go something like this: "Maybe other kids can make a difference. I can't. She is a leader. He is confident. She knows how to talk in front of other people. I don't. I'm not. I can't." We see so many kids who don't believe in themselves. They may feel compassion but have never experienced their compassion making a difference in someone else's life. They often simply haven't had the opportunity.

A Few Tips to Instill Compassion in Teens

- Give them opportunities, even when the opportunities seem far-fetched. If your child wants to raise a thousand dollars for Sudanese refugees, let her try. You don't have to go to either extreme of doing it for her or telling her it's impossible. Give her the opportunity. Listen. Let her gather friends at your house to talk about ideas. Honor her desire to help. She may well surprise you.

- Model compassion as a family, just as you would with your children. Let your teenagers be a part of what you do, even in the brainstorming phase. You could make it a weekly or monthly event that, as a family, you choose to show compassion to someone. You could rotate which family member chooses the beneficiary and then decide together what to do for them . . . bake cookies, order pizza to be delivered to their home, rake their leaves, etc.

- For Christmas give your teenage son or daughter a certain amount of money he can give to a charity of his choosing. Let him research several and report to you on what he chooses and why. Make sure the organization knows that he has chosen to give the gift himself and, if possible, let him have some firsthand experience of his money in action.

- Choose an organization like Compassion International where you can adopt children that your children can sponsor. They can write letters and develop a relationship with a child in an impoverished situation.

- If there has been a highly publicized national or international tragedy and your teen expresses interest or sadness, give her a chance to make a difference. You can brainstorm ways to do this as a family or even ways that her group of friends could get involved.

- Believe in them. Believe in them even when they're acting self-absorbed. Tell them that you believe in them. Tell them often and regardless of the situation. They need to know that you believe in them, even when they're at their worst . . . and maybe even especially when they're at their worst.

- Admire them for times when they show compassion or awareness for the emotions or needs of another. Tell them you're proud of them and respect who they're becoming. You can tell them out loud or even write a note or send an e-mail.

A Valuable Reminder

"There was once a man traveling from Jerusalem to Jericho. On the way he was attacked by robbers. They took his clothes, beat him up, and went off leaving him half-dead. Luckily, a priest was on his way down the same road, but when he saw him he angled across to the other side. Then a Levite religious man showed up; he also avoided the injured man.

"A Samaritan traveling the road came on him. When he saw the man's condition, his heart went out to him. He gave him first aid, disinfecting and bandaging his wounds. Then he lifted him onto his donkey, led him to an inn, and made him comfortable. In the morning he took out two silver coins and gave them to the innkeeper, saying, 'Take good care

of him. If it costs any more, put it on my bill—I'll pay
you on my way back.'

"What do you think? Which of the three became
a neighbor to the man attacked by robbers?"

"The one who treated him kindly," the religion
scholar responded.

Jesus said, "Go and do the same."

(Luke 10:30–37 *The Message)*

We know that the good Samaritan is a picture of compassion. The
priest, however, could be a picture of a fearful child or self-absorbed
teenager. What did he do when he saw the man left for dead on the side
of the road? He angled. He was afraid of his own overwhelming emotion. He became awkward and did nothing. The Levite did much of the
same. Nothing.

This is the rub for children and adolescents. They often do nothing. They do nothing out of their awkwardness and preoccupation
with themselves. They do nothing because they are afraid. They do
nothing because they don't honestly believe they can make a difference.
They don't know what to do, and so they freeze. They don't help the
Samaritan. They don't help with the dishes. They don't help their little
sister when she loses her shoes. And, then, when we confront them,
they shrug their shoulders and say, "What? What did I do?" And then
they angle across the street.

The funny thing about kids is that they often end up feeling good
about their lack of response. They haven't done anything wrong. They
just haven't done anything. They don't stand up. They don't step out.
They don't really hurt anyone or do anything bad, but they also don't
take action. They are much like the priest and angle out of the situation
that feels uncomfortable.

The Samaritan, however, was exactly who most children and teenagers don't want to be. He was not popular. He was from a group of people
others wouldn't want to hang out with. But, when he saw the man's
condition, "his heart went out to him." He felt compassion, and then he
helped him. He did something. He saw a need and responded to it.

First of all, we want our kids to see. We want to help them see past their fears, their preoccupation with themselves, and notice the person in the street, or the homeless shelter, or even the child that everyone else leaves out. We want them to feel compassion. We want their hearts to go out toward the people they care for—their friends, their grandparents, us. And we want them to act. We want them to learn to be Samaritans and stand up, give of themselves, offer who they are to others in compassion. They can. Your children can make a difference. And so can you. It's easy, as a parent, to lose your belief in your own difference-making ability. It's hard to find the time or energy to give of yourself. You're tired and overwhelmed, and so you do a little angling yourself. But you can and do make a difference every single day, especially in the eyes of the little one for whom you are reading this book. You make a tremendous difference. And your compassion leads the way for his.

A Sunday Drive

This is for young children and can be done once or on a regular basis. It can also be something you do whenever you sense your child needs a little nudge toward the value of compassion. It takes place as the child is getting dressed for the day. And you say something like . . .

"When you are getting dressed, what is the first thing you put on? (Child answers).

"In the Bible, God talks about things He wants us to put on, too. Colossians 3:12 says, 'So, chosen by God for this new life of love, dress in the wardrobe God picked out for you: compassion, kindness, humility, quiet strength, discipline' (*The Message*).

"What is the first thing God mentions?

"Do you know what *compassion* means? It means to see, feel, and do something for someone else. You put on compassion like you put on your socks. You decide to have compassion. And you can decide that for today." (Here you can have something they wear or put in their shoe to symbolize putting on compassion.)

"What 'putting on compassion' means is that when you see someone sitting alone at lunch, you go and eat lunch with them. Or, if you see someone fall down, rather than just feeling sad for her, you help her up. If someone is made fun of, you stand up for him and say, 'Don't make fun.'" (You can have your child come up with other examples.)

Then, at dinner that night, or when he is going to bed, talk about the compassion he is taking off. Have him tell you a story of compassion he showed that day. This tradition of taking off is something you can help the child look forward to—a ritual you develop to share that he learns to look forward to. You can even say things during the day like, "I sure can't wait to hear what happened today with the compassion you put on."

A Sunday Drive for Teens

Talking to your teenage son or daughter most likely isn't going to make a difference. We would suggest more of what we call a "backdoor" approach. Rather than teaching them about compassion, take a real Sunday drive. Pile in the car and head to their grandparents. As a family, work in their grandmother's favorite rose garden.

Teenagers often learn best experientially. They need to experience compassion rather than just hear about it. Sign them up for a mission trip. Take them to volunteer with underprivileged kids. Or, better yet, give them several options where they can serve and then let them pick. A church in our community regularly has a service they call "Church without Walls." On these Sundays, members pick a ministry, group, or even family in need and spend the day serving. You can implement your own church without walls as family. You can even take turns choosing where you will give, allowing your teenagers to take a turn. Teens blossom when they feel respected, and allowing them to have an opinion and make choices, even in giving, will help them feel more invested and take more ownership in the process.

The Value of Forgiveness

*If we claim that we're free of sin, we're only fooling ourselves. A claim
like that is errant nonsense. On the other hand, if we admit our
sins—make a clean breast of them—he won't let us down; he'll be
true to himself. He'll forgive our sins and purge us of all wrongdoing.*

—1 John 1:8–9 *The Message*

You round the corner to the playroom and see a familiar sight.
Carrie is sitting on the floor crying with her knees clutched up to
her chest. Jackson is sitting in front of the television, red faced and fuming. What's happened now? You attempt a fact-finding conversation. "He
stole the remote!" "I did not!" "She's been hogging the TV for our whole
lives!" "I have not!" That worked well. What do you do next? You have
no idea what really happened. You're left with sketchy truth from the
slanted rantings of two angry children. About all you know is someone
hurt someone else. And they actually probably both did. How do you
teach them to forgive? How in the world do you get them to apologize
without the proverbial, snotty "SORRY!" that they usually throw at each
other's feet?

Defining Forgiveness

Anne Lamott has said that "forgiveness means it finally becomes unimportant that you hit back."[64] This quote is especially true in the lives of children. They hit. They hit back. They hit with fists, feet, and words. They hit their siblings, their friends, their enemies, us, and sometimes even themselves. And then they defer blame.

In this chapter we're going to talk about forgiveness in two parts. The first is admitting wrong. It is your son having the humility to come to you and say he borrowed your iPod without telling you. It's your daughter acknowledging that she was the one who broke her sister's favorite toy. It involves the courage to ask for forgiveness and the humility to admit he needs it.

The second part of forgiveness is extending it. Your older daughter borrowed her sister's sweater without asking. She brings the sweater back and says she's sorry. Her sister's response is, "Whatever. You do stuff like that all of the time. I'm sick of it and sick of you." Extending forgiveness also involves humility and courage. It involves the humility to accept the offered hand of another and the courage to let go of the anger or hurt over the wrong. It does not mean your daughter forgets. It simply means she no longer holds it against her sister. It finally becomes unimportant that she hit back.

Forgiveness is an important topic. It's one that can affect our children spiritually, emotionally, and even physically. The Mayo Clinic published a report citing that forgiveness may be good for your health.[65] Holding a grudge evidently affects the cardiovascular and nervous systems. In one study people with personal grudges had elevated blood pressure and heart rates, increased muscle tension, and felt less in control. When asked to imagine forgiving the person, the health issues noticeably lessened.

Forgiveness is healthy. Forgiveness is crucial to understanding God. It helps their bodies, can heal their emotions, and causes their little unfettered spirits to grow.

Forgiveness in Children

What Forgiveness Looks Like

In some ways children forgive readily. On Wednesday you pick up your daughter from school in tears because Mary hurt her feelings. On Thursday morning she asks if Mary can spend the night that weekend. She's forgiven Mary much faster than you have. Your son operates the same way. The entire car ride home after school, he begs you for the newest PS2 game. When you've finally heard enough, you explode. You call him selfish and ungrateful. After a few hours of thinking, you decide to ask for his forgiveness. You do and he does immediately. You both cry, and he wraps his little arms tight around your neck.

Many children are also truth tellers. It may take them a while, but they will admit their wrong. They will come to you with furrowed brow and trembling lip and sincerely ask your forgiveness. In these early years your children will naturally ask for forgiveness, offer it to others, or even both. They are little lovers, after all—at least, some of the time.

Obstacles to Forgiveness

Melissa stole the cookie from the cookie jar. Who, me? Yes, you. Not me. Then who? Sissy stole the cookie from the cookie jar. Remember the rhyme? The cookie rhyme is a perfect picture of another way our children respond to forgiveness. "I did not!" "Billy yelled at me first!" "It's not my fault!" She stole the cookie. Not me. Then who?

We've mentioned a few of the positive things children often do naturally. They also defer blame. They don't want to get in trouble. They don't want to feel bad. They don't want you to know or see or hear what they've done. They're afraid their friends or teachers won't like them. They're afraid you won't love them. In their minds blame is a much safer response than admitting their wrong and asking for your forgiveness.

Children can thus operate out of fear, but they can also operate out of manipulation. He screams, "I'M SORRY," not because he feels it but because you have told him he can't go to a friend's house without apologizing. She works up her best attempt at humility and apologizes because she knows you are not supposed to be mad when she asks for forgiveness. Add to the list of natural giftings, a child's perceptive abilities. They are good (sometimes) at looking sorry or forgiving even when they're not if they think it's in their best interest to do so. In other words, they'll ask for and offer forgiveness so they don't have to talk about it, won't be in trouble, and life can go back to a fun state of normal.

We can also become an obstacle for them. We want our children to feel sorry, not just say it. We send them to their rooms until they're "really sorry" or can "say it like they mean it." As we've said throughout the book, we can't change the hearts of our children. Or their feelings. You cannot speak words or even give consequences that are powerful enough to bring about true repentance. But you can require them to say they're sorry with respect.

A Few Tips to Instill Forgiveness in Children

- Start with the basics. Teach your children about God's forgiveness of them and what that looks like with verses like Romans 5:8. We were still sinners, and Christ died. We acknowledge our need for forgiveness and he freely offers us his.
- Model forgiveness in your own life. Forgive her when she hurts you. Forgive your spouse or friends in front of her. Don't talk about grudges you're harboring in her presence.

To Help Them Learn to Ask

- Model humility. At times you will feel the need to ask your child's forgiveness or your spouse's forgiveness in front of your child. Help yourself know that we fail often and stand in desperate need ourselves, as adults.
- Don't overdo it. If you go to your child daily for forgiveness, he will start to feel like you are always messing up, and he's always having to forgive. You're in the wrong, and he's not. It's too much power. Be willing to ask for his forgiveness, but choose to ask in the times that it really counts.

- If you know that she has done something wrong, give her an opportunity to admit it first. "Ellie, is there anything you need to tell me?"
- If he denies it or tries to defend himself, stop him, reassure him that you love him, and that it's important he admit when he messes up, and give him another chance.
- If she still fails to own up to it, send her to her room until she can either talk to you about it or write you a letter admitting what happened.
- Keep several statements as a part of your regular conversations on forgiveness. "I love you no matter what." "You may have consequences, but nothing ever changes the way I love you." "It is important to me that you admit when you've done something wrong." These suggestions will help him know that you value honesty and repentance.
- Keep the feelings out of it. "Tell me you're sorry when you mean it" doesn't accomplish much. But she can tell you she's sorry with respect.
- Help her understand that to admit wrong doesn't mean to admit all of the wrong. If she and her brother are fighting, have them each say something they did. It can help her feel more comfortable telling the truth and present a valuable teaching opportunity that relationships always work two ways.

To Help Them Learn to Offer

- Help him understand that forgiveness is a decision first. We choose to forgive and let the feelings come later. We are motivated by God's forgiveness of us, not our warm feelings toward the other person.
- Help her know the difference between forgiving and being a doormat. She can forgive and still have boundaries. "Thank you for saying you're sorry. I forgive you, but I'm still not going to play with you at recess when you talk to me that way."

- Teach him the difference between forgiveness and reconciling. There may be situations where he can forgive, but it's not necessarily a child he needs to be in relationship with.
- Teach her that forgiveness is a process. She may have to forgive the same person over and over and over.
- Teach him that our forgiveness does not depend on the actions of someone else. We forgive because God calls us to, not because they're suddenly nice or say they're sorry.
- Have her talk about how she feels when she's hurt and how she would feel if she forgave the offender.
- Have him draw a picture of the same.
- If a sibling hurts her and asks for her forgiveness, help her with what she says back.
- If he won't forgive her, send him to his room until he can. He can do it verbally or in a letter. Again, he doesn't have to "say it like he feels it," but he can say it with respect.

Forgiveness in Teenagers

What Forgiveness Looks Like

"What? I didn't do anything." If you have a teenager, you've most likely heard these words or ones much like them. Teenagers may be a little more subtle in their blame shifting than their younger siblings, but they're just as crafty. They don't necessarily shift the blame, but they sure know how to avoid it. They didn't do anything. They weren't there. They didn't know they were supposed to. They didn't know they weren't. Our teenage friends don't want to admit fault, and they often don't want to release fault, either.

I (Sissy) was with a group of high school girls this week talking about others who had hurt them. They came up with a new buzzword; "Just you wait" was their decided response when someone had hurt their feelings. These are actually the same group of girls who abound in compassion. They believe that God loves them and forgives them with great mercy. But they also want a little vengeance from time to time.

So, what does forgiveness look like in the life of an adolescent? It looks like a high school brother and sister named Charles and Abbye. Charles is a senior. Abbye is a sophomore. Since seventh grade Abbye has had the same group of three best friends. To make a long story short, over the summer Abbye found out that one of her best friends had been having sex with Charles. All three of them (all four, actually) knew it, and none of them told her. What they did tell her was that they weren't really going to the party after all . . . or movie . . . or whatever event where Charles might show up. They were pulling away from her and toward him. And Charles just quietly kept the secret going. He didn't tell Abbye. He acted like things were completely normal whenever they were together. When Abbye found out, she was furious. She felt angry and hurt by her friends, by their actions and their lies. She felt betrayed by her brother. For a long time the hurt was really worse from him. When I met Abbye in December, she had come a long way.

"I guess now I'm just mad at my friends. My parents really let my brother have it. They told him he had betrayed them and me. They told him there was no reason I should ever trust him again and that this might just ruin our relationships for good. He came to me and apologized. I think he really meant it. Since that time he has been trying to make it up to me. When I'm in my room doing my homework, he comes in and talks to me about school. He asks me what's wrong when I seem sad. And, maybe best of all, he told those girls what he did was wrong, and he didn't want to hang out with them anymore."

Forgiveness from both sides. Charles had the humility and courage, after some strong prodding from his parents, to ask for Abbye's forgiveness. And she gave it to him. She had every reason to hold onto her grudge, but she didn't. She didn't because he's her brother and because she decided that the relationship matters more than her hurt.

Forgiveness can be a powerful action in the lives of teens whether they are asking for or offering it. They have the capacity to understand it at a much greater depth. They can understand the reasons for it and the impact of it. And many of them do know their need for it in ways they haven't before. We just want to get them past the obstacles.

Obstacles to Forgiveness

Do you remember when you first realized your own need for Christ? Perhaps when you were a teenager. It's the first time many of us really understood our sin. We were self-conscious. We were awkward. But we also realized that we failed. We hurt our parents. Sometimes we meant to; sometimes we didn't. We hurt our friends. We knew it even though we tried our hardest to cover it up. If we admitted we failed, we looked like a failure. If we gave away the fact that we were wrong, people might figure out that we were trying to be something we really weren't.

Your teenage children are floundering in the middle of those same concepts. It was different when they had a temper tantrum and you told them that Jesus forgave them and so did you. It was the way they acted. Now, when they fail, it feels like more a part of who they are. Does Jesus still forgive that? Does he really love them that much? They may know in their heads that his love for us is not dependent on their actions, but that truth is just trying to bump its way to their hearts.

In the meantime they cover up. They try to pretend they're not wrong, haven't done wrong, and don't even know anything about wrong. "What?" "I wasn't there." They still want you and God to be pleased with them, even though they may act the opposite. And their fear of admittance is one of their biggest obstacles to asking for and receiving forgiveness.

Teenagers also have a difficult time offering forgiveness. The oceans of emotions they feel on a daily basis cause them to hurt as they've never hurt before. A friend who betrays them, a girlfriend who breaks up with them, a parent who lets them down—all of these occurrences are earth-shattering in the life of a teen. Actually, most occurrences are.

Because they feel so much, their feelings often become their attitudes. I (Sissy) tell teenage girls often, "Just because you feel something doesn't make it true." But it sure feels like truth to them. We get it. It feels like truth to us, too. But our frontal lobes are more developed. We have wills that are powerful adversaries to our emotions. We can see truth beyond the feelings. But it is especially hard for teens with their under-developed frontal lobes and overdeveloped emotions.

What do they end up doing? Reacting. Teenagers often can live in a perpetual state of reacting. They get angry with you and yell back. They are hurt by a friend and leave her out of a gathering. They want to communicate their feelings but have a difficult time stepping back to evaluate how they want to respond. They lose sight of who they want to be in the midst of the emotions. They react and often seek revenge or just a passive-aggressive attempt to hurt the other. "Just wait," they say or act out.

What do we do? How do we help our teens move past the emotions and to the truth of forgiveness we've been teaching them for years?

A Tip to Instill Forgiveness in Teenagers

- Model forgiveness. It is especially important that in these years you live out what you're wanting them to learn. They will watch how you ask for and offer forgiveness in all of your relationship. They will even test you to see if you act on those principles with them when they don't deserve it. They long for your forgiveness. They long to see you act out God's forgiveness toward them and toward yourself. They're watching you even when it looks like their eyes are fixed on Facebook and their cell phone.

To Help Them Learn to Ask

- If you suspect that your child has done or is doing something wrong, be a good detective. Don't read his or her journal. If you find out because of a violation of his privacy, that offense will overshadow his own . . . at least to him. If you're suspicious, have him call you from a land line when he gets there. Drive by where he's supposed to be and see if his car is there. Call her friend's parents and verify her story. It is much better to catch them in the act than accuse them.
- Give him an opportunity to confess for himself. You can even prompt him with something like, "I know some things are going on, and I'd rather you tell me what they are." It can also help teens to know that their consequences are lessened by telling the

truth but compounded by lying about it.

- Allow your consequences to communicate more than your words. She has heard most of your lessons on repentance by this time in her life. She can tune out a lecture, but she can't ignore not seeing her friends or having her phone for a few weeks.

- Watch for saying he's sorry without saying it. A teenager may not verbally say the words "I'm sorry." At this stage the words may not be the issue. We know many kids, however, who act kinder and more respectful when they're grounded or given some type of consequences. Often this is because they really do feel bad about what they've done and want to make it up to you.

- If she's hurt you or another family member, give her some control over her form of an apology. You can still communicate that an apology is necessary, but she can choose how to offer it. She can write a letter to her grandmother whose feelings she hurt. She can wash her sister's car and leave a simple note. Teenagers need to feel some choices within our boundaries. The older they get, the more choices and less boundaries.

- Learn to ask thought-provoking questions, especially with older teens. If you know that your child has hurt someone, rather than starting a conversation with your thoughts, ask theirs. What happened with that certain friend? How has the friend acted toward them since? What do they think is going on inside of that friend? The less you impose your thoughts and judgments in the situation, the more they'll develop their own.

To Help Them Learn to Offer

- Teach less and listen more with every year of their adolescence. With your middle schoolers, use teachable moments. When they are hurt, teach them about forgiveness. Share biblical truths and principles. Tell them about the Mayo Clinic study. Help them understand that forgiveness affects them just as much as it affects the one forgiven. The older they get, the less they'll listen and the more you'll need to listen.

- Teenagers will need to understand concepts such as the differences in forgiveness and reconciliation, what reconciliation looks like, how to forgive someone and still stand up for themselves—those types of ideas. Offer your insight when they ask for it. Or you can even say, "I have some thoughts about what's happening if you'd like to hear them." Speak directly and to the point. Don't lecture. Their listening window will be short. If they want to know more, they'll ask.

- In his book *The Peacemaker*, Ken Sande outlines four principles of forgiveness: "I will not dwell on this incident; I will not bring this incident up again and use it against you; I will not talk to others about this incident; I will not let this incident stand between us."[66] Teenagers can comprehend these principles in ways that younger children couldn't (although they can learn them in age-appropriate language). These principles are great truths to teach your teenagers (when they're listening) and walk out in the way that you love them and others.

- Share your experiences. Talk about times you've had to forgive others. They can learn a lot indirectly from your experiences. They'll often appreciate your honesty without feeling like you're lecturing.

- Help them come to their own sense of forgiveness. If you know that your child has been hurt, give him every opportunity to talk about what he feels. In the beginning just listen. If he seems stuck, go back to those thought-provoking questions: "I know you've been really hurt by this. Have you thought about what you want life to look like now with that friend? Do you feel like the anger is affecting you?" Their forgiveness will be much more meaningful if they've come to it on their own.

A Valuable Reminder

It is unlikely that the pastor who wrote 1 John would dispute that there is a great deal schools, governments, and businesses, along with the courts and hospitals, can and need to do as we live together on this planet earth. But first of all he insists that we cannot ignore or deny the huge fact of sin and that we are sinners. At the core of who we are, there is something wrong, something wrong relationally, wrong personally between us and our neighbors and God. The only way to deal with it is by forgiveness. If we deny that we are sinners, other than in generalities or through euphemisms, forgiveness has no meaning for us. And so we are incapacitated for what we are created and saved to do best, to love.[67]

We cannot ignore or deny the fact that our children sin. It stares us in the face. It stares you in the face in the form of his disrespect and her disobedience. They are in desperate need of forgiveness . . . receiving and offering the forgiveness that Eugene Peterson speaks of in this quote. But are we aware of our need as parents?

I (Sissy) met with a high school student named Elizabeth who had been hurt by her best friend. These are girls of integrity and kindness who know the grace and forgiveness of Jesus. When Elizabeth confronted her friend with as much love and humility as possible, her friend diverted her. She got defensive and came up with excuses until she deftly changed the subject. Elizabeth's gracious response was, "I just don't think she's grown up that way."

How are your children growing up? What are they seeing modeled in your home? What are their friends seeing modeled in your home? As parents, it is easy to major in the sins of our children and minor in our own. We get caught up in trying to keep up. We want to keep up the appearance that we're good parents. We want to keep up the appearances that our children are good kids. We are and they are, at times. But then, none of us are. They act out and we act back. They make a teenage comment, and we give our own teenage response. When we're honest, we simply cannot deny the fact that we are sinners and something is wrong, as Peterson points out.

But we try. We try hard in our school and communities. We even try in our churches. And what happens when we deny our sin and don't receive his forgiveness is that we feel even more pressure to keep up. Our denial is reinforced by our guilt. And soon we end up pushing ourselves and our families to the point of perfectionism. It all ends up as pressure, and we all miss the free gift of his grace. The free gift, that is, that came as payment for our sin.

The greatest gift we can receive and the greatest gift we can offer our children is forgiveness. We honestly can't forgive others until we've received it ourselves. We love because he first loved us (1 John 4:19). We forgive similarly. As you admit your own sin and desperate need of God's forgiveness, he will meet you in that need. You then experience the freedom that enables you to forgive others, including your children. You live in the power—his power that enables you to do what you were created to do best . . . love.

We would encourage you to read Psalm 51:1–12 for further reminder and further hope in his redeeming love for you and for your children.

A Sunday Drive

On this Sunday we want you to do a little family reading. It can actually stretch over the course of several Sundays or just days in general. We have one friend who reads with her kids, even teenagers, at night before they go to bed. Another reads out loud to her family during dinner. Either will work. We want you to read C. S. Lewis's *The Lion, the Witch and the Wardrobe*. Read it even if you and they've seen the movie or read it before because in it is a powerful lesson on both types of forgiveness.

In this book, as many of you know, four children discover a magical land called Narnia. Narnia is filled with elves and creatures, gnomes and goblins, and a powerfully good lion named Aslan. Aslan is representative in the stories of Christ. One of these children, a boy named Edmund, makes a wrong turn in the story and falls into the clutches of a wily witch named the White Witch. As he is with her, he goes through many of the same experiences our children do (or even we do) when they've made a bad choice. He is isolated from those he loves. He has to continue to lie to cover up his choices, and so forth.

As the story unfolds, Aslan ends up paying a terrible price for Edmund's mistake—or sin. When Edmund revisits Aslan and his siblings, he is finally aware of his need for forgiveness. And they experience many of the emotions our children do when facing someone who has hurt them.

Read the story together. If your children are teenagers, be a little more casual about it than you would if they're young. The movie might even be an easier avenue to talk this way with teens. When you get to these parts, talk as a family (children answering first) about these questions:

- What do you think life was like for Edmund when he was with the White Witch? What was good about it? What was hard?
- Has anything like that ever happened to you?
- How do you think his siblings felt when he was gone? What about when they realized where he was?
- What was Edmund feeling about them when he was gone? What was he feeling about Aslan?
- What was it like when he came back and talked to Aslan? How do you think he felt? What was Aslan's response?
- How do you think Edmund was feeling when he saw his siblings?
- How did each of them respond to him? Why?
- Which sibling have you felt more like when someone has hurt your feelings?
- Why is it hard sometimes to forgive, like it was for Peter?

- Why did Peter finally forgive him?
- Why did Aslan forgive him? How was Aslan able to? What kind of price did he have to pay? See if your children can find a Bible verse that reminds them of this. Matthew 27:35–44 is where it is. If they're younger, you can give them a hint. How is Aslan like Jesus? What does he want us to do when someone hurts us?
- You can also watch the movie together and talk through it although the book goes into a little more detail and much more forgiveness-sharing truth.

> *You must go to them, Son of Adam.* Edmund shuddered. *No,* he begged Him, and he was very aware that his sudden change of heart was cowardly. But his eyes were wild with fear, and he turned back to Aslan. *They will hate me.* The sudden guilt was too much, and he wanted to run again. But Aslan considered him carefully, and he knew he had to do it. *I will be with you, child,* said the Lion. *You have nothing to fear.* Edmund felt a wave of something wash over him, and he realized it was courage, mixed with love. He turned once again toward his brother and sisters, and then he set his shoulders. They were waiting for him.[68]

The Value of Gratitude

The most generous God who gives seed to the farmer that becomes bread for your meals is more than extravagant with you. He gives you something you can then give away, which grows into full-formed lives, robust in God, wealthy in every way, so that you can be generous in every way, producing with us great praise to God.

—2 Corinthians 9:10–11 *The Message*

*A*s we write this chapter, it has been four days since one of the most devastating events of our lifetimes: the Haitian earthquake of 2010. Daily more relief workers and funds are coming to the aid of those who are injured, have lost their homes, lost their work, and lost their family members. It is undoubtedly a tragedy of catastrophic proportion. Such tragedies remind us of all we have to be grateful for.

Another tragedy was one that we had the humbling privilege of being intimately acquainted with. On September 13, 2001, we received a call from a local church to travel to New York. They wanted the two of us and our friend and coworker, David, to spend time with a sister church there, meeting with those who had been affected.

Our trip was not at all what we had imagined. Meeting led to meeting, and we ended up spending most of our time either on the streets or in firehouses. Blocks away from the site, hordes of people lined the streets holding up posters of loved ones saying, "Have you seen this person?" They would wave them as the emergency workers drove to and from the rubble. The sorrow and fear on the streets were palpable.

The firehouses were filled with flowers and food of all kinds. Every firehouse had its doors open to the street with pictures posted of their brothers who had fallen. At each firehouse we visited, appreciative citizens stood in lines just to shake the hands of the firemen.

Everywhere we went that week, every conversation we had, every face we looked into was filled with the grief of what had happened. But there truly was a prevailing sense of gratitude . . . gratitude for those who had survived, gratitude for the 346 emergency workers who gave their lives that day, gratitude even for those who had been lost. Gratitude wove its way through the tragedy of that event and the hearts of all who were touched by it. It will, in Haiti, as well. It is, even now, as they're still counting the lives lost.

Defining Gratitude

Gratitude is a responsiveness to what you see and hear—even what you feel. Your friend surprises you with a gift, and you're grateful. You notice a sunset and are filled with gratitude. Your daughter draws you a picture. Your teenage son tells you he loves you for no reason. You see and are grateful.

But, first, to be grateful, we must see. Maybe that is why tragedies bring about a sense of gratitude in us. They shift our sight from our busyness and criticalness. They shift our thoughts from all that isn't to what is around us—even for a moment. They make us stop and look, listen and feel. And we are grateful.

Gratitude in Children

What Gratitude Looks Like

In Mark 10:13–16 Jesus calls a child up to him from the crowd. He calls and the child comes. In other words the child responds. But, first, he must have seen and heard Jesus.

Children do this naturally. They see. Your daughter is filled with wonder at the caterpillar crawling across the ground. They hear. Your son is thrilled to hear Rudolph come on the radio. They feel. The first time your son heard the story of the cross, he was sad for Jesus and couldn't believe Jesus would actually do all of that for him. They see, they hear, they feel, and they respond.

Their responses may not take the form of words. That's where we can help them learn to communicate gratitude verbally. But they express it through their eyes and squeals of excitement. They say it through their mouths that form little O's and smiles. We can learn a lot from children in the ways they see, in the ways they respond, and in their inherent sense of gratitude.

Obstacles to Gratitude

Some days, however, your son is not so grateful. Instead he is shrieking in the checkout line at Kroger because he wants a candy bar more than he's ever wanted anything in his whole life. Your daughter is not so grateful when her grandmother gives her the "wrong" doll for her birthday. Your son stomps around the house yelling you "never" let him stay up late and "always" make him clean up his room. Their responsiveness can be both a blessing and a curse . . . for them and for us.

The most typical obstacles to gratitude in children are the sense of entitlement we talked about earlier in the book as well as other emotions that take over their little bodies and hearts—competitiveness, jealousy, impatience, selfishness. They can be just as overcome by these feelings as they are by the sweet gratitude we talked about earlier. They are responsive and they are impulsive. They are just as likely to feel surges of joy as they are swings of terrific anger. So, what do we do? How do we encourage their responsiveness in positive moments and discourage their impulsiveness in the negative?

A Few Tips to Instill Gratitude in Children

- When you see your child stop and look or listen, ask her what she's noticed. Have her describe it to you and how it makes her feel. You can spontaneously thank God with her for whatever it is.
- Tell your child how much you love his eyes and ears, how he sees things that you sometimes don't as an adult. This will help encourage and validate that sense of wonder.
- Take the time to listen when he notices. Don't hurry him along or try to shift the conversation just because it's not convenient.
- Thank God for the food before you eat meals.
- Randomly pray in the car on the way to school or in the kitchen, to tell God your gratitude. This will help them learn that gratitude is not only what happens at a meal or bedtime.
- Play gratitude games. For example, everyone at dinner can go around and list several things they're thankful for. You can give a "silver lining" award to the child who sees the good even in hard circumstances. Keep gratitude calendars as a family. Play gratitude charades.
- Model gratitude. If you find yourself making more critical comments than you do grateful, you may want to shift gears yourself. Tell your children things you're thankful for in your own life. Let them hear you express appreciation about and to others.
- Tell your kids how much you appreciate them. Thank them when they do things. Tell them how much you appreciate certain traits and characteristics that you see inside of them.
- Stop every once in a while. Pull over in a pretty field. Walk outside and look at the stars. Take the time for gratitude.
- Practice going without certain things. For a week make your bread rather than buy it. Walk somewhere close, rather

than driving. Little sacrifices can help your children learn to appreciate what they do have.

- Write thank-you notes. Write thank-you notes to your children when they give you gifts and insist that they write notes for gifts they receive. They'll moan and grumble, but they'll also learn a powerful lesson in acting out our gratitude. My (Sissy's) grandmother always told me that children who don't write thank-you notes don't receive gifts. I still write thank-you notes to this day!

Gratitude in Teenagers

What Gratitude Looks Like

Uh-oh. This one doesn't sound familiar, either . . . gratitude and teenagers. How often does your son say, "Mom, thanks for driving me to soccer practice. It really means a lot that you took the time out of your schedule." Or, "Dad, thanks for working so hard to provide for us. I know you worry about making sure we all have enough, and I have everything I need." Hmmm . . . not so much.

Their gratitude comes out more in the form of a quietly grunted "Thanks" when you put his laundry back in his room. Or maybe even a gentle "Thanks, Mom, that was fun," when you take your daughter and several friends out to dinner. More likely, when your teenager is feeling grateful, he'll just smile a little more. She'll sit on the kitchen counter when you're cooking. He'll stay a little longer in the living room before going upstairs. Teenagers have a hard time expressing gratitude; they have lots of obstacles. But they do at times still have grateful hearts. We just have to have our eyes open to see their subtle showings of gratefulness.

Obstacles to Gratitude for Teenagers

For gratitude to take place, we first have to see. Our senses have to be awakened to all that's around us. We have to notice the beauty or the kindness. What do teenagers see most of the time instead? Themselves. Because of all that we've continued to talk about that is going on inside of them developmentally, they are tremendously shortsighted. Their awareness often begins and ends with themselves. She sees that she doesn't look cute. He hears his own voice crack. Their preoccupation with themselves and their own insecurity blocks their awareness. At camps we tell our teenagers often to "wake up!"

We want them to wake up to the world around them. We want them to see and hear and experience God's goodness in their lives. At camp we can tell them to "wake up." But it's a little harder for you to tell them at home. Your direction can end up as an obstacle for them. Because, not only are they shortsighted; they're also independent . . . or at least trying to be. They're trying to find themselves, become their own person, discover "who they are." And, so, when you as their parents tell them to be grateful, what happens most of the time? They do the opposite.

Because teens are trying to establish their independence, they often think they have to pull away from their parents and the things you value. They will come back. But for a time separation takes place—not just from you, as a person, but from the things you believe. So, how do you continue to teach them gratitude? What can you do, as a parent, to wake them up and remind them of the importance of gratitude?

A Few Tips to Instill Gratitude in Teenagers

- Let's circle back around to the back door. If you are teaching them directly, they're most likely going to tune you out. Think through what it means to be both unpredictable and relational in your teaching. How do you catch them off guard with a sense of gratitude?
- Model gratitude. Be aware of what you communicate in front of them and to them. Think about how you talk about your friends and your acquaintances. How do you handle it when someone disappoints you? Remember that they're watching.
- Express gratitude to your teenagers. Tell them how thankful you are. Don't overdo it because, again, they can start to feel too much power. Be unpredictable and let your words count.
- Ask questions. If you can tell your teenager is moved by gratitude, ask her questions. Find out what she feels and why.

Make sure she knows you respect her ideas and feeling and truly
are interested. Feeling respected by you helps free her to share
her thoughts and feelings.

- Make gratitude a family event. Have notecards at the dinner
table for everyone to write a note to someone they are thankful
for . . . just because.
- Have a Saturday morning where you go together to Target or
another store to buy things for a care package for someone
you're each thankful for.
- Enlist their help with their younger siblings. "I'm really trying
to teach your brother to be thankful. Will you help me?" Let
him give you ideas that he thinks would help. He'll be more
conscientious of the idea and his little brother.
- Give them room to be thankful. Don't force the issue.
Newsweek.com reports that kids who feel more autonomy
actually show more gratitude. Give them some choice in their
gratitude and in their independence.

A Valuable Reminder

> Open your eyes and there it is! By taking a long and
> thoughtful look at what God has created, people have
> always been able to see what their eyes as such can't
> see: eternal power, for instance, and the mystery of his
> divine being. So nobody has a good excuse.
> (Rom. 1:19–21 *The Message*)

I (Melissa) woke up early this morning and was in the kitchen at my
lake house. I had a CD of hymns playing. I was making my coffee, listening to "This Is My Father's World," and thinking about this chapter on
gratitude. I truly felt grateful. And then I opened the refrigerator.

Over New Year's, I let some friends come up here while I was out
of town. A few more of them came than I expected. (I'm already losing
my sense of gratitude, aren't I?) When I opened the refrigerator door,

I couldn't find what I wanted. They had eaten it . . . along with a lot of my other favorite things. And my gratitude went out the window.

Later this morning I walked up to my room, still thinking about gratitude. I looked out at the lake with the sun coming in through the windows. It was beautiful and I felt grateful. Then I looked down and saw a tarp with leaves piled up on top of it. I asked someone to get rid of that tarp several months ago. My gratitude went out the window.

I couldn't appreciate the man who works so hard around my house. I didn't remember all he has done. I only saw what he hadn't done. I wanted to offer my friends something by letting them use my lake house. And then I got mad and tried to grab it back. Gratitude is like this for me. It's back and forth. I feel so thankful for my life and my house, and then I notice what's wrong with it.

A demandingness (yes, I just made up that word, but you know what I mean) overtakes my gratitude—a need for control, a grabbing, entitled type of attitude. I want my eyes to see, but too often I see what isn't as opposed to what is. I notice what I think I should be given rather than what I have. I guess I'm not too different from the children we're talking about after all.

Maybe what awakens my senses the most, as well as theirs, is Jesus. Maybe what I really need is what is unseen but still powerfully present. Dan Allender says, "The greatest gift is not what I see but how I am seen by the living God. Then my gratitude knows no limits."[69]

Jesus sees me, knows me, and loves me in spite of my selfishness and need for control. He loves me, has redeemed me, and calls me his own. I serve a God who is grateful for me no matter what. That is the kind of gratitude I can teach, share, and reflect to children. This is my Father's world, and I have so much to be thankful for. And so, I would guess, do you.

A Sunday Drive

The Old Testament is filled with offerings. God commanded his people to make offerings of all kinds—burnt offerings, guilt offerings, sin offerings, fellowship offerings, and a host of others. There were also thank offerings. God wanted those offerings to serve as a visual reminder to his people of his faithfulness.

Offerings were like the altars that Jacob, Samuel, and others built in the Old Testament. When these Old Testament men had completed a victory or heard from God, God often had them build an altar to remind them. "Samuel took a stone and set it up between Mizpah and Shen, and called its name Ebenezer, saying 'Thus far the LORD has helped us'" (1 Sam. 7:12 NKJV).

Today, we don't build altars. Sure, there's one at church, but we don't really think about the meaning behind it. Offerings are another issue entirely. The offering plate passes at church or a concert and we groan. Our kids hear us complain about being asked for money for this fund or that. We rarely take the opportunity for our offering to serve as a reminder.

In this Sunday Drive we encourage you to make an offering, build an altar, or both. How could you, as a family, talk about what offerings mean and make a regular offering to remember God's faithfulness? It could be a great dinner conversation.

Where could you set up your own Ebenezer? What could you put together on display to remind you of how God has helped you?

Come up with one or several visual reminders of God's faithfulness. Talk about them regularly. Add to them as the months and years go by.

> This service that you perform is not only supplying
> the needs of God's people but is also overflowing in
> many expressions of thanks to God. Because of the
> service by which you have proved yourselves, men will

praise God for the obedience that accompanies your confession of the gospel of Christ, and for your generosity in sharing with them and everyone else. And in their prayers for you their hearts will go out to you, because of the surpassing grace God has given you. Thanks be to God for his indescribable gift! (2 Cor. 9:12–15)

The Value of Integrity

God can't stand deceivers, but oh how he relishes integrity.

—Proverbs 11:20 *The Message*

*W*e have a parenting seminar called Raising Kids of Character that we offer with our colleague, David Thomas. We speak to a variety of churches, schools, and parent groups in our community and beyond. When we do, we ask parents what the character traits are that they most want to see in their children. Without question, honesty is always one of those included. Teaching our children to tell the truth is of the utmost importance. But every once in a while, a parent will raise their hand and use the word *integrity*.

We don't talk about integrity as often as we do honesty. Maybe it's because we don't fully understand it. Maybe it's because examples of integrity seem to be fewer and farther between. Whatever the reason, we miss an opportunity to teach our children rich truth when we don't speak of integrity. Honesty is undoubtedly an important character trait for our children to learn. But integrity can be foundational to who our children are.

Defining Integrity

Integrity and honesty are similar. *Honesty* means "telling the truth." *Integrity* means "living out the truth." You can be honest and not have much integrity. But it is difficult to live with integrity and not be honest. Merriam-Webster defines *honesty* as "a fairness and straightforwardness of conduct." In other words, telling the truth. *Integrity* is defined as a "firm adherence to a code of especially moral or artistic values." Integrity encompasses many values, including honesty. To be honest is to make a choice to say what you mean. *Integrity* means "to make daily choices to live out what you believe."

I (Sissy) will never forget a mom of a girl I was counseling who told me that my eyebrows were entirely too dark for my hair color. She was honest, but I'm not sure her words were spoken with integrity. From my perspective integrity mixes truth with love. And it doesn't just speak it. Integrity walks truth and love out in daily life.

I have a friend I would describe as having integrity. Pepper is honest and straightforward, but she also is exceedingly kind. She desires to makes choices to live and speak in the way to which she believes God has called her. I have no question that if I asked her a question she would do her best to tell me the truth. She would tell it with love and grace. If I were to ask Pepper about my eyebrows, I can imagine that she would smile and say, "Sissy, I have always thought your eyebrows striking, although they are definitely darker than your hair." But, more than that, I think she would tell me that who I am has nothing to do with the color of my hair or my eyebrows. I think she would move toward something deeper.

How does this translate to children? How do we teach them to speak with honesty? To mix that honesty with love? And to make decisions based on how God has called them to love in the ways they both speak and live?

Integrity in Children

What Integrity Looks Like

We know what honesty looks like in children. It looks like a child who, when you ask if she's done her homework, says no if no is the honest answer. It looks like a daughter who admits to taking her brother's blanket. Or a son who tells you he forgot to brush his teeth . . . three days in a row.

Honesty is definitely important. We want our children to speak the truth. We want them to be honest with us. We want them to be honest with their teachers and coaches, their piano instructors and art teachers. But sometimes their version of the truth can be a little more than we need to hear.

A classmate calls your daughter to ask her to play. Your daughter, who doesn't really like this classmate, responds with, "No, I don't want to." She was honest. Better yet your son tells his teacher that "my mom and dad think you're teaching me math the wrong way." Or he even tells you, "Mom, you're getting fat." Children can be brutally honest. What we want children to learn is to make decisions based on what it means to live out whom God has called them to be. They speak the truth in love. And they live out of our high calling to love others. (See John 13:34–35; Rom. 12:10; 13:8; and Gal. 5:13, to name just a few.)

At every one of our summer camps, we give the kids an opportunity to speak to each other. They give each other beads, bracelets, or bandannas . . . something to serve as a reminder of what they have meant to each other over the week. A child comes to the front of the room and is allowed to call on the kids who raise their hands to speak.

Last year a fifth-grade boy called on his fourth-grade sister, Patricia. "Scott," she said, "sometimes you say things that hurt my feelings when you're in front of your friends. But I want you to know that I love you. I watch how you care about people here at camp. I'm proud of you and proud I'm your sister." Patricia was honest, but more than that she spoke to her brother with integrity. She made a hard decision to speak to him in front of a roomful of his friends. She didn't only speak words of love.

She also spoke words of truth. She reminded Scott of who he really is and called him to something deeper. Patricia is just beginning to live out the concept of integrity, even though she's probably not yet sure what it means.

Obstacles to Integrity

The first obstacle is simply that integrity is a hard value to understand for any of us. We have defined and redefined it between the two of us just in writing this chapter. Children are concrete thinkers, and integrity is not a concrete concept. They can understand honesty. They can understand love. But we want them to speak the truth in love. We want them to walk out what it means to love someone and stand up for themselves at the same time. Your daughter may be more likely to say to a bully, "No one likes you. Everyone thinks you're mean." Your son may be more likely to smile and shrug it off with, "That's okay." Rather than swing from one side to the other, we want them to live in the balance between the two. We're still trying to learn that as adults.

Another obstacle is that children want to please. Your children will lie to you about their homework because they don't want you to be disappointed in them. They'll tell their piano teacher they've practiced every day this week. They won't stand up at school for someone being made fun of because they don't want to stand out. Children want to be liked and to have friends. They long to be delighted in. And it can be terrifying for them to speak truth in light of that kind of longing. We know . . . we might have been there a time or two ourselves.

Integrity is hard no matter the age. It takes more thoughtfulness than just honesty. It takes more time. It takes a strong commitment to a calling to love. For our children, maybe more than anything else, it takes us. It takes our willingness to teach them truth, to love them with honesty and consistency and a deep desire to pursue our own integrity.

A Few Tips to Instill Integrity in Children

- Start with honesty as a building block. Your children need to know how truth is different from a lie. They need to understand that lying is wrong and that there are consequences for it. Simply and generally, children continue to lie when they get away with it. It is up to you to teach them that they can't and won't.

- Make your home a place where your children feel secure and loved—no matter what. Children who are constantly criticized have a difficult time with integrity because they are desperate to please. Enjoy your children. Tell them often how much you love and delight in them, no matter what their age.
- Teach them verses on the type of love Jesus has called us to. Use him as an example for truth telling in the name of love.
- Model for them what it looks like to speak truth in love by the way you talk to your spouse, friends, and even your children.
- Teach them the word *integrity* at a young age. When different situations come up, ask them: "What would someone with integrity do in this situation? How can you love this person and be honest with him or her? How can you live the way Jesus calls you to live?"
- Tell your children that they can talk to you about any situation in which they don't know what to do. If they get in a situation and can't figure a way out with integrity, come up with a family buzzword. If your ten-year-old son is at a friend's house and they start to watch a PG-13 movie, he can call you and say, "Could you buy me some pickles?" or something like that. You would know either that he needs to talk to you or that you need to come and get him without having to say it.
- Pursue integrity yourself with as much integrity as you can. Obviously we all fail. We're sinners. Your children need to understand this, as well, so that integrity doesn't become synonymous with perfection. When you fail, do so with honesty (age-appropriately) and start again. You will earn their respect and strengthen their desire to live with integrity themselves.

Integrity in Teenagers

What Integrity Looks Like

Of all the values we've discussed so far, we can easily think of teenagers who have integrity . . . or, at least, who are trying. Surprised? We are, too. Most of these kids are in high school. For middle schoolers integrity feels a little more difficult. We'll talk about why in a minute. But we know more than a handful of high school girls and guys who are trying to be who God wants them to be. They truly desire to love others, even when that means speaking difficult truth.

Kate hangs out with a group of kids who are bad news. The guys smoke a lot of pot and drink a little. The girls drink a lot and smoke a little. You can imagine how things go from there. Kate doesn't want to live this way anymore. She developed a relationship with Jesus at camp this summer that made her want to live differently. But she can't seem to break away from those friends and doesn't know how to be who she wants to be with them.

Kate has been in the same small group at Daystar for several years. The girls have heard story after story about how her "friends" at school treat her. They stab her in the back, pressure her, and make her feel pretty lousy about herself. Her group friends have had it.

"Kate, you have got to break away," Maddy said.

"I've been there. I know it's hard. But you're not going to be able to do it while you're hanging out with them," Libby told her.

"I'm not really sure you want to," Brooke boldly said. "I think a part of you does, but it's still more important to you that those girls like you. You're going to have to decide what's more important: who you want to be or who those friends want you to be."

That's what integrity can look like in the life of a teenager. Brooke has made her own share of mistakes. She has had friends just like Kate's and had to go through a couple of months with no friends when she pulled away from them. But now she knows how much better she feels to live differently. She would tell you that she doesn't have to worry about being caught by her parents. She doesn't have to lie to cover things up.

And she doesn't have to feel bad when she closes her eyes at night. She feels close to Jesus and is proud of who she's trying to become. We're pretty proud of her, too.

Obstacles to Integrity

Integrity for teens definitely has obstacles. Especially in middle school, their strongest concern is what other people think. They're embarrassed to be seen at the movies with you, their parent. They want to be dropped off a block away from the mall so no one sees them get out of your car. (How do people think they get there, anyway?) They truly think they are being watched by a mass of people at all times who are sitting back and judging everything they do. We tell young teenagers that no one is thinking about what they're doing because everyone else is worried about what everyone else is thinking about them.

I (Melissa) was talking to a group of eighth-grade boys. I was telling them how I knew a boy in fifth grade who stood up to the class bully who was making fun of one of his friends. One of the eighth-graders said, "I just can't imagine myself doing that." The funny thing was that the boy who did it was actually him just three years ago. When I told him that, he was shocked. He had no memory of the event and couldn't even imagine himself in that situation.

Another obstacle for teenagers is the same one Kate is facing today: peers. Most of the kids we know who are trying to live with integrity have friends who are also trying to live with integrity. It is hard to stand alone at any age but especially in your teenage years.

Perfectionistic pressure is another obstacle for many teenagers we know. Some kids do their best to make the kinds of decisions they believe God calls them to make. And some kids feel pressure to make every decision perfectly. Rather than experiencing more of Christ and his love for them, these kids just experience more anxiety. They have to make the "right" decision at all times. They have to do it for God and for everyone who is watching their choices. It may be their parents or their friends. Many of these girls and guys are in some type of leadership position. The concern is what happens when these kids fail, and they will fail. They end up feeling like a failure instead of forgiven.

A last obstacle to integrity in teens that we'll mention goes back to that impulsive issue they've got going on. Even the kids who really love Jesus make bad decisions. (Sounds familiar, too, doesn't it?) A girl on our summer staff was leading kids to Christ right and left, speaking in front of parent groups, and secretly smoking cigarettes in her car. Part of it might be because she knew her youth director smoked. But it also had to do with the fact that kids are still becoming. They are in process. You will be so proud of a choice your teenager makes, believing he truly is pursuing integrity. And then he'll sneak out with a group of his friends. You will believe your daughter has finally gotten it, and then you'll hear she's had oral sex. They are growing up. They are growing and becoming. And they most definitely need our patience, love, and grace to help.

A Few Tips to Instill Integrity in Teenagers

- Remember the back door. Teach with words in small, unpredictable moments.
- Choose your words. Teenagers only listen to the first paragraph or two out of your mouth. Think about that paragraph before you speak it and don't go on and on.
- Choose your battles. Don't place the same emphasis on sneaking out that you do on a messy room. We'll talk more about the messy room in the next chapter. You may have to bite your tongue on a few issues to make it count on others.
- Teach with consequences in the big moments. There may be a few years in your teen's life when consequences speak the loudest. They won't make bad choices because they don't want to get in trouble. That's fine. Use consequences and stay consistent with them.
- Ask them questions. Help them learn to think through decisions on their own. What do you feel is right? What do you believe? Who do you want to be in this? How do you want others to

see you? are all great questions to help them focus on who they want to be.

- Give them a safe place. Help them find a group of kids who they can wrestle with as they learn what integrity means. A group will also bring in an added and often more powerful (at least in their teen years) level of accountability.
- Remember they're watching. Pursue integrity. Be honest about your mistakes. Reflect to them in your words (although short) and choices that Jesus is the author and perfecter of our faith (Heb. 12:2).
- Give them role models. Choose another adult (or allow them to choose one) whom you trust and can be a model and sounding board for them during their teen years.
- Allow them to fail. Teenagers will mess up. Don't limit their choices so much that they don't have opportunities to make mistakes. Widen your boundaries and give them consequences when they go too far. They will learn a lot from those failures.
- Remember your own teenage years. How did you learn? Who were you trying to be? Thinking back on who you were during those years can help you love them with a little more humility and a lot more grace.

A Valuable Reminder

Tome is the Hebrew word for "integrity" that is used most often in the Old Testament. David uses it as he cries out to God in Psalm 7:8, "Judge me, O LORD, according to my righteousness, according to my integrity, O Most High."

Tome, in this sense, has several meanings combined into one idea. It means "honesty, genuineness, completeness, soundness." It comes down to a heart condition that includes blamelessness and uprightness. The word *integrity* describes a life that comes together.

How is your life coming together? What about your parenting? It's easy to read any parenting book, including this one, and be discouraged. Model compassion. Model kindness. Pursue integrity. Love your children. Give them grace and patience and hope, and speak truth in love. But we're not there when your seven-year-old daughter screams in your face. We don't know how hard it is to be a single mom and raise a son who is not only twice your size but ten times as angry. Actually we do know a little because we sit with moms and dads like you every single day. And we would never want them or you to be discouraged.

In an article called "Being a Person of Integrity," Mark D. Roberts says, "I really don't want to be judged according to integrity in my life or the lack of it, because there are so many pieces in my life that don't fit. My integrity falls short."[70] So does ours; so does yours. And so did David's even as he was praying the prayer from Psalm 7. But David was also called a man after God's own heart.

Roberts goes on to say, "Integrity is a result of God's work in us in which the Spirit helps us to be conformed to the image of Christ." We know there are so many pieces in your life that don't fit. They aren't all coming together in the ways you had imagined or hoped, as a person or as a parent. There are days when you feel proud of the decisions you've made, the words you've spoken, and the way you have parented. And then there are days where you feel the same kind of failure we're talking about with teens.

You can still pursue integrity, even on those days. The reason you can is because your integrity has more to do with God's work than it does yours. David was a man after God's own heart because it was God's spirit at work in him. It's by Jesus' grace and his Spirit in you that you are freed to pursue integrity.

We may sound confusing. On one hand we're echoing the words of Titus 2:7–8: "In everything set them an example by doing what is good. In your teaching show integrity, seriousness and soundness of speech that cannot be condemned." On the other hand we're saying, "You can't do it." We really don't believe you can. But what you can do is desire integrity. You can pursue Christ and pray that his Spirit will bring all of the pieces together. You can parent your children from a heart that knows your integrity is found in Jesus. And you can speak to them the loving truth that their integrity is found in him, too.

Mark Roberts said, "I'm thankful that you judge me in light of the integrity of Christ. In this knowledge I am free to approach you, to honor you, to live for you. Nevertheless, I pray that by your spirit, you will make me a more complete person. One in whom all the pieces fit together neatly. May my heart match my words and deeds. May I live in such a way that people are drawn to you because of me."

A Sunday Drive

Have you ever made a puzzle? That's what we want you to do in this Sunday Drive. You'll need:

- Some type of thick poster board, even foam board—one for each family member
- Several pairs of scissors
- Markers
- Magazines to cut out photos or real-life photos you don't mind using
- Different types of craft paper with various patterns that can be used as backgrounds for each of the pieces

Talk to your kids about the Hebrew word *tome* and the definition of *integrity*. It's when the pieces of our lives start to come together . . . what God calls us to and who we believe he's called us to be. Each family member is going to create his or her own integrity puzzle. This can be as simple or as elaborate as you and your family choose to make it.

1. Start with your board. Draw and then cut out different pieces of the puzzle, large enough that each one can contain a sentence or a cut-out picture.
2. Make personal pieces. Each piece can have a characteristic your child wants to be: compassionate, kind, patient, loving. They can also have pictures or drawings that reflect those

characteristics. (Teenagers will like magazine clippings for it to look more like a collage.) You can also use the craft paper as background for each piece.

3. Make Scripture pieces. Write Scriptures at the bottom of the page on a puzzle piece. Ask your children what they think about each one and how it fits with integrity. Have them tell stories of when they've seen that verse played out and how it can help them personally. Share your own stories and thoughts.

4. Put the pieces together and have each family member share about his or her puzzle.

- Integrity protects us. "In my integrity you uphold me and set me in your presence forever" (Ps. 41:12).
- Integrity gives us security. "The man of integrity walks securely, but he who takes crooked paths will be found out" (Prov. 10:9).
- Integrity guides us. "The integrity of the upright guides them, but the unfaithful are destroyed by their duplicity" (Prov. 11:3).
- Integrity pleases God. "I know, my God, that you test the heart and are pleased with integrity" (1 Chron. 29:17).

The Value of Responsibility

Whatever you do, work at it with all your heart, as working for the Lord, not for men, since you know that you will receive an inheritance from the Lord as a reward. It is the Lord Christ you are serving.

—Colossians 3:23–24

o the Right Thing." You may have seen the ad campaign from Liberty Mutual. In 2006 they filmed a commercial with people doing things for strangers. The response from an appreciative public was overwhelming. Since that time, they've started the Responsibility Project with a Web site and entire ad campaign targeting this value: responsibility. The ads feature everything from a cartoon character who is considerate to others in his office, to a father who invites a boy without a dad to play basketball, to a man who walks around looking for ways to give to strangers. He takes shopping bags to people who have left them at restaurants, pays parking meters, and stops traffic for kids to cross the street.

If you were to film a "Do the Right Thing" ad for your children, we're guessing it would look a little different. Sure, it would include compassionate clips where your son helps an elderly woman across the street. It would cut to blazing candles with your daughter's smiling face as she takes her dad the sunken birthday cake she made for him. It would show a group of teenagers with yours in the middle having good, clean fun by playing a game of Frisbee. But there would be other scenes, as well. "Do the Right Thing" would include your daughter making her bed, your son picking up his shoes he left in the living room with a smile on his face. Your teenage daughter would put her laundry away rather than throw her clean clothes on the floor. It would show children of all ages doing what they're told within a reasonable time limit. It would show them following through on their promises, their chores, and even their homework.

Defining Responsibility

Responsibility comes from the root word *respond*. How do your kids respond to responsibility? They definitely respond when they don't want to do something . . . "Not right now, Mom." "That's Charlie's job." Or, "Why should I clean up my room just so the cleaning people can clean it again?" The trick to responsibility is to teach them to respond differently. We want our children to respond in a respectful and timely manner. Plus we just want them to do what we ask.

Teaching your children responsibility can bring up a whole host of issues. From our offices, the top ten list would include:

1. Making their beds
2. Cleaning up their rooms
3. Helping around the house
4. Doing their homework
5. Organizing their time
6. Keeping curfews
7. Saving their money
8. Keeping up with (and not losing) their things
9. Turning off their game systems, cell phones, and computers
10. Having a quiet time

We spend a *lot* of time with parents talking about these issues of responsibility. I (Sissy) wish I had my own allowance for every time I talked with a family about ways children could earn theirs. The bottom line, however, is that you want your children to learn responsibility. You want them to learn to share the load, follow through, clean up, help out, and be on time. You want them to learn to be responsible citizens of your home now and wherever they choose to park their messy selves in the future.

Responsibility in Children

What Responsibility Looks Like

We have a friend who was sent to the first grade in a jacket, tie, and carrying a briefcase. Although his parents meant well, this is not the kind of responsibility we're talking about. What we're talking about is children who pick up after themselves, clean up their toys, make their bed, brush their teeth, come downstairs for dinner when called, mow the lawn, do the dishes, take their grandmothers to run errands, put a little of their birthday money in savings. Okay, probably no child would do all of those things or at least do them heartily. But we have heard of a few kids who are at least beginning to get the concept.

In the August 2009 *O! Magazine*, Marie Howe wrote an article called "A Hard Times Companion." In it Ms. Howe talked about how she didn't get a job she was hoping for, forcing her and her eight-year-old daughter to downscale and move to a small apartment in Manhattan. As a mom, she decided to take the change as an opportunity to find means of entertainment for the two of them that weren't so costly. They started reading Laura Ingalls Wilder's *Little House on the Prairie*.

She describes the experience, how it started with their feeling bad for the Ingalls family, how they couldn't relate to the cold winters and lack of food. They thought their indomitable spirits a little, well, cheesy. But, as they delved deeper into the pages and the lives of the Ingalls, Marie and her daughter started to change. She describes the change that gradually took place:

> It was several weeks of reading before I noticed how
> the uncomplaining dignity of those people was slowly
> entering us. My daughter and I, almost unconsciously,
> began to slow down when we were at home. She

began to read her schoolbooks out loud to me as
I cooked dinner. (I cooked dinner! We are New
Yorkers, used to eating out or ordering in.) And we
started to refer to our housework as chores."[71]

Pa and Ma Ingalls would have been proud of Marie Howe and her daughter. So would John Boy—oh, wait, wrong prairie family. But both shows, *The Waltons* and *Little House on the Prairie* that were popular when many of us were growing up outlined the importance of responsibility. Today's shows look more than a little different.

Obstacles to Responsibility

No more Bill Cosby talking about walking to school uphill both ways in the snow. Now we've got Hannah Montana and Zack and Cody throwing more than a little bit of attitude at their parents. We see parents constantly who make their children take breaks from television because of the attitudes of children represented there. The media definitely are not helping our children learn responsibility.

Our schedules aren't helping too much, either. You want your daughter to take out the trash every Wednesday. But Wednesday morning rolls around, and you're late for school because the kids were up too late at soccer practice and play rehearsal. Or you want your son to memorize three Bible verses a week. But by the time you remember or have time to find the verses for him to memorize, the week is almost over. One of the biggest obstacles to responsibility can be the muchness, manyness, and busyness of the lives we live in today's culture. The Ingalls didn't have a lot they had to do after school—chores, homework, the occasional baseball game with a homemade bat. We have piano lessons, travel soccer practice, art lessons, dance team, Spanish tutoring, a group project in history, and youth group. None of those events are bad in themselves, but they add up to a lot of time spent outside the home. It's hard to help out around the house when you're simply not in it.

Another obstacle to responsibility is how unfun it sounds. What child wants to pick up his toys? Okay, I (Sissy) think I was Type A enough to enjoy even things like that when I was little. But most children don't. I (Melissa) would have liked to sweep the garage if I could pretend I was sweeping a saloon in the old west. I (Sissy) do remember how much I enjoyed going to the bank as a young girl. My bank brilliantly had Acorn savings for children where you had your own ledger and got a toy every time you deposited money. They made saving fun. For most children responsibility isn't fun. There is some truth to that—even for us, as adults—but we can do some things to make responsibility a little more appealing.

A Few Tips to Instill Responsibility in Children

- Make things visible. Young children remember better if they can see it. Have a poster in their room or a whiteboard with their chores on it.
- Create a chart where they get a check when they accomplish something. Enough checks can earn a reward or their allowance. This can make it a game or something to work toward that's fun.
- Turn up the music. If you're having a Saturday morning cleanup as a family, turn on some fun tunes and dance while you're sweeping. You'll all enjoy the process.
- Be patient. Children really don't remember and don't understand instructions. They often need our help and gentle explanations.
- Give lots of praise and encouragement. Help them know how much you value responsibility.
- Start young. As soon as a child can walk, he can pick up his toys. As young as three or four, they can make their beds (we won't worry so much how it looks for now). At age five, they can help clear and set the table.
- Give them choices in chores. Have a list your children can choose from where they feel some degree of choice in the matter.
- Give a child something to take care of. If you don't have one, your son or daughter is probably clamoring for a pet. Start with

a plant. Tell them that you're going to start small and work your way up. If they take good care of the plant, give them a fish. Then a hamster. And so forth. That way they will see that their responsibility paid off, and they have something to love and love them in return (not the plant).

- Don't rescue them. If your child has forgotten his lunch, don't take him McDonald's. He will either go hungry or become resourceful enough to get his own lunch. Either way works. If your daughter has forgotten her homework, let her pay the consequences. She will remember much better the next time around if she is the one who learns the lesson, rather than you.

- Help your child with an organizational system for their homework. Go together to the store and pick out an organizer or binder. Come up with a schedule together for how much homework he or she has and how long it will take him. Teach him to budget his time. Let him be a part of the planning, rather than you figuring it all out for him.

- Teach a child to manage money. Dave Ramsey has great programs for children where kids learn to have money to spend, money to save, and money to tithe.

- Let your children save for something. Let them pick out an item they really want and save toward it. You can even match their money, if you'd like, but let them have the impetus to work toward it.

- If a young child is having trouble keeping up with his things, give him a warning. It can help to have a visual warning, such as a note posted on his mirror that can be a reminder. The next time give logical consequences. If he leaves his shoes out, he can shine his dad's shoes. Or maybe he loses the privilege of wearing those shoes for a day. If she leaves her backpack out, she can carry her sister's backpack the next day for her.

- Tie a reward to a responsibility. "I'd love to take you to get a new library book when you finish cleaning your room." "I'd be happy to take you to softball practice when you've unloaded the dishwasher." Those kinds of comments help kids learn that responsibility does have rewards and that they're not simply entitled for you to take them wherever and whenever they want.

- Read Foster Cline and Jim Fay's *Parenting with Love and Logic*. The subtitle is *Teaching Children Responsibility*, and they do a great job of teaching parents to teach children this important value that we can't even begin to cover in one chapter.

Responsibility in Teenagers

What Responsibility Looks Like

Why do I have to clean my room when it's my room? Do you remember thinking these kinds of "deep thoughts" when you were a teenager? Teenagers question everything, including your attempts to teach them responsibility. They "already know" or "they heard you before" when their actions say just the opposite.

What does a responsible teenager look like? It looks like Jacob, who volunteers with our younger groups at Daystar. Jacob has gotten a speeding ticket or two, but Jacob makes fairly good grades, he comes in on time (most nights), and he makes pretty good choices. And he gives of his time to help a ministry he believes in.

Responsibility looks like Erin. Erin is a football cheerleader. She feels a lot of pressure and has to take a "personal day" from school sometimes (with her parent's permission). When she gets really tired and overwhelmed, her parents tell her she's got a bad attitude. But she's committed to staying pure with her boyfriend. And she's been elected vice president of her class.

One of the things teenagers say to us in our offices a lot is, "I just wish my parents could see that I'm a good kid." Typically these kids don't drink. They don't use drugs, and they're not having sex. They're not "doing what all the other kids are doing at school." Now we know this doesn't make these kids perfect. They still have bad attitudes, get speeding tickets, and bomb tests from time to time. But they are trying. They are swimming upstream against a culture that is pretty tough to handle.

Obstacles to Responsibility

I (Melissa) remember when I was in high school, I ran for vice president of my class. When I was elected, I did a horrible job. I wasn't any good because I didn't want the responsibility. I just wanted to win the election. Teenagers often don't want responsibility. Or at least they only want the responsibilities they choose. Your daughter may be an officer in three clubs and have a room that looks like a tornado hit it. Your son might be incredibly consistent with his grades and inconsistent with his curfew. They pick and choose based on their interests. This need for control may work for them but often doesn't work for us.

"Maturity" can also be an obstacle to responsibility for teenagers. "My mom still treats me like I'm ten." Your son thinks he's too old for chores. Your daughter doesn't understand why she has to clean her room when it's her room, after all. Teenagers want answers. They want to know the whys, in good ways, in that they are searching for answers to big questions like what they believe and why. But they also want to know why they have to do certain things.

We have a rule at camp that girls go through the line first at mealtime. I remember a boy who came to camp for the fourth year when he was a seventh-grader. He had heard that rule every meal, every day, every year for four years. But when the counselor made the announcement, he quickly came back with, "But why do the girls get to go in front?" In reality, it was a good question and a great teaching opportunity.

A Few Tips to Instill Responsibility in Teenagers

- At this point in their lives, responsibility can't be taught directly. You've said all you need to say and all they're going to hear in the matter. You teach by your actions and their consequences.
- Teenagers are old enough to understand the importance of responsibilities. Talk through the reasons for certain responsibilities and consequences for not following through.
- Give them opportunities to make mistakes. Teenagers need to know boundaries ahead of time. They need to know what is expected of them and what will happen if they fail to meet those

expectations.

- Expect of them. Hold your teenagers to standards. Give them a curfew. Set limits. Don't let "teenagers be teenagers." They do not know how to set their own limits, especially in the younger years. They need your guidance and boundaries.
- Widen those boundaries with every year. As your child gets older, give him more freedom in his choices from bedtime to screen time to curfew. He needs more choices so that he can make mistakes he can learn from. You'd rather him make mistakes at home than when he's eighteen and no longer living under your roof.
- Give her more responsibilities as she grows, too. Let your sixteen-year-old help with the laundry. Let him mow the yard and help cook meals. To whom much is given, much is required . . . even around the house.
- Reward the choices they are making. If your child is one of those swimming upstream, if she's making good choices for the most part, reward those choices. She will feel more trusted and want to earn more of your trust, in return.
- Don't wait for a response. If you've told your teenager something once, don't repeat yourself. He has nine times out of ten heard you. They just forget to respond or don't want to give you the pleasure. Tell him once and then implement consequences if he's missed it. He'll listen a little better the next time.
- Have them choose one activity that is not some type of sport, lesson, or academic endeavor to learn responsibility. It can be a place to volunteer regularly, a part-time job, or any other idea they choose (the operative word here is *they*).
- The older they get, give them more responsibility over their lives and their calendars. By the time your daughter is a senior in high school, she can schedule her own tutoring appointments, take her own medicine, and even make her own haircuts. She can also have the responsibility to cancel those in a timely fashion or pay the consequences if she doesn't. This can help

prepare her greatly for life without your master calendar.

- Read *Parenting with Love and Logic for Teens* by Foster Cline and Jim Fay. Once again we don't have enough room in this chapter to include all we'd like to in teaching adolescent responsibility, but they've done a great job! We recommend their book wholeheartedly.

A Valuable Reminder

On November 7, 2009, Florida was playing Vanderbilt. Tim Tebow, Florida's quarterback, had under his eye in black, Colossians 3:23. "Whatever you do, do your work heartily, as for the Lord rather than for men" (Col. 3:23 NASB).

That verse is like a charge. It's a charge to get up and go. It's a call to do the work that's placed before us heartily. In this verse *heartily* means "with all of your mind, soul, body, the seat of your feelings and desires— to put your whole self into it." Do your work heartily.

When children ask us why they should do something or "who really cares?" God does. The verse reminds us that we do our work heartily for the Lord. And his charge to us comes with a promise. It is a promise that we'll receive a reward. It's that simple. You will receive the reward of the inheritance. We will as we parent and love them with responsibility, and they will as they learn to live with responsibility. It is the Lord Christ whom we serve.

A Sunday Drive

This Sunday Drive is on the family body. It is to help come up with a plan by which everyone can contribute to the household and share the load. Start off reading the following verses:

> The body is a unit, though it is made up of many parts; and though all its parts are many, they form one body. So it is with Christ. For we were all baptized by one Spirit into one body—whether Jews or Greeks, slave or free—and we were all given the one Spirit to drink.
>
> Now the body is not made up of one part but of many. If the foot should say, "Because I am not a hand, I do not belong to the body," it would not for that reason cease to be part of the body. And if the ear should say, "Because I am not an eye, I do not belong to the body," it would not for that reason cease to be part of the body. If the whole body were an eye, where would the sense of hearing be? If the whole body were an ear, where would the sense of smell be? But in fact God has arranged the parts in the body, every one of them, just as he wanted them to be. If they were all one part, where would the body be? As it is, there are many parts, but one body.
>
> The eye cannot say to the hand, "I don't need you!" And the head cannot say to the feet, "I don't need you!" On the contrary, those parts of the body that seem to be weaker are indispensable, and the parts that we think are less honorable we treat with special honor. And the parts that are unpresentable are treated with special modesty, while our presentable

parts need no special treatment. But God has combined the members of the body and has given greater
honor to the parts that lacked it, so that there should
be no division in the body, but that its parts should
have equal concern for each other. If one part suffers,
every part suffers with it; if one part is honored, every
part rejoices with it.

Now you are the body of Christ, and each one of
you is a part of it. (1 Cor. 12:12–27)

As a family, sit down with several pieces of paper, a poster board, and
markers. The body parts mentioned in the verses were hand, foot, eye,
and ear. Talk about what this verse can mean for your family—how you
all work together to make up a family, just as these body parts make up
the body of Christ. Take each family member, one by one, and talk about
what that person brings to the family that is different from anyone else.
Remember to stay positive. Don't let one person receive more positive
feedback than another. Try to keep it even.

Next talk about chores that need to be done in your household.
Divide them into different body parts. (You can add to the list of four,
if need be.) A hand job is dusting, for example. A foot job might be
sweeping. Make a list of as many body parts as there are people in your
family.

For each week, have a different family member act as a different
body part. Place that body part on his or her door for the week as a
reminder. Then you can get together at an appointed time each week
and swap jobs. Talk about how that person made a good foot or hand or
eye. This can be not only a lesson in responsibility but also how important each family member is to the whole.

The Value of Patience

So don't lose a minute in building on what you've been given,
complementing your basic faith with good character,
spiritual understanding, alert discipline, passionate patience,
reverent wonder, warm friendliness, and generous love,
each dimension fitting into and developing the others.

—2 Peter 1:5–7 *The Message*

I (Sissy) am counseling a twelve-year-old girl who has just been diagnosed with her fourth brain tumor. Four. In twelve years. Holly is one of the strongest children I have ever met. Her smile is irresistible, her compassion is moving, and her spirit is undaunted. I am staggered by the strength this little girl shows continually in the face of fear. The day after they found that the fourth mass was not only a tumor but was growing, she came into my office.

I met Holly that October. She came in just after they had found the mass. The doctors told her that it could be another tumor, but she would have to wait and have a repeat scan on January 20. On that date they would know what it was and if it was growing. And so Holly waited.

At least weekly we filled the waiting time with conversation. She worried some and prayed more. She read her Bible and wrote stories. I suggested she read the Time Quartet by Madeleine L'Engle, starting with *A Wrinkle in Time*. Like any good counselor, I wanted to help distract her.

Turns out she just started reading the book, right as the awaited date rolled around. When she came into my offices on January 21, one of the first things she said was, "I love *A Wrinkle in Time*! I think my life theme, right now, is something that Meg believed. One who has never known unhappiness can never know what true happiness really means." Those words are this young girl's response to her fourth brain tumor.

We also talked about patience—her phenomenal patience over the last four months. All I could say to Holly was, "You have got to be one of the most patient people I have ever known. Waiting like this sure puts things in perspective. When you've had to wait like this, other kinds of waiting, like to find out what you made on a test, probably feel pretty insignificant."

"Definitely," was her strong and sure response.

Defining Patience

Most of us can't even begin to relate to the kind of patience Holly has. In fact, it's probably hard to think back over a time in your life when you've had a lot of patience. What comes to mind much more easily is when you haven't had patience, when you've been frustrated or worried, impulsive or demanding.

It is easy to think of patience as simply a willingness to wait. We've all done that. We've waited on a mechanic to change our tire, a potential employer to return a call, a word back from a doctor. Some waiting is harder than others. But Merriam-Webster takes *patience* a step farther. It defines being patient as "bearing pains or trials calmly or without complaint." Oh, that's a whole 'nother ballgame, as we'd say in the South.

When you are waiting, how often do you bear the pain without complaint? How often do you stay calm when an appointment is taking much longer than expected? Or an important return call? Even a slow car in the fast lane?

If you're anything like we are, your patience is not quite so quiet.

You gripe and grumble. (We do.) Sometimes, you shout. (We do that, too). You complain to the manager. (Actually, only Sissy does that.) You complain to yourself. (Melissa?)

And what about those children of yours? When your son wants a new toy in Wal-Mart, does he keep that information to himself and wait quietly? What about when your daughter wants to have a friend over to spend the night? What about your teenager who wants a car or even just a little later curfew? Patience and kids of all ages just don't seem to get along very well.

Patience in Children

What Patience Looks Like

Impatience starts as early as your child's first breath. He cries when his diaper needs to be changed. She cries when she wants to eat or sleep or be held. And what do we do? We pick him up. We feed her or rock her or change her or do basically anything we can to soothe her. Of course we do. His cries, in those early stages, are his only ways to communicate his needs. And we meet those needs as quickly as we can, just as we should.

A year (or earlier than that) later, and what was a survival instinct begins to have an undercurrent of demand. It's part of why the terrible twos really can be kind of terrible. He is used to having his needs met immediately. He continues to communicate his needs, expecting that you'll jump. But you no longer jump. You're trying to teach him patience, just as you should.

Patience is not like compassion or kindness. Kids don't have a natural inclination toward it. If anything, their leaning is not just leaning; it's running in the opposite direction. They DO NOT want to wait, and when they do, it's sure not calmly or without complaint.

Obstacles to Patience

Do you remember Psychology 101? Sigmund Freud was the guy we all talked about and wondered about. He divided the psyche into id, ego, and superego. In basic terms, you could consider the id the seat of impulses; the superego, the seat of conscience; and the ego, the mediator between the two, using reason and common sense. In his theory infants were ruled by their ids. He describes the id as responsible for our basic drives. It is selfish and ruled by the pleasure-pain principle: striving for one and avoiding the other. It has no sense of time, is completely illogical and emotionally immature, and does not understand the word *no*. Does sound a little like the toddler under your roof, doesn't it?

Children start there. The primary obstacle to patience is that it simply is not inherent in their little psyches. They want to have fun. They want to eat. They want to play or draw or get down RIGHT NOW! We have to, with great patience and our own modeling, teach them what patience means.

Boys' and girls' lack of patience comes in different forms. David Thomas, Stephen James, Michael Gurian, and any other expert on the subject of boys would use the word *impulsive* as one of their primary characteristics. For boys, this impulsivity often stands in direct opposition to their patience. He wants something and he grabs it. He gets angry and lashes out, maybe even physically. He needs to go to the bathroom in the middle of the night at camp and goes off the balcony of his cabin rather than walking the twenty steps to a real bathroom with plumbing (occurred on more than one occasion and with more than one boy at our camp). Melissa has dead shrubbery to prove it.

We were recently teaching a Raising Girls seminar. The man in charge of the seminar kindly told us we needed a new name. "Raising Girls is too boring," he told us. "You should call it 'Sugar and Spice.'" Cute idea, but we would guess you have moments with your daughter when everything isn't so nice. Instead, we like the words one mom used in our office to describe herself—cute and demanding. Girls do their best to be cute in an endearing sort of way and are often demanding, in a not so endearing sort of way. They demand that you pick them up, buy them this, take them there, get them that. We would go so far as to say that what impulsiveness is to boys, demandingness is to girls. Both are major obstacles to their practice in patience.

A final obstacle for both boys and girls is hinted at in a song you may remember from the seventies. It's from an album (and yes, they were albums back then) called *Music Machine*. It's sung by a snail named

Herbert, whose friends get really frustrated with his speed—or lack thereof. The snail slowly sings, "Have patience. Have patience. Don't be in such a hurry. When you get impatient, you only start to worry. Remember, remember, that God is patient, too, and think of all the times when others have to wait for you."

Worry is one of those obstacles of patience that is particularly gripping for children. They're afraid they won't get what they want. Or they're afraid of more substantial options like you won't come home or they will get hurt or won't be loved. Patience starts with trust, which is also a learned behavior in the lives of our children. If they don't trust, they worry. And if they worry, they often become loudly impatient. (See the section on anxiety in chapter 6.)

A Few Tips to Instill Patience in Children

- Buy seed for a plant, raise tadpoles or even sea monkeys (yes, these are real). Bake together. Activities that slowly cause something to grow help children understand and experience the value of patience. It can also provide you with great teaching opportunities along the way.
- Teach them to wait in small increments in their early years (start with fifteen seconds and build slowly). Teach them to wait for a snack, for you to come wherever they're beckoning. Patience is like a muscle and develops gradually and with consistency.
- You can set a kitchen time or even anchor time with "when your dad comes home" or "after you finish your homework." It helps children to have a concrete time frame rather than a vague understanding of time.
- When your child is waiting, help him find options of things he can do. It can help him to know that he can fill his time while waiting without becoming frustrated.
- If she (or he) says something in a demanding voice, simply have her say it again. Help her know that you will not respond to a demand, only a request. Have her restate until it comes out respectfully.

- Look at your child when he's talking to you. Give him your full attention rather than your hurried, impatient response.
- Don't give in to instant gratification. Continually getting what they want right when they want it teaches them impatience rather than patience.
- Let your child work toward things. If he wants a big ticket item, tell him you'll match every dollar he saves. If she wants to buy an expensive gift, tell her you'll help with the last little bit or simply allow her to save for it.
- Help your child learn to problem solve one step at a time. If he's frustrated, sit down with him and talk through options. What's the first thing he can do? The second? Make a list that will help calm him down and think through the situation.
- If you feel like you've already lost some ground in the patience war, you can be honest with your child. "It's obvious to me, by the way that you're acting, that I haven't done a great job on teaching you patience. This is something we're going to work on together."
- Be a patient parent. It is difficult to tell a child to "be patient" when you're yelling. Count to three. Take time out. Breathe . . . whatever you need to do to respond to your impatient child with patience.
- Model patience in your own life. If you're waiting for a promotion or to find out some type of news, pray together as a family. Give God control of the situation and pray that you can walk out what it means to wait calmly and without complaint. (This also counts in traffic.)
- Acknowledge and reinforce their patience.

Patience in Teenagers

What Patience Looks Like in Teenagers

It is hard to decide if teenagers are patient. He can wait forever to find out his grades. She wants to take an hour and a half every day to fix her hair and put on her makeup. They love long road trips (as long

THE VALUE OF PATIENCE • 211

as they're with their friends) and don't mind being stuck in traffic if they've got their iPod (and friends). Teenagers can have seemingly limitless amounts of patience. They would describe themselves as laid back, mellow, "chill," but then the wind blows a different direction.

Obstacles to Patience (aka Demandingness and Impulsivity Grow Up)

Melissa is the much more patient of the two of us. Maybe it's because she's the middle child, and I was the only child for sixteen years. Maybe it's because her personality is a little more laid back. Whatever the reason, I would almost go as far as to say she has patience and I don't. But I'm trying to learn. It just takes too long.

I remember being a teenager myself and taking my sister to a play date. She was a toddler and I was a teen. I don't really remember what I was doing, but I definitely remember her words in response, "Thithy [that's Sissy in three-year-old Kathleen language], why do you always have to be in such a hurry?" I was, especially when it came to something I deemed important.

Teenagers can be "chill" and all of that, unless it's something that matters to them. Your son may love a long road trip with his friends and iPod, but he will get irate with you if you're late dropping him off to meet up with those friends. Your daughter may be thoroughly enjoying her time with Estee (Lauder) and Max (Factor), but her impatience will go through the roof if you interrupt and ask her a question. He'll wait on his friends for hours and become angry with you within minutes. She is impatient with your questions, your comments, your eating, even your breathing on some days.

If we go back to the Freudian theory, it's as if the id is in control in the earliest years of your child's life. Then during elementary school the superego steps up to the plate. He is kind, conscientious, and thoughtful. Then she hits thirteen (or even eleven). The id quickly begins its comeback.

As we've said over and over and over, teenagers are selfish. As their selfishness increases during their adolescence, their patience often decreases. They will act impatient with you, their siblings, their teachers, and in rare windows of times, their friends (although they would never tell them). Mostly, however, they're impatient with themselves. They're frustrated they're not prettier or more athletic, stronger or braver or kinder or skinnier or any other attribute they think all of their friends possess more than they. And so they get frustrated. You're the safest person in his life, so it's easiest for his insecurity to come out as impatience. She knows you will always love her, and so she snaps at you when she's really feeling bad about herself.

We are aware that we're making teenagers sound like their selfishness or impatience only arises out of their own insecurities. They are also, however, impatient at times simply because they're impatient. They're also still battling those old ideas of impulsivity and demandingness.

Now the gender lines have blurred. Most teenagers are impulsive—boys and girls alike. They make rash decisions and don't think through outcomes. They do things in excess—drive too fast, eat too little, drink too much (even caffeine-ladened drinks like Jolt). I (Melissa) recently talked to a thirteen-year-old who snuck out at midnight and walked three miles to meet up and make out with a guy friend of hers. Just one of so very many stories of impulsivity in the lives of teens.

What about demanding? If you have a teenager, you know—or at least live the answer more than we do. How does he approach you when he's lost his jacket and wants a new one? We would guess that he doesn't come to you and say, "Mom, I know you do so much for me, and I sometimes don't do a good job of keeping up with my stuff. But it's cold, and I really need a new jacket." Instead, "Mom, I lost my jacket" or, better yet, "Somebody must have taken my jacket, and I need you to get me a new one today." They command, order, and outline exactly what we need to do for them and when.

A Few Tips to Instill Patience in Teenagers

- Start early. Teenagers whose parents have taught them patience in their early years have a better understanding and sense of trust when they have to wait. Better understanding, not full; however . . . they are teenagers.

- Allow them to struggle. Much like Holly in the beginning of the chapter, children and teenagers who have had trials in their lives gain perspective. They learn that answers often don't come easily or immediately, and they better learn to handle themselves in the process.

- Expect some impatience. Their frustration with themselves really will feel overwhelming to them at times. Know that some of that frustration will spill over to you. Don't respond to every eye roll or show of attitude.

- Give them some room to be teenagers, but draw a line. You can even tell them that you know they're angry, but you're not the enemy and so you aren't going to let them keep talking to you that way. They can and often need consequences when their impatience with you becomes really hurtful. If kids are allowed to get away with the worst that they can be, they often will believe the worst about who they are.

- Don't take their impatience personally. You really are not the cause and source of all of his problems in life, even if he tells you that you are. The reality is that he doesn't believe it either. He just needs an outlet, and you happen to be standing in front of him. Remind yourself of this and have other people in your life who can remind you, as well.

- Continue to model patience. She will try your patience and push your buttons in these years like never before. But, again, it's hard to teach her patience or punish her for her impatience when you're acting the same way.

- Watch for signs that more is going on. If the emotional outbursts persist, you may want to take him to talk to someone. As we've said before, teenage depression can look a lot like anger and impatience.

- Slow down the pace of your household. It's hard to be patient if everyone is moving frenetically to and fro. Slow down. Enjoy each other. Eat meals together and not in a hurry. Take time to watch a movie or play a board game. Go for walks. Watch old home videos. Tell stories about when your children were younger. Light candles and read out loud. They may act like you're corny and they're embarrassed. But teenagers often tell us they secretly enjoy those quaint, warm, corny times.

A Valuable Reminder

The words "passionate patience" are used on three different occasions in *The Message*. In Revelation 3:10 and Romans 5:3, "passionate patience" is said to keep us safe, forge virtue, and bring about an alert expectancy in us for whatever God is doing. Second Peter 1:5 says this: "So don't lose a minute in building on what you've been given, complementing your basic faith with good character, spiritual understanding, alert discipline, passionate patience, reverent wonder, warm friendliness, and generous love, each dimension fitting into and developing the others" (*The Message*).

When we think of patience, we usually think of it as more passive than passionate. Our kids don't want to be patient because they think it's boring. In all honesty it sounds a little boring to us, too. After all, we live in a fast-paced modern world. If anything describes our society right now, it's that we're in a hurry. We're continually thinking of the next thing: the next test your child isn't ready for, the next tennis match to drive carpool to, the next family vacation to pack for, the next pile of bills to pay. We don't end up being passionate in this moment because we're already anticipating the next. It's as if we live in a state of perpetual restlessness.

But, somehow, 2 Peter 1:5 tells us to hurry and have patience in the same sentence. "So don't lose a minute in building on what you've been given," and then Peter includes a commendable list of characteristics, including "passionate patience." Don't lose a minute building passionate patience. Sounds a little like the idiom, "Hurry up and wait." But, in reality, what it's saying is just the opposite.

When you think back on the people who have most impacted your life, what would you say about them? Do you see any commonalities, whether it was a coach or teacher, youth director or mentor? Maybe it was someone who taught you to water-ski or a tutor who really helped you understand math. We would guess one phrase would describe them all: they took the time. They took the time to listen; they took the time to help; they took the time to encourage you; they took the time to love you.

I (Melissa) remember overhearing a conversation between a twelve-year-old and her mom about Sissy. As they were walking away from Sissy's office, she said, "Mom, I know Sissy talks to a lot of kids. But when I'm with her, she makes me feel like I'm the most important one." Sissy took the time.

Passionate patience is about taking the time. Kids respond to someone who is present with them, listening to them, alive to the moment and what God has in it. Passionate patience is not passive in any way. Think about the love chapter, 1 Corinthians 13. The first description of love is that it's patient. What your children long for, what we long for, is for someone to be passionately patient with us not just in math lessons and ski school but in who we really are. You want someone who has the passionate patience to love you as you are and have hope for what God is forging inside you. Your children want the same thing. So don't lose a moment. Pray that Jesus will continue to build in you his passionate patience. And pray that God's Spirit will help calm your restlessness and make you alive to the moment and all that he has for you and for them in it.

A Sunday Drive

"Lissa, let's get a Pepsi and go down to the creek." When I was growing up, I had the immense pleasure of going fishing with my Granddaddy Jack. We would get ice-cold Pepsis, our poles, some worms, and head down to the creek. I don't remember catching many fish, but I remember how good it felt to spend an afternoon with my grandfather. My older brother didn't come with us because he was usually home building a model of some kind of car or airplane.

Kids don't build models much anymore or go fishing. It takes too long. Their activities move faster and typically don't require assembly.

Their dollhouses come prepackaged by rooms. Mine (Sissy's) was a kit that my mom and dad built shingle by shingle and electrified themselves. I would get a new piece of furniture for an A on my report card or a birthday. I loved that dollhouse and spent hours playing in it as a young girl and decorating it as I got older.

In this Sunday Drive we want to give you a few suggestions to help your kids take the time and learn a little of what passionate patience looked like in the vintage days.

- Build a model with your child. It can be a model of anything that interests them. Ehobbies.com has a great variety of cars, trucks, helicopters, and even rockets.

- Teach your child or teenager to fish. It can be in a creek, on a lake, or even on an ocean. Don't worry if they object. What they learn now, they'll often come to love later. Sissy and Kathleen grew up deep-sea fishing with their dad and still make sure they get to fish with him on any trip that goes near the ocean.

- Create a hideout with your child. I (Melissa) loved to do this, too. Decide the items you'll need, draw out plans to make it as elaborate as you want, and build it together.

- Build a dollhouse together. Greenleafdollhouses.com, Dollhousesdear.com, manhattandollhouse.com, and even Wal-Mart and Target carry dollhouse kits to build and furniture to fill them.

- If you have a teenager, help him or her come up with a moneymaking scheme for the summer (that will involve time). We know boys and girls who teach tennis lessons and run their own camps for neighborhood kids. You can act as an advisor, and they can learn a lot of passionate patience working with children.

- Use your own imagination and theirs. Come up with something you can do together that takes time and maybe teaches a little patience in the process.

The Value of Confidence

With your help I can advance against a troop;
with my God I can scale a wall.

—Psalm 18:29

S he loves to shop," this mother of a thirteen-year-old told me (Melissa) recently. "The problem is that she has a meltdown every time we go shopping. It starts when she walks in the dressing room and sees the mirror. By the time she comes out to show me the clothes, she's in tears. 'I hate it. I look bad in it and I hate it.' She quickly moves from being angry with herself to angry with me. The last time we went, I said, 'Okay, Sarah. Sometimes when we're shopping, you start to feel really bad about yourself. You end up getting really mad at me. That doesn't work so well for either of us. What do you want me to do this time if you start having a meltdown?'

"'I want you to say, "Sarah, suck it up and keep shopping."'

"We walked in the mall. She picked out several tops, a dress, a new pair of jeans and headed to the dressing room. I was on alert. She came out with the same dejected, discouraged look on her face.

"'I look awful,'" was her first comment. We digressed from there.

"'Sarah, suck it up and keep shopping. You're beautiful and wonderful and a joy to have as a daughter.'

"'MOM, DON'T DEVIATE FROM THE SCRIPT!'"

Sarah's mom went on to say that Sarah hates it when she compliments her. "She didn't like it that I said nice things about her." She also said that when Sarah started yelling again, her mom lost it. "I yelled back. I told her she was being downright mean. Sarah burst into tears and told me that the worst thing I can do when she's already feeling horrible is to tell her something bad about herself. It only makes her feel worse. That's the last thing I would ever want to do."

Defining Confidence

Do you have moments when you see confidence in your child? Maybe when she has a new ballet skirt and twirls through the den? Maybe when he makes a basket and shouts the "yeaaaaa" of cheering crowds. Those are the moments we feel good knowing that our children feel good about themselves.

But then there are other moments—the moments your daughter comes home from school and tells you that the other girls told her she couldn't play with them anymore because she was "different." When your son comes home from school with his head down and goes straight to his room. You know something happened but have no idea what. Moments when you find laxatives in your daughter's drawer or discover that your son is cutting himself. Those are the moments when you would do anything to get back the smile of the twirling ballerina or the shouts of the basketball star.

You want your child to have confidence. You want him to feel good enough about himself to try new things. You want her to have the confidence to pick up the phone and call someone to spend the night. You want him to lift his head and her to accept a compliment without brushing it away. You want them to believe in themselves and who God has created them to be. You want them to know that they have so much to offer. And you want them to have it through every stage of their life, even—maybe especially—if you don't.

Confidence in Children

What Confidence Looks Like

Children lack self-consciousness. Connor, in particular, lacks self-consciousness. Connor's in the second grade and is coming to Daystar because his parents are going through a divorce. This fall Connor was around while we were promoting our fall fund-raiser, the Bike Thing. For several weeks before the event, Kathleen (our assistant development director and Sissy's now grown sister) goes to each of the groups to talk about the Bike Thing. Groups consist of second- through twelfth-graders, boys and girls, with an average of six to twelve kids per group. Kathleen tells them stories and gives them incentives to ride and raise money to help underwrite counseling for those who can't afford it. One day Connor caught on.

"Kathleen, where are you going?"

"I'm going to the groups to tell them about the Bike Thing."

"I'll come and help," was Connor's quick response.

Kathleen spoke to four groups that night. Connor gave his input at every group, telling them the Bike Thing was "really cool and they should all do it." When they finished the fourth, Connor turned to Kathleen and said, "Okay, what time to do you need me tomorrow?"

"Connor, I can't go to the groups tomorrow. I have a meeting."

"Okay, then I'll do them myself."

Connor stood in front of groups of his peers and groups of kids seven and eight years older than himself. He had no self-consciousness doing so. A teenager wouldn't want to stand in front of other teenagers and talk about the Bike Thing or anything else. But Connor did. And he did so with confidence.

I (Melissa) had a note in my box from Connor when I came back from the Christmas holidays. It had a drawing (I think) of Connor at the Daystar house. It said,

> *Miss Melissa,*
> *I've missed working at Daystar. I'm glad to be back.*
> *See you soon.*
> *Connor*

Like Connor, many children have a natural confidence. They try new things and meet new people with much more ease than their adolescent counterparts. Of course, some children are shy around people they don't know. But for the most part younger kids have a swagger and skip in their steps, especially around those they love. As for those they don't know as well, many children believe others will think they're just as smart, funny, and cute as you do.

Obstacles to Confidence in Children

We do see children in our offices who aren't confident. We see children who believe they're fat. We see children who believe they're dumb or stupid. We see children who think they're trouble or just plain bad. The obstacle to confidence in these children is criticism. Children don't usually grow up believing these things about themselves. For a child to believe he's trouble, he's most often been told that he is. A girl who believes she's fat has probably heard it from other lips first.

You are mirrors for your children. Other kids are mirrors for your children . . . even the mean ones. They are highly impressionable and highly gullible. They believe what they're told, even if it's about themselves.

Other children struggle with confidence because of a situation going on around them. As we've said before, they don't understand their feelings. If a circumstance causes your son to be angry, he may see himself as "bad." For example, a little boy we know lost his dad to suicide. He is angry that his dad can't take him to baseball games and come to his school programs. Of course he's angry. We know that, but he doesn't. Other little boys who are angry are "bad," so he must be, too.

Children's perceptive abilities can further this confidence problem. Your daughter notices that you're upset. In her limited understanding, she is the center of her world and yours. She, therefore, must have caused you to be upset. Your son notices that you don't come home much anymore. He thinks it's because he broke your favorite mug. As you have most likely read, children whose parents divorce often believe they caused the divorce. Again, they are the center of their own universe. So, if something is going wrong in their universe, it is most likely because they caused it. You can imagine how this would affect a child's confidence.

We know a few children who don't fall into these categories but still seem to be lacking in confidence. *Seem* is the key word here. These are often the children who hide behind their parent's pant leg or won't look an adult in the eye. One mom told me (Sissy) that she thought her daughter would crawl inside her skin with her if she could when they're in social situations. It may not, however, be that this child lacks confidence. Shyness and a lack of confidence are not the same. A child can be shy in public and a complete clown at home. He can be reserved on the playground and aggressive on the basketball court. Your child's personality may make him feel more comfortable in academic arenas than social. He may seem more like himself when playing sports or in art class than with a group of his peers. Don't confuse an introverted personality with a lack of confidence, although one can, at times, lead to the other.

A Few Tips to Instill Confidence in Children

- Start early. Give your baby plenty of opportunity to attach. Interact with him or her often, beyond just necessary caretaking. Smile at him. Make noises at her. Read to him. Play with her. Be affectionate. Babies thrive on affection and engagement. They feel good about themselves and about you when they feel connected to you.

- Be aware of your own confidence level. If you struggle significantly with insecurity, he or she will, as well. Or he will see you as weak and feel that he has to be strong. He needs you to love him from your own sense of security. We all struggle with that every day. But there is a security in Christ that can free you to parent with more confidence in who you are and hope in who God is still creating you to be.

- If you are struggling emotionally, talk to someone for yourself and for your child. As we said, they read your emotions and can often feel responsible for them. How much would it have helped your parents be free to parent you from a place of love and confidence if they had someone to talk to? Be open to giving your child the same gift.

- Encourage your child. Don't just praise his successes because he can begin to tie his confidence to his own success academically, athletically, or in any arena. Rather than just telling him how smart he is (although you can tell him that, too), point out positive character traits you see. Tell him when you see him act lovingly. Tell her when she shows gentleness or strength.

- Don't ignore their failures. Children are often aware when they fail. They may try to pretend they're not, but this is often for your benefit even more than theirs. They don't want to let you down. If your child makes a bad grade or misses a goal, don't ignore it. You can ask them how they felt about it and acknowledge the miss, but still stress the positive. "I know you were frustrated when you missed that ball, but I thought you had a great attitude and did a good job supporting your teammates. I'm proud of how you played, but I'm really proud of who you are." They will feel more known and loved when you see where they fail and love them still. They will also learn to place their confidence in more than just their perfect performance.

- Enjoy your child. In our girls classes we say that girls who are delighted in feel that they're delightful. This goes for boys, too. Set aside moments just for play rather than instruction. Enjoy them. Get on the floor and play a board game. Stand up and play Wii. Playing with them helps them know that you love them and that you like them, as well.

- Be aware of comparing your children. To tell Susan that her sister understands how important grades are does not make Susan care more about her studies. It usually makes her care less.

- Give your child responsibilities. It helps him feel that you believe he's capable when he helps, even if he drags his feet.

- Validate her feelings. Ask questions to help her talk about what she feels. Telling a child she "shouldn't" feel sad or angry doesn't help the situation and often makes her second-guess herself. Listen to her feelings and help her think through them. She's sad, and how does she want to handle the sadness? What can she do that helps her feel better? You want her to learn to trust you and herself.

- Create a secure home environment. As your child gets older, his confidence will come under attack at school. It doesn't need to be under attack at home, too. Be aware of sounding critical.
- Help your child find something where he can feel good about himself. He doesn't have to be the star, but he might be good at athletics, academics, or arts. He might be good with younger children and could help volunteer with underprivileged kids.
- Don't assume you understand your child. Your child is growing and developing as a person. What she thinks and feels changes, too. Ask her questions to continue to stay connected and know what's important to her.
- Believe in who he can be. Remember that God is doing a good work in your child, even when it's hard to see. He needs you not only to remember but to help remind him.
- Encourage independence. Allow your child to wander and explore life on his own (within safe limits). With each growing year, give him a little more room to make his own decisions.
- Let him dream. If your child wants to be an astronaut, help him learn more about NASA. If she wants to be president, take her to Washington, DC, for a family trip. Even if you're not sure he's capable, he needs you to dream with him and believe that anything is possible. It might just be (unless he really is a bad singer and wants to do something like try out for *American Idol* and embarrass himself).

Confidence in a Teenager

What Confidence Looks Like

We have been racking our brains trying to think of teenagers with confidence. All we can think of are the stereotypical teens in movies like Danny Zuko from the seventies, Ferris Bueller from the eighties, *Clueless's* Cher from the nineties, Regina in *Mean Girls,* and Anna in *Freaky Friday* from the last decade. They're cool, confident, and secure. And they are not at all typical teens.

We don't know kids like any of those in the movies. We know kids who try. In our office we have our share of Danny, Ferris, and Anna wannabes. They wear the right clothes, use the right slang, and throw the right amount of attitude at their parents. In fact, we see kids who don't get along with their parents because they're not "supposed to" when they're teenagers. For one reason or another, these kids feel like they don't fit. They don't measure up. They're different. And so they compensate by adopting the image.

Some movies show a much more realistic picture of teenagers. Akeelah from *Akeelah and the Bee,* Simon and Joe in *Simon Birch,* Peter Parker in *Spiderman,* Mia in *The Princess Diaries,* and our good friend Edmund from *The Lion, the Witch and the Wardrobe* are kids who are not only struggling with their confidence but are struggling to be more than the typical teenage image. Those are the kinds of teenagers we know and see in our offices. If you haven't seen these movies, any of the above would be a crash course on the confidence of teens: the first set, who they often wish they were on the outside; and the second, how they feel about themselves on the inside.

Obstacles to Confidence

Parents build a child's confidence in childhood. In adolescence they protect it. If there was ever a time confidence needs protecting, it's in adolescence. Think back on your own teenage years. How did you feel about yourself? How did you think others felt about you? Are you embarrassed when you look back on ways you acted or choices you made? How many of those choices were fueled by your own insecurity? Many of them likely had more to do with the way you wanted people to see you than who you really were.

Confidence is hard to come by in these twelve to eighteen years. For some kids it starts even younger and lasts even longer. (*When does it stop?*

you may be thinking.) Most kids will say that the zenith of insecurity was in the seventh grade.

We speak to seventh-grade girls across the country as a part of an event called You and Your Girl. We love having time with girls we've never met before . . . hearing their hearts, sharing truth, and watching them learn what confidence truly looks like. In the first part of our talk, we tell them a few secrets about confidence. The first has to do with their brain development, and it's an idea we discuss at length in *Raising Girls*. Somewhere between the ages of eight and twelve, your daughter's brain growth surges. The connections in her brain are growing so fast that her brain can't handle it. It's almost as if her brain short circuits. The two areas that short-circuiting affects are her memory and her confidence. Therefore, you will pick your daughter up from school. She will hug four girls on the way to the car. As you drive away, she'll burst into tears because "no one likes her." Her brain is literally malfunctioning.

Boys are experiencing surges of testosterone like never before in adolescence. These surges will prompt a heightened interest in their sexuality, as well as a desire for strength. Both can make boys doubt themselves. Boys often don't understand the changes taking place in their bodies or their minds sexually. They feel guilty for the dreams they have and the images that pop into their heads. Unless they have had appropriate conversations with adults they trust, they may feel as though they're doing something wrong or they are "bad."

In terms of their strength, testosterone makes boys more aggressive physically and emotionally. They want to assert themselves and test their strength. They push the boundaries and argue. They challenge authority and do so with anger. In fact, boys will feel and experience more anger in these years than before, as a result of their changing hormones.

Adolescence is confusing for us. But it's even more confusing for them. You may feel like an alien has invaded your home, but at least it hasn't invaded your body. The confidence level of boys tends to fluctuate more than girls. Girls may fluctuate some, but, on a scale from one to ten, with one being low and ten being high, they stay mostly in the three to seven range. Boys, on the other hand, shoot from two to ten . . . quickly.

Boys feel bad about themselves and struggle with self-doubt and insecurity. But they'll also have moments of grandiosity. They will flip from feeling like they are Superman to the guy whose name we can't even remember who only gets to take his picture. (Okay, we know, it's Jimmy Olsen.)

Basically the changes in their brains and bodies are at the top of the list of things that impact confidence of teenagers. Number two on the list, or maybe even number one and a half, is their relationships. Boys and girls alike say that relationships can make their day or wreck it. A fifteen-year-old girl smiles at your son in algebra, and he's on cloud nine. A fifteen-year-old girl frowns at your daughter, and she can't think about anything else for the rest of the day.

If teenagers were consistent, if they were loyal in their friendships and didn't make a big deal out of things, relationships wouldn't necessarily be a major obstacle to their confidence. But what word would you use to describe the relationships of the teenagers living under your roof? We would use the word *drama*. Something is always going on. One girl is mad at another. A guy has been talking about a girl. She broke up with him. He likes her. We could go on and on and on and fill the rest of the pages of this book. That would be miserable for all of us. We've already lived that phase of life, thankfully. But they're still in the midst of it. And the ups and downs and ins and outs of all those dramatic relationships will have a major affect on the confidence of your son and daughter.

Appearance used to be something we talked about for girls more than boys. Today, however, boys are worrying and even primping just as much as girls. At a recent parenting event, we talked about how insecure teenagers can be. A father raised his hand and said, "What do you do if your child thinks he's fat? I tell him he's not and that he looks great, but he says I'm only saying that because I'm his dad." We used to get this question only from parents of girls. Today it's an issue for boys, too. As we said, eating disorders for boys are on the rise. Guys are having their hair highlighted and eyebrows plucked. There is pressure for boys and girls alike to look thin, beautiful, handsome—airbrushed, basically.

There is not enough time or paper to talk about all of the things that can affect your teenager's level of confidence. So many factors are at play in how they see themselves. But that is what they are doing the most—seeing themselves. And that's where we can help.

A Few Tips to Instill Confidence in Teenagers

- Get her mind off herself. Volunteer as a family. Have her pick something she can do with her time that gives to others. It will not only change her perspective, but it's also one of the best ways to help her feel better about herself.

- Use the back door to encourage him. If your son says he's fat, tell him that he looks great to you. But come at it from a different direction, as well. When he's away at school, cut out pieces of paper and write on each the positive qualities you see in him. It will get his attention and serve as a visual reminder of all that he has to offer beyond what he looks like—even while he's looking at himself.

- Find a group of kids who can encourage her and walk with her through these turbulent years.

- Have other adults who can speak truth into his life about who he is and how God sees him.

- Be aware of her strengths and weaknesses. Don't have expectations she can't fulfill. Make how hard she tries more important than how well she performs. Point out her strengths. Acknowledge her weaknesses, but help her know that she's so much more.

- Create a safe place. It is easy to dwell on the negatives in these years. It's easy to comment more on his weaknesses than his strengths. It's easy to nag. But you want home to be a place for him where he doesn't have to worry about the image. He needs at least one place where he can feel safe and free to be himself, albeit his respectful, appropriate self.

- Trust her. Teenagers who deserve trust thrive on it. If she's making good choices, let her know that you believe in her and the choices she's making. Give her a little more rope and a little more responsibility every year. Teenagers want to be respected by you, and your trust helps them feel that way.

- Continue to enjoy him. He will feel unenjoyable a lot in these years—to you and even to himself. But it continues to matter. He feels more likable when he knows that he's liked, not just loved.
- Remind her often of how God sees her. You don't have to do this verbally. You can make signs for her room and slip notes in her lunch. But she can't hear too much how God loves and delights in her.
- Model your own understanding of grace. If you talk about how well you did in school when she's struggling or how well you handle your anger when he's lost control of his, he'll only feel bad about himself. Help him know that you know that you mess up, too.
- Place your confidence in Christ. It will free her to hear you talk about Christ's work in you rather than your work on yourself.

A Valuable Reminder

We've done it again. We already told you to have compassion, kindness, and integrity as parents. Now we've told you to have confidence. Easy for us to say. We have no idea how you were parented. We have no idea how critical your spouse is or that you don't have a spouse and are having to go this alone. We have no idea how hard your children are and how much you feel to blame. *At least I can relate to my kids on the days they feel lousy,* you may think. You feel pretty lousy yourself.

But we want more for you. We want more for your children. Scripture contains countless visual pictures of confidence. In Psalm 18 David says he can jump over a wall. He's that confident. Psalm 3:3 calls God the "lifter of my head." Philippians 4:13 says, "I can do all things through Christ who strengthens me" (NKJV). All things. All things includes the exhausted toddler moments, the dramatic teenager moments, and everything in between. It includes the days when you feel bad about yourself. It includes the days when you feel bad about your spouse. It includes the days when you have no hope in who you are and no hope in who your children are becoming. All things.

How do you get to a place where you feel that kind of confidence? What we do more often is go back and forth between two extremes.

The first extreme is described in Isaiah 29:16: "You turn things upside down, as if the potter were thought to be like the clay! Shall what is formed say to him who formed it, 'He did not make me'? Can the pot say of the potter, 'He knows nothing'?" Romans 9:20 goes on with this idea: "But who are you, O man, to talk back to God? 'Shall what is formed say to him who formed it, "Why did you make me like this?"'"

Have you ever had those moments in your parenting? We'll call them unworthy moments. It's when you think things like, "I am not the right parent for this child." "I have no idea what God was doing when he gave me a child with ADD." Or, "I have no idea why he thought I would be able to raise children as a single parent." You probably also have those unworthy thoughts about yourself in general. We do.

But we have the other extreme, as well. Rather than feeling like we're unworthy, we get to feeling a little proud of ourselves. Luke 18:9 says, "To some who were confident of their own righteousness and looked down on everybody else, Jesus told this parable. . . ." We see a lot of parents in this category, as well. They're parents who don't trust any other parents. They are parents who feel like their children will turn out "good" because they've parented them "well." They are often parents who end up disappointed.

The problem with the second scenario is that the focus is on the parents. They might say they could jump over a wall, but it would be by their own strength. Confidence—real, humble confidence—is rooted in the love of God. It is grounded in the fact that it is him who lifts our heads. I can do all things through Christ. "With God's help," the verse actually says, I can jump over a wall. Each of those Scriptures relating to confidence has to do with his ability, not ours.

It's a little confusing because we want our children to feel some confidence in their abilities. We want them to see their strengths, but we also want them to know where those strengths and abilities originated.

The pot knows that the Potter made it to hold liquid. It doesn't question that ability. It's not arrogance on the part of the pot. It's fact. It's just not really about the pot. It's about the Potter.

Your strength as a parent, your confidence in who you are, comes from the Lifter of your head. He can lift your head. You can jump over a wall and three piles of laundry. You can do all things through Christ who strengthens you. And so can your child. The kind of confidence he needs is the knowledge that not only does he have good gifts but an even deeper knowledge of the Giver of them all (James 1:17).

A Sunday Drive

This Sunday Drive starts with the Disney-Pixar movie *Up*. We don't care how old your children are or if they've seen it before. We want you to watch it again, together. (You can blame it on us and this silly book we wrote.)

Pay special attention to the book that Ellie gave Carl. You're each going to make your own Book of Adventures.

You can either prepare the books ahead of time, or you can make your own together. But we want you to fill them with the following:

1. Write down your fears (this is particularly for your children). Have them write down what they are afraid of and the reasons behind their fear. They might need help with the reasons such as "I don't like for you to leave my room at night because I'm afraid of the dark and being by myself."

2. Write down your response to those fears. Write out a logical response of why they don't have to be afraid as well as a scriptural one.

3. Write down small victories you've each had in those areas. Leave room to add more.

4. Start to write down adventures you take as a family or each take individually. It could be as small as cooking a meal or as large as

hiking to a camp that is only accessed by trail. It could be horseback riding or speaking in front of the classroom. It could be joining a new club or making a new friend.

5. Revisit the books regularly. Add to them and share them with each other.

The Value of Manners

*A new command I give you: Love one another. As I have loved you,
so you must love one another. By this all men will know that
you are my disciples, if you love one another.*

—John 13:34–35

or Christmas my (Sissy's) sister was given the book *How to Be a Hepburn in a Hilton World: The Art of Living with Style, Class and Grace.* We could call a boy version *How to Be a Wayne [John] in a West [Kanye] World: The Art of Living with Courage, Class and Chivalry.* We're going to roll all of those ideas into one subject: manners.

For many kids manners are a lost art, as are grace and chivalry. Boys don't open doors. Girls don't write thank-you notes. Kids would probably think "close your plate" was some kind of slang for "shut your mouth."

I (Sissy) remember my first date with a guy named Jay as a freshman in college. We went to church and then out to lunch. It was raining, and he carried the umbrella for both of us. As we were crossing the street, I almost tripped over him as he moved from my left to my right side. "What are you doing?" I asked him. "I'm walking on the side of oncoming traffic." I was impressed and Emily Post would have been, as well.

Defining Manners

Today most of us have lost many of the old manners that my beau (that old vintage word, again) showed. Men don't lay their coats on the road to protect the woman with them from being splashed by a puddle. They don't remove their hats in elevators. Families don't leave their doors open on Sundays for friends to drop by. Someone who did all of these things would look odd.

Manners that are still customary today, however, include a man who opens the door. They include a napkin in the lap and an RSVP on an invitation. They have even evolved into texting and technology. Manners differ from person to person and family to family. As Emily Post has noted, *Manners are a sensitive awareness of the feelings of others. If you have that awareness, you have good manners, no matter what fork you use.* This chapter is not meant to be a guide as to the social mores of today's children and teenagers. But we want it to be helpful in terms of teaching your children of all ages an awareness of others.

Manners in Children

Children are not born with manners. Instead, they're born burping out loud, using the bathroom in inappropriate places and often at inappropriate times, and with an innate desire to walk around the house naked (once they start walking).

What Manners Look Like

Manners can be taught and caught by children. Last year at camp, Chelsea, one of our valiant interns, and I (Sissy) were in my room choosing worship songs for the night. One of the third-graders knocked on my door and came in. She had her broom and said, "I hate to interrupt the two of you. I know worship the first night is very important. But I feel that sweeping is, too. If you'll just excuse me for a moment."

Chloe had to have heard these words before. Children don't speak in "excuse me for a moment" types of language. Her mother couldn't have told her beforehand how to interrupt counselors planning worship when you want to sweep. She had heard her mom speak similarly, and she followed suit.

Although it's easy to feel like manners are a thing of the past, we do meet many kids like Chloe. We meet boys who speak first and respectfully. We meet girls who say "please" and "thank you." We have boys shake our hands and girls who wait for the child who is last in line. Children can be taught this kind of awareness of others.

Obstacles to Manners

At our camp we try to teach some semblance of table manners. Rather than grab a roll, we have the kids ask for one. But it doesn't come naturally. Grabbing is second nature to children. This never comes out more than when it's time to sign up for which boat they ride on during the day. We have five boats at our camp (which takes place on a lake, by the way, so water sports is one of our primary activities). There are fast ski boats and slow pontoons. You can imagine how many of the second-through fourth-graders want to ride on the pontoon. Instead they grab. "I want to be on Melissa's boat." Or they'll even take a step further in their grabbiness and say, "I want to be the first on the banana today!"

In those situations we typically send the kids who have demanded the fastest boat or water toy on the slowest boat. They ride the pontoon for the day. The kids who are mannerly and aware of others ride the MasterCraft.

Another obstacle for children and manners may be the parents themselves. We live in an age where many parents value self-expression over anything else. They want their children to feel free to say what they feel regardless of the cost. These children end up struggling with even more impulsivity and a real lack of awareness of others.

Manners aren't cool anymore, either, at least according to the media. Think about *The Simpsons* and *Family Guy*. They are crass and filled with disrespect. Come to think of it, even the Disney channel dishes out its share of ill-mannered kids. And think about their heroes. You don't have to think long or hard to come up with the names and shenanigans of some of the celebrities our culture builds up and then tears down.

Unfortunately the behavior is not limited to any particular celebrity or those in a particular field of media. The reality is that if it's not them, it will be someone else.

How to Instill Manners

- Start early. Baby sign language has signs for please and thank you. They can begin as toddlers to learn the basics such as how to introduce themselves and greet others. They can learn how to act as a host when guests come over.
- Remind them of the Golden Rule. When your child feels hurt by someone else, have them talk about what happened and how they felt. Ask them how they would like to have been treated and what they will do when the situation is reversed.
- Reinforce the positive. Instead of pointing out every thing he did wrong, tell him the things he did right. It helps him know what to aim for and builds his confidence, too.
- Don't label your child a "slob." Instead, point out the behavior they can change and how to change it.
- Make manners fun. One night a week (or month), have a formal dinner with fancy table settings and a special meal. Practice table manners and polite conversation.
- Give your child a polite word or phrase to use when answering the phone.
- Help them know the difference between speaking volume at home and in public.
- Limit their exposure. Watch what your children watch. Check to see if the manners shown on their shows are ones you would mind your child emulating. If not, you may need to get a little more creative with your channels. If you don't want to restrict their viewing, at least talk about the differences in what they are watching and what you expect.
- Let kids help. If you are having friends over for dinner, let your son serve the hors d'oeuvres. If you're eating out, let him order his own food and even help you figure out the tip.

- Value privacy and help them value it, as well. Knock on your son's door and require him to knock on yours. Help him know not to go through other people's things or listen in on their conversations, whether in person, on the phone, or online.
- Play fair. Children need to learn the importance of playing fair, whether in an organized activity or over a board game. Their grabbiness will often get in the way, and they will need your instruction and often consequences to intervene.
- Thank the giver. Thank-you notes are not required if the giver is there when your child opens the gift. If they are not, however, your child should write a note, either online or by hand to express her appreciation.
- Some degree of table manners will help your child function throughout his life. He doesn't have to keep his left hand in his lap at all times. But many relationships are formed and maintained over meals, and those relationships will struggle if his table manners are rude.
- Teach children not to interrupt. It's too much power for a child to feel that you will stop your conversation to answer her every time she says "Mom" or "Dad."
- Magic words still work. You can teach your child that certain words have special powers. "Please" makes adults more likely to do what you ask, and so forth (although this can become manipulative at a later age).
- Model manners. They will learn as much by what they watch in your behavior as what they hear in your words.
- Go to www.emilypost.com for more information and for resources for children of all ages and parents.

Manners in Teenagers
What Manners Look Like

> "Wally, if your dumb brother tags along, I'm gonna—
> 'Oh, good afternoon, Mrs. Cleaver. I was just telling

> Wallace how pleasant it would be for Theodore to
> accompany us to the movies.'"

Does that voice sound familiar? Those are the words of Eddie Haskell from the TV show *Leave It to Beaver*. Eddie was one of the most polite teenagers in the history of television . . . at least around adults. He could smile and schmooze his way out of almost anything. Or, at least he tried. Eddie isn't really our model for manners in teenagers, but he does have some characteristics in common with even the most mannerly teenagers we know.

Mark has been coming to Daystar for about four years. He volunteers during the summers with our younger kids camps. In his own counseling group, he is considered a leader for both his wisdom and his kindness. Mark stands out among his peers as a young man who many parents would like their sons to be like.

Just recently I (Melissa) talked to Mark about a guy who would be joining his group. "This guy has been really depressed. He doesn't have any friends, mostly because he's more mature than the other guys in his school. He really needs a group of guys who can support him and be his friends. Mark, I think you'd be great with him. Will you help the other guys welcome him?"

"No, I don't think so. I don't really want anyone else in our group."

Lauren was one of the most compassionate teenagers we've ever met. She, also, was a leader with her peers and with the younger kids. One summer when she was thirteen, Lauren made her mission at camp to lead as many of her friends to Christ as possible. She probably was instrumental in seven or eight kids accepting Christ, just in the course of a five-day period. Lauren had a sensitivity to both the needs of her peers and the movement of God's Spirit. But her strong compassion was only to be rivaled by her atrocious table manners.

When Lauren was sitting next to you at a meal, she would lean over you to grab a piece of bacon. She bent low over her plate and shoveled food in her mouth. If someone asked her a question, she didn't hesitate to answer with a mouthful of food. When she was finished, she would then rise up, smile, and burp louder than we thought was humanly possible. Her sensitivity to and awareness of others included compassion but not table manners.

So, what do Eddie, Mark, and Lauren have in common? They have compartmentalized manners. They are wonderfully aware in certain areas of their lives and not at all in others. They know how to be polite when it comes to adults but are disrespectful and boorish around their friends. Maybe they know how to eat with grace but don't know how to extend it to others. They're mannerly one moment and act like monsters the next. What about your adolescent? Where is he strong in his awareness? Where is she weak? And why is their awareness so compartmentalized?

Obstacles to Manners in Teenagers

When you think back over the words we've used to describe teenagers over the last few chapters, which one would you guess blocks their awareness the most? You're right—selfishness. Their innate selfishness makes them use manners most often when those manners benefit them, aka, Eddie Haskell.

"A new girl started our school last week," Callie told me (Sissy) in counseling recently. "I guess she's trying to make friends. She follows our group around, and it's driving me crazy. I haven't talked to her yet. I don't really know what to do about it. I mean, what am I supposed to do, go up to her and say, 'Hi, I'm Callie. It's nice to meet you,' just because she's new?"

The answer to that one is pretty obvious. Yes, Callie. You speak to her because she's new. But making new friends, in Callie's mind, doesn't benefit her. In fact, it might even embarrass her.

The insecurity of teenagers is another obstacle to manners. Have you ever tried to walk through a group of teenagers in public? It could be at a mall or movie theater (two of their favorite hangouts). They don't look at you or speak to you. None of them would typically say, "Sorry, are we in your way?" They might even snicker as you go by. Even when we're the adults and they're the kids, a group of teenagers can feel intimidating. Think how much more intimidating it feels to them.

Picture taking your son out to dinner on his fourteenth birthday. You are walking into the restaurant and run into a couple you haven't seen in several years. You introduce them to your son. He politely offers his hand and says, "Hi Mr. and Mrs. Jackson. It's nice to meet you."

Picture the same scene, but you've added three of his friends to the birthday festivities. You walk into the restaurant, see the couple, and try to introduce the boys. They become awkward. One puts his hands in his back pockets. Another jerkily nods his head in the couple's direction. Another just looks down. And your son, who knows much better, quietly grunts out a "hey." Maybe he even shakes their hands, but he would not typically not greet them with the warmth, enthusiasm, or freedom he would have if his all-important peers weren't watching.

The last obstacle we'll mention here is sheer laziness. We haven't really talked much about that, but teenagers are pretty strong in the laziness department. Maybe it has to do with what interests them and that manners basically don't. Your daughter takes a long time to get around to her Christmas thank-you notes. Your son doesn't open the door, mostly because he doesn't feel like it. Forget standing when a woman walks into the room. That takes entirely too much energy. But you can try a few backdoor tricks—oops! we mean tips—to raise their awareness.

A Few Tips to Instill Manners in Teenagers

- Make it fun. If you have a son, take him on a "date" (for moms). Role play with him how a guy acts and then have him practice. Talk to him about how girls feel when guys are chivalrous. Keep it light and fun, though. He'll respond much more if it feels enjoyable and playful than if he feels like you're lecturing. Dads, do the same for your daughters.

- Give a compliment; teach them to take one. Teens have a really hard time accepting compliments. It's usually because they're embarrassed by the attention, but they end up drawing more attention to themselves by hmmph and hmming around. Instead of lecturing, keep it light. "Hey, I had a thought. I know you get kind of embarrassed when people say nice things to you. The best way to get the conversation over with is to smile and say thanks. I'll really embarrass you by reminding you later what they said because I'm sure whatever compliment they gave you was right."

- Keep the thank-you notes coming. Maybe it can be more enticing by letting them pick out stationary they like (Okay, that would probably only be enticing for girls). You can be playful by writing your child a thank-you note for writing his thank-you notes and telling him that it really does mean a lot to people. Also, you can prompt his grandmother or other adult friends to tell him how much it means. This helps reinforce the behavior without your having to be the one reinforcing.

- A smile is worth a thousand words. Teenagers can be awfully surly. Again, they're so much in their own heads that they forget their face is connected to their bodies. Whatever they are feeling shows on their faces. Remind your child how important a smile is. But you can come at this one lightly, too, "Smiles, everyone, smiles"—although you might have to show them a YouTube clip of "Fantasy Island" for them to get it.

- Shake on it. Hopefully, they've learned at a younger age how to shake someone's hand. If not, there's no time like the present. Practice greetings and handshakes.

- Give her the benefit of the doubt. If she acts rude, don't assume it's because she means to. A response like, "You know, I think I've messed up. I know you didn't mean to be rude to your grandmother this afternoon and tell her you were ready to leave. I just don't think we've gone over how to exit gracefully." If she really didn't know, she'll appreciate (Okay, maybe she'll begrudgingly listen to) the input. If she was just being rude, she'll be embarrassed and hopefully act different next time.

- Clarify your expectations and stick to the basics. Explain what is a requirement in your family, like "please" and "thank you" and speaking when spoken to. You don't want to be in continual power struggles with your teen. It may be that you have to choose your battles in the manners department, too.

- Discipline if necessary. In choosing your battles, you will probably have to let some things, such as a few grunted responses, go. But, if he crosses a line with you or is outright rude in public, it can be appropriate to give him consequences such as taking away his phone or a night out.
- Bring in other voices. Have other role models for her. Send him to cotillion or some type of class with other teenagers where he learns manners from other teachers besides you. Table manners were a part of my (Sissy's) summer camp, as was charm class. When my lack of manners affected my entire tribe's points at the end of camp, I paid attention.
- Buy a manners book aimed at teenagers. If your child loves to read, it will be a great reinforcement of what you and all those other voices have been teaching. If not, we have parents who actually reward their kids for reading certain books.
- Model, model, model. I (Sissy) talked to a teenage girl who recently told me that just after her dad finished lecturing her on table manners, he scooped a crumb off his necktie and ate it. They're watching more now than ever. If you're not modeling manners, they'll not only feel like you're hypocritical but also feel very entitled to act the same way.

A Valuable Reminder

It was Thanksgiving at camp. (We know Thanksgiving in June sounds strange, but we have Thanksgiving and Christmas at our summer camps.) We had just finished eating and a group of high school kids were cleaning the kitchen. Just as I (Melissa) rounded the corner, I saw James stick his fingers in the pecan pie and pull a large, drippy piece up to his mouth. I hollered, "JAMES!" Caught Karo-Syrup handed, he looked sheepishly at me and said, "I didn't mean to."

How many times have you heard those four words from the lips of your children? "I didn't mean to shove my brother." "I didn't mean to yell." "I didn't mean to take the last bite." "I didn't mean to _____."

You can fill in the blank, and probably lots of them, with the apathetic explanations of your children and teenagers.

What does "I didn't mean to" really mean anyway? It's his way of saying, "I didn't do it on purpose." He probably really didn't. It was a knee-jerk reaction. It was an impulsive decision. He didn't mean to eat the pie. It was unintentional. But it was also unaware.

Jesus advocates something different throughout Scripture. He calls us to be intentional. He calls us to be aware. And he calls us to be both at the same time.

The words "one another" are used throughout Scripture as a command. The Bible says:

- Teach one another. (Rom. 15:14)
- Serve one another. (Gal. 5:13)
- Don't lie to one another. (Col. 3:9)
- Pray for one another. (James 5:16)
- Don't judge one another. (James 4:11)
- Don't provoke one another. (Gal. 5:26)
- Get along with one another. (1 Cor. 1:10)
- Carry each other's burdens. (Gal. 6:2)
- Submit to one another. (1 Pet. 5:5)
- Offer hospitality to one another. (1 Pet. 4:9)
- Fellowship with one another. (1 John 1:7)
- Encourage one another. (1 Thess. 5:11)
- Live peacefully and humbly with one another. (1 Thess. 5:13)

Toward the end of his ministry on earth, Jesus gave this command to his disciples: "A new command I give you: Love one another. As I have loved you, so you must love one another. By this all men will know that you are my disciples, if you love one another" (John 13:34–35).

Love one another. Be intentional. Be aware. Have manners. We love intentionally because Jesus first did so with us. We don't normally think of it this way, but he had manners. He was perfectly aware. He loved unfailingly. He was intentional. I don't think the Bible has one record of Jesus saying, "I didn't mean to," even as a child.

Our call is to love with intention. Our call is to have an awareness of other people that gives off the aroma of Christ. By this others will know that we are his. They will know that our children are, as well. When your son says, "Mom, do I have to say 'thank you' to my Aunt Robbie?" or your daughter asks, "Why does anyone care if I put my elbows on the table," the answer is that our call is to be intentionally aware of other people. Jesus has given us a new command. And it's one that sheds new light on this value of manners.

A Sunday Drive

For Children

We want to make manners and this "one another" idea fun. Here are a few ideas:

1. For girls, have a tea party. Invite some of her friends over. Let the girls read from a book about etiquette. Practice walking with books on your head. Write thank-you notes to someone special. Have scones or cucumber sandwiches and talk in silly but proper voices. We have done this at our camps, and not only did the girls love it, but they learned a little about manners in the process.

2. For boys, conduct a "man school." We did this one at camp, too. The guys met by the fire pit every afternoon. They learned to build fires, shake hands, tie knots, and how to treat a girl. They talked about how being a man really means having strength that makes others feel taken care of. They even wrote a song about it.

3. Have your kids write a "One Another" rap song. Use the words of these verses and let them make up a rap they can perform at your next family gathering. They can start off by sharing what they've been learning about manners.

For Teenagers

We want to capitalize on how they hear each other's voices often louder than they hear ours as adults.

1. This one involves an adult who can pull together a group of kids. A youth director would be ideal because kids tend to relate to and respect youth leaders in church. Have that leader make a fill-in-the-blanks list ahead of time, with sentences such as:

- When someone talks with their mouth full, I feel _____.
- When no one speaks to me when I walk in, I feel _____.
- When someone burps across the table, I feel _____.

Obviously he would have to stress to the kids that they are to answer honestly, not sarcastically. Then he could compile a list and read it out to the kids. To hear that their peers think it's gross when someone talks with their mouth full will drive home the point that you've been trying to teach them for years.

2. Help your teenager start a "one another" club. A group of kids could either anonymously or publicly get together once a month to be instruments of change in their group. They could pick out different "one anothers" to stress each week or just be intentional with their classmates and teachers. They can also volunteer with other organizations. It will help them understand the importance of awareness and boost their confidence at the same time.

3. Let your children host a supper club or progressive dinner in your home. (A progressive dinner is one where they go to one home for appetizers, another for the main course, and so on.) I (Sissy) did this with my group of friends in high school. We rotated houses and cooked the meals ourselves. We had a great time and felt very grown up. They can invite friends and even boyfriends. We have noticed at Daystar, too, that boys' interest in cooking is on the rise. A group of guys might be interested in inviting a group of girls over to make them dinner or even dessert. Present the option and offer to help them in the process.

Part 3

Timeless Truths

Take Heart

*And they called the blind man, saying to him,
"Take heart. Get up; he is calling you."*

—Mark 10:49 ESV

*T*his has been a convicting book to write. We're not sure how they've affected you, but the past few chapters have gotten to us. I (Melissa) have seen that I try to please people out of my own need to avoid conflict and sacrifice my integrity. But only sometimes . . . okay, actually, a lot. I (Sissy) have continued to see how impatient I am with people and with God, who is infinitely patient with me. Basically we've ended this section of the book aware of our own sin. And, as discouraging as it can be, we think you might be feeling a few of the same pangs of conviction that we are.

One of the greatest gifts you can give your children is to look at your life . . . and your stuff. Your kids will have the power to bring that stuff up like no one else. I (Melissa) recently met with a mom in just that situation.

Her husband disappeared six years ago. Her three boys were used to having their mom all to themselves. She, however, was ready to have a man in her life who would rather spend time with her than a video game. She wanted to start dating. Her boys, however, were not happy about the idea. They were ten, twelve, and fourteen and believed they had every right to act like her parents. One night the boys were eating their dinner as she picked up her purse to head out the door.

"Where are you going?" one of them asked.

"I'm going out with a friend."

"Which friend?"

"Someone you don't know."

"Where are the two of you going?"

Her patience was waning, "I'm not really sure yet."

"What time will you be home?"

She snapped. "I WILL COME HOME WHENEVER I'M READY! IT'S NONE OF YOUR BUSINESS WHAT I'M DOING ANYWAY!" she yelled.

She humbly recounted the story and ended with, "I think I said the wrong thing."

This single mom tried to have patience, but her boys knew how to push her buttons. They may have even thought that if they made dating difficult enough, she wouldn't do it. But her response made her look like she was a teenager, too. She stooped to their level.

Kids will do that to you. You will find yourself talking in the same tone of voice, having the same sassy attitude or the same irritation they have with you. Your stuff will come out, and you'll find yourself behaving in ways you never would behave in front of another adult. In fact, if people were watching, they might think *Freaky Friday* was taking place under your roof. You're acting more like you're fourteen than forty.

In reality, that might be part of the problem. Research suggests that trauma in the life of growing children can cause them to be stuck in their own development. When we talk about kids' development with groups of parents, the same thing happens every time. Some man or woman comes up and says, "You know, I think I never grew out of my adventurous or my narcissistic years." You may have found that in the pages of this book, as well. Maybe you realize that you never developed your own sense of compassion. Or, when we described how teenagers compartmentalize their manners, you realized how much you do the same thing. It may not have been due to a trauma at some point in your life. It could just be that you didn't know how to grow up in that area or never had anyone to help you.

You can't remove yourself and your life from your parenting. As your children stomp around your house, they will inevitably step on your stuff, your pain, your sin, your unhealed wounds from your own childhood. They will remind you of areas in your life where you struggle. They will remind you of things you missed when you were growing up. You will be left discouraged, disheartened, and feeling childish. The timeless truth we want you to hear is take heart.

"Take heart" is a phrase that is used throughout the Psalms and the New Testament. Psalm 27:14 tells us to "be strong and take heart and wait for the LORD." Psalm 31:24 says, "Be strong and take heart." In Matthew 9:2 Jesus tells the paralytic, "Take heart, son; your sins are forgiven." In John 16:33, he says, "But take heart! I have overcome the world." To take heart means to have courage. Rely on what God has placed inside of you. Take heart. These words were also used in Mark 10 to a beggar named Bartimaeus.

Bartimaeus was blind. He was sitting on the side of the road begging. You can imagine how he felt. How many days had he sat in the same place hoping for a little change? How long had he waited for someone to help him? Bartimaeus was stuck. He was stuck and he couldn't see a way out. But, then, Jesus walked by. Jesus and his disciples were leaving Jericho and walked by the place where Bartimaeus happened to be stuck.

"Jesus, Son of David, have mercy on me!" Bartimaeus shouted. He said it again, "Son of David, have mercy on me!" Have you ever had that kind of desperation? Maybe you've wakened in the middle of the night and felt stuck. That's when it usually happens to me (Melissa). I wake up feeling not just convicted but disheartened about my own lack of integrity. My first thought is, *Jesus, have mercy on me.* I need help. It usually is in the middle of the night, for me, or at least in the middle of some kind of darkness. Bartimaeus knew the feeling. And so, I would guess, do you.

Jesus then turns to the crowd and says, "Call him." When they do, the words they use to call blind, stuck Bartimaeus are, "Take heart. Rise. He's calling you."

That's the kind of heart we want you to take as you come to the last section of this book. Rise. You may feel like you're walking around in your own darkness. You're stuck in your sin or pain. But the crowd is calling out to you. Your children are calling out to you. God did not make a mistake when he made you the parent of your children . . . even with your insecurities, pain, and darkness. Your sin and your awareness of that sin will help your children know Jesus as much or more than the words you say to them. But, in the midst of that sin and your awareness, we want to say, "Take heart." Rely on what God has placed inside of you, and there is so much. Take heart. Have courage. Rise. You can do this. Jesus is calling you.

Have Life

I have come that they may have life, and have it to the full.

—John 10:10

"I promise I used to be fun before I was a mom." She said these words in the middle of a counseling session with her sixteen-year-old daughter. Her daughter was berating her for being too serious, too strict, too anything but fun. She wanted me to know that hadn't always been the case.

At a parenting seminar, we were telling parents how important it is for them to have their own lives, interests, and pursuits separate from their children. "You need to go on dates with your spouse. Go on trips with them. Go on a trip with a group of friends. Having a world outside of them helps your children know they are not the center of your universe." At the end of the talk, a father came up to us and said, "I can't remember the last time my wife and I went out to dinner without our kids, let alone on a trip. They definitely know they're the center of our universe." This kind of power is too much for them and too draining on you.

How do you take art lessons when you barely have time to get them to theirs? How do you spend time with friends when you're making cookies for their next gathering? You don't have time to be in a men's accountability group or play tennis. Your time is your children's. And as a result, you are exhausted. You've lost your sense of fun. You've really lost your sense of you.

How did it happen . . . this losing your life in the lives of your children? It may have dawned on you slowly. Or, maybe it even was a little on purpose. A friend of mine (Melissa's) recently told me that she is not ready for all of her children to be in school because she realizes she has hidden behind them for too many years. All she knows is how to be Kaye, the mom . . . not just plain Kaye, anymore. It doesn't feel safe.

But your children need you to be plain Kaye, and they need you to remember that plain Kaye isn't so plain, after all. In her book *Plan B*, Anne Lamott talks about this idea: "My friend Mark, who works with church youth groups, reminded me recently that Sam doesn't need me to correct his feelings. He needs me to listen, to be clear and fair and parental. But most of all he needs me to be alive in a way that makes him feel he will be able to bear adulthood, because he is terrified of death, and that includes growing up to be one of the stressed-out, gray-faced adults he sees rushing around him."[72]

Let's go back to our friend Bartimaeus. We left him right after the crowd had said, "Take heart" (Mark 10:49 esv). The next verse says, "Throwing his cloak aside, he jumped to his feet and came to Jesus" (Mark 10:50).

Nothing about Bartimaeus at that point was gray faced. When the people told him that Jesus called him, he responded. Not only did he respond, but he responded with great life. He threw his cloak aside. He didn't just slowly gather his things so that he could take them with him when he went to talk to Jesus. Perhaps he threw aside the only possession he had. His response was so immediate that it really looked a lot like trust. He doesn't want anything to hinder him. He knows that Jesus has called, and he trusts that whatever happens next will be in his presence.

Once he threw off that cloak, Bartimaeus jumped to his feet. He had energy. He had life. The trust, in actuality, lightened him. Bartimaeus is now free to be who he is and bring that person to Jesus.

The timeless truth we want you to hear is to have life. Jesus is calling you. He wants you to throw off the gray face. Your children need you to live in a way that makes them not only want to be alive themselves but to be alive in Christ. Laugh with them. Play with them. Dance as you're doing the dishes. Race them to the car. Tell a joke. Teach them the song that was your favorite when you were their age. Don't sit in some counselor's office and say, "I used to be fun before I was a mom, or a dad, or a grandparent." Throw off your cloak, trust Jesus, and be you. Be the you Jesus really made you to be. Your kids will be grateful, and you will be free to jump up and go to Jesus with energy and life.

Seek Hope

We rejoice in the hope of the glory of God. Not only so, but we also rejoice in our sufferings, because we know that suffering produces perseverance; perseverance, character; and character, hope. And hope does not disappoint us, because God has poured out his love into our hearts by the Holy Spirit, whom he has given us.

—Romans 5:2–5

Do you know what happened after Bartimaeus went to Jesus with all of that life and energy? Jesus asked him a question. Jesus asked the simple question, "What do you want me to do for you?" (Mark 10:51).

If God asked you the same question, what would your answer be? On some days you might say, "Give me energy." On others, "Give me patience." On others, "Give me a sense of humor." On others, "Give me more days just like this." But we would guess what you really want on most days is hope.

The parents whose daughter was diagnosed with her fourth brain tumor undoubtedly want hope. The father of the boy who was expelled from school for having marijuana in his locker, the grandparents of the girl who lost her mom, the mother of the boy who can't seem to find any true friends—besides wanting their children not to suffer, the thing they want most is hope. And, according to Scripture, the two are closely related.

Romans 5:2–5 outlines for us the path to hope. In his letter to the Romans, Paul says, "We rejoice in the hope of the glory of God. Not only so, but we also rejoice in our sufferings, because we know that suffering produces perseverance; perseverance, character; and character, hope." Suffering to perseverance to character to hope.

Sometime, if Jesus were to ask, we would say we wanted our children's happiness more than hope. Of course Holly's parents want her to be healed. Of course you don't want to see your child suffer. You hurt when you see him scratch his knee, let alone suffer the heartbreak of losing his best friend. In these moments we still want you to seek hope.

Your children will suffer. You can't prevent it. A father of seven children, ranging in age from eight to twenty-three recently told me (Melissa) that he had learned a couple of things in all these years of being a dad. "The main thing is that you aren't in control."

Your children will suffer. Sorry. We said it again. She will have her feelings hurt by friends. Over and over and over. He will have his heart broken by her. She will make bad choices. He will miss opportunities. They will both fail . . . probably a lot in their growing up years. They will hurt physically, emotionally, and spiritually. But that suffering is the very thing God will use in their lives to build perseverance and character. We see kids every day who are stronger and more tender, wiser and more hopeful because of the pain they've been through.

Protect them when and if you can, but don't prevent them from the experiences God will use to draw them to himself. Wendy Mogel has a tremendous book called *The Blessing of a Skinned Knee*. The blessing of a skinned knee or hurt heart is that your children will learn to depend on God, rather than you to get them through. They will learn that they can suffer and survive. They will learn that God can be present with them even in pain. And that knowledge will lead to perseverance, which will lead to character, which will lead to hope. Seek hope. Trust that God has your child in his hand. Trust that he will use all things to bring about his or her good.

The final line of that verse is "and hope does not disappoint us." Your children will. Write that down. _____ will disappoint me. (Fill their names in the blank.) _____ will disappoint myself (the correct answer here is I). Your children will fail. They will struggle. You will struggle and fail, too. But the one thing that won't disappoint you is Jesus. Hope will not disappoint you because he has poured out his love into your heart. He wants good for your children. He wants good for you. He loves them and you more than you can ever imagine. And his hope, his life, his love will not disappoint you or them.

Give Love

*Watch what God does, and then you do it, like children who
learn proper behavior from their parents. Mostly what God does
is love you. Keep company with him and learn a life of love.
Observe how Christ loved us. His love was not cautious but
extravagant. He didn't love in order to get something from us
but to give everything of himself to us. Love like that.*

—Ephesians 5:1–2 *The Message*

We've gone and done it again. Take heart. Have life. Seek hope.
Now, give love . . . not just love, but extravagant love. That's
right. Jesus has loved you extravagantly; now go and do the same for
those little toddling three-year-olds, the adventurous eight-year-olds, the
narcissistic fourteen-year-olds and the independent seventeen-year-olds
living under your roof.

Parenting is a sacred trust. God has entrusted you with these impressionable children for a few short years. We have two final truths we want
you to know in this chapter: One is that you matter more than you
have any idea. The other is that you don't matter nearly as much as you
thought.

You matter so much. They watch and listen and emulate you, even when they act like they're not. You are their first friends, their first teachers, their first ministers, and their first great loves. They will learn from you everything from how to tie their shoes to what it means to trust God. You matter more than you have any idea.

But, then again, you don't really matter so much. When our *Raising Girls* book came out, we did a two-hour live radio program. It was late afternoon and we were on the phone with an interviewer from K-something or other from Florida, or maybe Georgia . . . we don't really know. We did this whole, really long interview about girls. We finally reached the hour-and-fifty-nine-minute mark, and the music swelled in the background. For his final question the interviewer said, "So what you ladies are saying is that if a parent follows all of the principles in this book, their children will turn out right?"

Things quickly fell apart. I (Sissy) started yelling to make myself heard over the strain of music. "That would be wonderful, except for the fact that we live in a fallen world." (*Oh, great*, I thought, *that was a hopeful note to end on*.) I think the interview cut off somewhere in the middle of me yelling about it really being good news.

It is. You don't matter nearly as much as you think. You can't directly change the heart of your child. You can't instill all of these vintage values and create the perfect child. You can't take heart and have life and seek hope and love extravagantly. But he can. God can and does do all of these things. He is the reason we have vintage values. He can directly change the hearts of children. You can pray. You can enjoy them. You can trust that God will bring the good work he's begun in you and them to completion. It's his job, not yours. That is truly good news.

Mostly what God does is love you. And that frees you to parent in a way in which mostly what you do is love them. Keep company with him and learn a life of love. His love is not cautious but extravagant. Love like that.

Notes

1. Eugene Peterson, *A Long Obedience in the Same Direction* (Downers Grove, IL: InterVarsity Press, 1980, 2000), 106.

2. Nielsen Company, "Breaking Teen Myths," *Consumer Insight* (August 2009), http://en-us.nielsen.com/main/insights/consumer_insight/August2009.

3. C&R Research Center on Media and Child Health, "Hot Topics: Cell Phones," CMCH Mentors for Parents and Teachers, http://www.cmch.tv/mentors/hottopic.asp?id=70.

4. Steve Simon, "Elementary School Gets Smart Phones: Gadget Given to Local Fifth Graders," 39 Online.com (October 2, 2009), http://www.39online.com/news/local/kiah-elementary-school-smart-phones-story,0,2801382.story.

5. Valerie Strauss, "Is Your Kid 'Sexting'?," The Answer Sheet: A School Survival Guide for Parents (and Everyone Else) (September 3, 2009), http://voices.washingtonpost.com/answer-sheet/sexting/is-your-kid-sexting.html.

6. Dan Neil, "Up to Speed: Texting While Driving and the Subtext," *Los Angeles Times* (September 29, 2009), http://latimesblogs.latimes.com/uptospeed/2009/09/texting-while-driving-and-the-subtext.html.

7. Vicki Courtney, *Logged On and Tuned Out* (Nashville, TN: B&H Publishing Group, 2007).

8. Harris Interactive, "Video Game Addiction: Is it Real?" (April 2, 2007), http://www.harrisinteractive.com/NEWS/allnewsbydate.asp?NewsID=1196.

9. Scott Alexander, "Video-Gaming with Your Kids," Parents.com (September 30, 2009), http://www.parents.com/fun/entertainment/gadgets/video-gaming-with-your-kids/.

10. Dave Rosenberg, "Sesame Workshop: Video games good for kids," Software, Interrupted, cnet News (June 25, 2009), http://news.cnet.com/8301-13846_3-10273382-62.html.

11. Tracy McVeigh, "Computer Games Stunt Teen Brains," *The Observer,* Guardian.co.uk (August 19, 2001), http://www.guardian.co.uk/world/2001/aug/19/ games.schools.

12. Harris Interactive.

13. Stephen James and David Thomas, *Wild Things: The Art of Nurturing Boys* (Carol Stream, IL: Tyndale House Publishers, 2009).

14. "Youth and General Internet Use," Statistics, Enough Is Enough: Making the Internet Safer for Children and Families (September 29, 2009), http://www. enough.org/inside.php?tag=statistics.

15. Janis Wolak, et al., "Unwanted and Wanted Exposure to Online Pornography in a National Sample of Youth Internet Users," *Pediatrics* 119 (2007), 247–57.

16. "Protecting Kids Online," *Washington Post* (July 1, 2004), http://www. washingtonpost.com/wp-dyn/articles/A19307-2004Jun30.html.

17. Amanda Lenhart, "Adults and Social Networking Websites," Pew Internet and American Life Project (January 14, 2009), http://www.pewinternet.org/ Reports/2009/Adults-and-Social-Network-Websites.aspx.

18. Claire Cain Miller, "Who's Driving Twitter's Popularity? Not Teens," the *New York Times* (August 25, 2009), http://www.nytimes.com/2009/08/26/technol-ogy/internet/26twitter.html.

19. Jack Loechner, "What Parents Don't Know," Research Brief from the Center for Media Research (August 27, 2009), http://www.mediapost.com/ publications/?art_aid=112100&fa=Articles.showArticle.

20. Fox News.com Survey: Teens Use Instant-Messaging to Avoid Awkward Moments (November 15, 2007), http://www.foxnews.com/printer_friendly_ story/0,3566,311785,00.html.

21. Topline Findings from Omnibuzz Research, Hotsheet: Teenage Research Unlimited, Polly Klaas Foundation 2006, http://www.pollyklaas.org/internet-safety/internet-pdfs/PollingSummary.pdf.

22. Daniel Foggo, Claire Newell, and Martin Foley, "Paedophiles Use Skype 'loophole' to woo children," TimesOnline (May 6, 2007), http://technology.time sonline.co.uk/tol/news/tech_and_web/the_web/article1752240.ece.

23. John Walsh, "New Study Reveals Parents Need Better Cybersmarts," National Center for Missing & Exploited Children and Cox Communications Parental Internet Monitoring Survey, *Take Charge News* (May 23, 2005), http:// www.cox.com/TakeCharge/pr_05_05_23.asp.

24. Elizabeth Goudge, *The Blue Hills* (New York: Coward McCann, 1942), 29.

25. Centers for Disease Control and Prevention, Adverse Childhood Experiences Study, http://www.cdc.gov/nccdphp/ace/prevalence.htm.

26. Andrea J. Sedlak, et al., "National Estimates of Missing Children: An Overview" in National Incidence Studies of Missing, Abducted, Runaway,

and Thrownaway Children, Washington, DC: Office of Juvenile Justice and Delinquency Prevention, Office of Justice Programs, U.S. Department of Justice (October 2002), 5.

27. "Teaching Skills, Instilling Confidence Best Ways to Prevent Child Abduction," Mayo Clinic (October 4, 2004), http://www.mayoclinic.org/news2004-rst/2452.html.

28. Sedlak, et al., "National Estimates of Missing Children: An Overview."

29. Melissa Trevathan and Sissy Goff, *Raising Girls* (Grand Rapids, MI: Zondervan, 2007), 68.

30. Melissa Trevathan and Sissy Goff, *The Back Door to Your Teen's Heart* (Eugene, OR: Harvest House, 2002), 15.

31. Tamar E. Chansky, Ph.D., *Freeing Your Child from Anxiety* (New York: Broadway Books, 2004), 26.

32. Rick Nauert, Ph.D., "Anxious Parents, Anxious Kids," Psych Central, http://psychcentral.com/news/2009/06/05/anxious-parents-anxious-kids/6333.html.

33. Foster Cline, M.D., and Jim Fay, *Parenting with Love and Logic* (Colorado Springs, CO: Pinon Press, 2006), 23.

34. Chansky, *Freeing Your Child from Anxiety,* 26.

35. Anne Lamott, *Grace Eventually* (New York: Riverhead Books, 2007), 6.

36. Fyodor Dostoyevsky, *The Insulted and Injured* (Whitefish, MT: Kessinger Publishing, 1915, 2005), 172.

37. Erik Erikson, *Identity and the Life Cycle* (New York: W. W. Norton and Company, 1959, 1994), 57.

38. Gerald May, *Addiction and Grace* (New York: Harper One, 2007), 4.

39. Center for Disease Control, "Healthy Youth!" www.cdc.gov/HealthyYouth/alcoholdrug.

40. Richard J. Fantus, MD, FACS, "Underage and Under the Influence," Vol. 94, No. 5, *Bulletin of the American College of Surgeons*, www.facs.org/trauma/ntdb/fantus/0509.pdf.

41. The Century Council, "Underage Drinking Research," #898, www.centurycoucil.org/learn-the-facts/underage-drinking-research.

42. National Institute on Alcohol Abuse and Alcoholism, "Alcohol Alert," http://pubs.niaaa.nih.gov/publications/aa59.htm.

43. Center for Disease Control, "Healthy Youth!"

44. Mike Galgloff and Mike Allen, "Rise in Heroin Use among Youth Alarms Officials," *The Roanoke Times*, www.roanoke.com/news/roanoke/wb/195771.

45. Teen Drug Abuse, "Statistics on Teenage Drug Use," www.teendrugabuse.us/teen_drug_use.html.

46. Greater Dallas Council on Alcohol and Drug Abuse, "Candy Flavored Cigarettes Gain Popularity," www.gdcada.org/stories/print/bidi.pdf.

47. Debra Bradley Ruder, "The Teen Brain," *Harvard Magazine* (September–October 2008), http://harvardmagazine.com/2008/09/the-teen-brain.html.

48. Teen Drug Abuse, "Statistics on Teenage Drug Use."

49. Debra Bradley Ruder, "The Teen Brain."

50. Guttmacher Institute, "Facts on American Teens' Sexual and Reproductive Health" (September 2006), www.guttmacher.org/pubs/FB-ATSRH.html.

51. Laura Sessions Stepp, "Study: Half of All Teens Have Had Oral Sex," *Washington Post* (September 16, 2005), www.washingtonpost.com/wp-dyn/content/article/2005/09/15/AR2005091500915.html.

52. Marcia Herrin, EdD, MPH, RD, and Nancy Matsumoto, taken from an excerpt from *The Parent's Guide to Eating Disorders*, www.bulimia.com/client/client_pages/exerptpgd2.cfm.

53. AnneCollins.com, "Eating Disorders in Pre-Teens & Teens," www.annecollins.com/weight_loss_tips/anorexia.htm.

54. National Association of Anorexia Nervosa and Associated Eating Disorders, www.anad.org/getinformation/abouteatingdisorders.

55. Trevathan and Goff, *Raising Girls*, 187.

56. Sharri Roan, "Turning the Hurt toward the Self," *Los Angeles Times* (December 8, 2008), http://articles.latimes.com/2008/dec/08/health/he-cutting8.

57. Dr. Seuss, *I Had Trouble in Getting to Solla Sollew* (New York: Random House for Young Readers, 1965), 7, 58.

58. See http://en.wikipedia.org/wiki/Anxiety.

59. See www.worrywisekids.org.

60. See http://en.wikipedia.org/wiki/Major_depressive_disorder.

61. Colleen Raezler, "Texas QB: 'I Always Give God the Glory,'" *Newsbusters* (January 2, 2010), http://newsbusters.org/blogs/colleen-raezler/2010/01/08/texas-colt-mccoy-i-always-give-god-glory.

62. See http://www.merriam-webster.com/dictionary/compassion.

63. James and Thomas, *Wild Things*, 17.

64. Anne Lamott, *Plan B* (New York: Riverhead Books, 2005), 47.

65. Mayoclinic.org, "Learning to Forgive May Improve Well-Being" (January 2, 2008), www.mayoclinic.org/news2008-mchi/4405.html.

66. Ken Sande, *The Peacemaker* (Grand Rapids, MI: Baker Books, 2004), 209.

67. Eugene Peterson, *Christ Plays in Ten Thousand Places* (Grand Rapids, MI: Wm. B. Eerdmans, 2005), 319.

68. C. S. Lewis, *The Lion, the Witch and the Wardrobe* (New York: HarperCollins, 1998).

69. Dan Allender, *Leading with a Limp* (Colorado Springs, CO: Waterbrook, 2006), 146.

70. Mark D. Roberts, "Being a Person of Integrity," *Daily Reflection and Prayer, The High Calling of Our Daily Work* (January 24, 2009), http://www.thehighcalling.org/Library/ViewLibrary.asp?LibraryID=4941.

71. Marie Howe, "The Hard Times Companion," *O!, The Oprah Magazine* (August 2009), 117–19.

72. Lamott, *Plan B*.